KU-161-251

Aldham Robarts LRC

Liverpool John Moores University

SITY

LIVERPOOL JMU LIBRARY

3   1111   01078   4898

LIVERPOOL
JOHN MOORES UNIVERSITY
AVRIL ROBARTS LRC
TEL. 0151 231 4022

FASHIONING INEQUALITY

Gender in a Global/Local World

Series Editors: Jane Parpart, Pauline Gardiner Barber
and Marianne H. Marchand

Gender in a Global/Local World critically explores the uneven and often contradictory ways in which global processes and local identities come together. Much has been and is being written about globalization and responses to it but rarely from a critical, historical, gendered perspective. Yet, these processes are profoundly gendered albeit in different ways in particular contexts and times. The changes in social, cultural, economic and political institutions and practices alter the conditions under which women and men make and remake their lives. New spaces have been created – economic, political, social – and previously silent voices are being heard. North-South dichotomies are being undermined as increasing numbers of people and communities are exposed to international processes through migration, travel and communication, even as marginalization and poverty intensify for many in all parts of the world. The series features monographs and collections which explore the tensions in a 'global/local world', and includes contributions from all disciplines in recognition that no single approach can capture these complex processes.

Also in the series

Setting the Agenda for Global Peace
Conflict and consensus building
Anna C. Snyder
ISBN 0 7546 1933 8

Fashioning Inequality

The Multinational Company and Gendered
Employment in a Globalizing World

JUANITA ELIAS
University of Manchester, Department of Government

ASHGATE

© Juanita Elias 2004

All rights reserved. No part of this publication may be reproduced, stored in a retrieval system or transmitted in any form or by any means, electronic, mechanical, photocopying, recording or otherwise without the prior permission of the publisher.

Juanita Elias has asserted her right under the Copyright, Designs and Patents Act, 1988, to be identified as the author of this work.

Published by
Ashgate Publishing Limited
Gower House
Croft Road
Aldershot
Hampshire GU11 3HR
England

Ashgate Publishing Company
Suite 420
101 Cherry Street
Burlington, VT 05401-4405
USA

Ashgate website: http://www.ashgate.com

British Library Cataloguing in Publication Data
Elias, Juanita
    Fashioning inequality : the multinational company and
    gendered employment in a globalizing world. - (Gender in a
    global/local world)
    1. Women clothing workers - Malaysia 2. Offshore assembly
    industry - Employees - Malaysia 3. Women - Employment -
    Malaysia 4. Women - Malaysia - Social conditions
    5. Investment, Foreign - Social aspects - Malaysia 6. Women
    clothing workers - Great Britain 7. Clothing trade -
    Economic aspects 8. Globalization - Social aspects
    9. Globalization - Economic aspects 10. International
    business enterprises - Social aspects
    I. Title
    687'.082'09595

Library of Congress Cataloging-in-Publication Data
Elias, Juanita.
    Fashioning inequality : the multinational company and gendered employment in a globalizing world /
    Juanita Elias.
        p. cm. -- (Gender in a global/local world)
    Includes bibliographical references and index.
    ISBN 0-7546-3698-4
        1. Sexual division of labor--Malaysia--Case studies. 2. International business
    enterprises--Social aspects--Malaysia--Case studies. 3. Subsidiary
    corporations--Malaysia--Personnel management--Case studies. 4. Clothing
    workers--Malaysia--Case studies. 5. Working class women--Malaysia--Economic
    conditions--Case studies. 6. Globalization--Economic aspects--Malaysia--Case studies. 7.
    Clothing trade--Great Britain--Personnel management--Case studies. 8. Corporations,
    British--Malaysia--Case studies. 9. Investments, Foreign--Malaysia--Case studies. 10
    Feminist economics. I. Title: Multinational company and gendered employment in a globalizing world. II.
    Title: Gendered employment in a globalizing world. III. Title. IV. Series.

HD6060.65.M4E44 2003
331.4'887'09595--dc22   2003062697

ISBN 0 7546 3698 4

Printed and bound in Great Britain by MPG Books Ltd, Bodmin, Cornwall

Contents

List of Figures

List of Tables

Series Editors' Preface

This series critically engages debates on globalization through focusing upon gendered processes and identities at the intersections of global and local sites. Volumes in the series are defining new global/local spaces where previously silent voices are being heard, and books such as *Fashioning Inequality: The Multinational Company and Gendered Employment in a Globalizing World* are entering the debates. In *Fashioning Inequality*, Juanita Elias argues convincingly for replacing discourses about the progressive firm with a gendered political economy perspective on multi-national corporations. Her innovative Malaysian case study reveals that contrary to the arguments of mainstream and liberal approaches to international relations, the multi-national firm does not have a progressive impact on the gendered labour force in host states. By focusing on localized social practices, Elias traces the complex ways in which gendered and racialized inequalities in local culture are replicated within the firm. This conclusion runs counter to arguments in international political economy that posit the firm as a vehicle for translating progressive modernizing values into new global sites. In Elias' innovative case study a reversal occurs; the firm shores up rather than transforms local inequities. In addition to its important critique of the assumptions in the international relations and political economy literature, the book makes a significant contribution to the interdisciplinary regional literature on gender and work in Southeast Asia. However, the implications of this study pose challenges to global political economy and development initiatives in all regions of the world. The compelling new synthesis of relevant literatures is far-reaching. Of particular interest for researchers of gender and work and international political economy, the book also provides new insights for scholars attuned to global issues in a variety of disciplines including sociology, anthropology, economics, political science, international development, labour studies, and management studies.

Jane Parpart, Pauline Gardiner Barber and Marianne H. Marchand

Acknowledgements

The writing of this book has depended on the help of so many people and organisations. I would like to thank the Economic and Social Research Council (ESRC) for funding the research that formed the basis of this book, and I would also like to thank the European Commission's European Studies Programme who, through their ASEAN-EU junior research fellowship scheme, helped to fund my fieldwork.

I could never have written this book without the help of two individuals; Shirin Rai and Peter Burnham at the University of Warwick. Through their unique joint supervision style, they helped me to develop a much-needed critical perspective on gender issues in the global political economy. Thanks again to Shirin for encouraging me to develop my original PhD thesis into a book.

Of course there are many other people whose constructive feedback was most useful in developing this research; my PhD examiners Georgina Waylen and Annie Phizacklea, and my father Peter Elias deserve particular mention. I am also grateful to Ken Peattie and Georgina Waylen for their comments on the original book proposal and to Timothy Shaw in encouraging me to send this proposal to Ashgate.

The institutional support of the ESRC Centre for Business Relationships Accountability, Sustainability and Society (BRASS), Cardiff University, must also be acknowledged. During my employment as a research associate at the centre I was given the time to produce this book manuscript, many thanks to Frances Hines for making this possible. Louise Croker and Lauren Darby at BRASS also provided crucial last minute help, reading through and commenting on the initial drafts of the manuscript.

I am extremely grateful to all of those at Ashgate who have been involved in the publication of this book and for the comments of the anonymous reviewer who provided incisive, constructive feedback that contributed immensely to the development of the manuscript.

This study would not have been possible without the cooperation of many people at the case study firm, UK-Apparel. I am grateful to all the managers and members of staff in both the UK and Malaysia who gave up some of their time to speak with me. In addition to all those who were interviewed at UK-Apparel, I am grateful to all those people who helped me both indirectly and directly in completing the fieldwork. The many NGO members, government officials and trade unionists who spoke with me in Malaysia and the staff at various think tanks, universities and archives (in the UK, Malaysia and Thailand) who helped me to track down resources utilised in this book, my thanks to you all. In particular, I am most grateful to the following people that I met during my time in Southeast Asia; Lai Suat Yen, Meredith Weiss, Chelle Izzi, Sarah Bewley, Ceclia Ng, Mary

Asunta, Agile Fernandez, Premish Chandran, Anne-Marie Reerink and Sunai Phasuk.

A big thank you to my family and friends who have supported me during the researching and writing of this book. In particular, Kate, Cathy, Sarah, Phil and my parents Peter and Helen.

Manchester, December 2003

List of Abbreviations

BN	*Barisan Nasional*
CAD/CAM	Computer Aided Design/Computer Aided Manufacture
CMT	Cut, Make and Trim
CPM	Communist Party of Malaysia
DFID	Department for International Development
EC	European Community
EOI	Export Oriented Industrialisation
EPU	Economic Planning Unit
EPZ	Export Processing Zone
EU	European Union
FDI	Foreign Direct Investment
FTZ	Free Trade Zone
GAD	Gender and Development
GATT	General Agreement on Tariffs and Trade
HPAE	High Performance Asian Economies
HR	Human Resources
ICA	Industrial Co-ordination Act
ILO	International Labour Organisation
IMF	International Monetary Fund
IPE	International Political Economy
IR	International Relations
ISA	Internal Security Act
LFPR	Labour Force Participation Rate
LMW	Licensed Manufacturing Warehouse
LSD	Light Sewing Division
M&S	Marks and Spencer
MCA	Malaysian Chinese Association
MFA	Multi-Fibre Agreement
MIC	Malaysian Indian Congress Party
MIDA	Malaysian Industrial Development Authority
MNC	Multinational Corporation
MP	Malaysia Plan
MSDC	Malacca State Development Commission
MTMA	Malaysian Textiles Manufacturers Association
MTUC	Malaysian Trade Union Congress
NACIWID	National Advisory Council on the Integration of Women in Development
NDP	National Development Policy
NEP	New Economic Policy
NIC	Newly Industrialising Country

NIDL	New International Division of Labour
NPW	National Policy for Women
OPT	Outward Processing Trade
PAS	*Parti Islam Se-Malaysia*
PIA	Promotion of Investment Act
PMFTU	Pan Malaysian Federation of Trade Unions
PSO	Pre Sewing Operator
QC	Quality Control
QR	Quick Response
RM	Malaysian Ringgit
Sdn. Bhd.	*Senderin Berhad* (Private Limited Company)
T&C	Textiles and Clothing
TNC	Transnational Corporation
UKALM	UK-Apparel Ladieswear Malaysia
UMNO	United Malays National Organisation
UNCTAD	United Nations Commission on Trade and Development
UNCTC	United Nations Centre for Transnational Corporations
UNDP	United Nations Development Programme
UNIDO	United Nations Industrial Development Organisation
WID	Women in Development

Introduction

In recent decades, the economies of Southeast Asia have demonstrated remarkable growth rates, associated in part with the expansion of their manufacturing base. In order to facilitate this expansion, a high proportion of female workers in these countries have entered industrial employment, usually in jobs associated with the manufacture of goods for export. The link between export-led growth and increases in female employment has been well documented in the literature on gender and development in Asia, although these approaches have tended to focus attention on the experiences of women workers in the so-called "world market factories" (Arrigo, 1980; Lee, 1998; Lie & Lund, 1994; Salaff, 1981; Wolf, 1992). The research presented in this book considers the role of the firm itself, specifically the multinational firm, in the generation and perpetuation of the gendered patterns of recruitment and employment that have accompanied the shift towards export-led development. The book utilizes case study research based upon a British garment sector multinational corporation (MNC) that has invested in Malaysia,[1] focussing on how company recruitment and employment strategies intersect with local social divisions based upon gender, ethnicity as well as age, rural-urban divides, class and education.

I suggest that the firm benefits from the operation of gendered divisions of labour in order to mobilize a supply of low cost female labour to work as production operatives in this labour intensive sector. More specifically, via its recruitment strategies, the firm plays a role in the construction of these gendered and racialized inequalities. This process of construction reflects, on the one hand, how the firm has drawn upon pre-existing local inequalities. But, on the other hand, the construction of women as low cost labour is something that is happening at a global level across the (highly globalized) garment sector. There is, therefore, value in looking at how the process of foreign direct investment (FDI) is shaped by a gendered set of assumptions concerning the need to seek out a productive, low cost feminized workforce that operates at both the global and the local level. Such an approach therefore builds upon the large feminist literature concerning economic development in Asia, and thereby, raises specific questions regarding FDI and the process of global economic integration more generally.

---

[1] The case study firm and its Malaysian subsidiary will be referred to in this book as UK-Apparel PLC and UK-Apparel Ladieswear Malaysia Sdn. Bhd. (UKALM). For reasons of confidentiality, these are not the actual names of the firms. Similarly, where names of UK-Apparel and UKALM employees appear in the book, these names have also been changed.

Re-evaluating the firm in International Political Economy

In mainstream studies of the process of globalization within International Political Economy (IPE), the MNC is given a central role. The firm is conceptualized as an agent for globalization, drawing previously isolated areas of the world into an integrated global economic system organized around the institution of the self-regulating "free" market (Barnet & Cavanagh, 1994; Lairson & Skidmore, 1997; Ostry, 1992). This liberal approach rests on the traditional distinction between state and market, with firms, as market actors, taking on the role of an external progressive force for change in states that would otherwise be locked into "backward" economic, social and cultural practices. Consequently, Liberal IPE perspectives take a very positive view concerning the impact of FDI on countries in the developing world (Casson, 1992: 12-13; Dunning, 1993: 445-471). MNCs are credited with generating economic development and employment, providing technology transfers (Dunning 1993), and in raising labour and environmental standards through the operation of corporate codes of conduct (UNCTAD 1994, Luinstra 2001, Ellis, 1999). Viewed as a gender-neutral rational-economic actor, the firm is also seen to play a role in undermining gender inequalities and hierarchies in local societies (UNCTAD 1994, 1999). In this book, a critique of this liberal IPE approach to the MNC (referred to throughout as the "progressive firm" perspective) is provided, in favour of an approach that suggests that MNCs are not external actors generating "progressive" change, but rather, they actively engage with local states and societies in order to benefit from entrenched social practices such as gendered and racialized divisions of labour.

Company recruitment practices are highlighted as a particular mechanism through which firms engage with the gendered divisions and hierarchies that exist in local societies. In this sense, the MNC perpetuates structures of inequality, deeply embedded in the local political economy of the host state. For example, it is shown that the firm targets a specific group of the local population for recruitment for low wage, low status assembly line work (definable in terms of their gender, ethnicity, class, educational and marital status). Locally produced inequalities are then replicated within the capitalist firm. Thus the argument is made, that we need to rethink the idea that firms have a progressive/modernising impact on the societies that they invest into. More generally, by bringing issues of gender relations and gender inequalities into how we think about IPE, we can see that the liberal view of global economic integration has neglected to look at how different groups of people are affected quite differently by the process(es) of globalization.

The critique of the liberal IPE perspective is rooted in the case study material of company recruitment practices (presented in the later sections of this study). But the critique also draws upon certain theoretical arguments associated with the traditions of economic sociology and feminist economics that have undermined many of the core assumptions of economic liberalism (for example, the idea that markets arise spontaneously, the result of interactions between rational acting individuals, or the separation between state and market, and the 'public' and the 'private' spheres). In particular, any analysis of a "market actor" such as the MNC, must recognize how gendered assumptions are built into this liberal model of the firm that dominates IPE thinking. An emphasis on the gendered cultural context within which states, firms and markets operate and the discursive mechanisms through which this gender culture is reproduced therefore, lies at the heart of this study. This emphasis reflects the theoretical underpinnings of this study which draws upon the work of economic sociologists, primarily Karl Polanyi (1957), in developing a gendered political economy (Cook, Roberts, & Waylen, 2000: 3) approach to the study of FDI. In a direct challenge to mainstream liberal political economy, Polanyi emphasized the way that markets are (normally) embedded in systems of social relations (Lie, 1991: 219; Polanyi, 1957: 46; Swedberg, 1987: 65) and this concept of social embeddedness provides a space for looking at how gender divisions, and other forms of social division (and inequality), are fundamental to the functioning of a market system.

State led development, gender and FDI

Furthermore, Polanyi's work, *The Great Transformation*, which charted the rise of a market oriented society in the mid-19th century, is useful in that it emphasizes the role of the state in the shift toward a market economy (Polanyi 1957: 139-140). This is a theme that is developed in the book through an analysis of how Malaysia sought to attract FDI as part of its export-oriented development strategies. The significance of the state in East and Southeast Asia in the shift towards export-led growth generates clear parallels with Polanyi's account of the rise of market society in the 19th century. It is interesting, therefore, to look at how the Malaysian state has sought to create a market in young female (and Malay) labour in order to suit the demands of a multinationally dominated export-industry.

But the selection of a case study firm that invested in Malaysia goes much deeper than these general assertions regarding the role of the state in gendered economic development strategies. Indeed, the presentation in the mainstream development literature of an economic model based upon export-orientation and the opening up of the economy to FDI is based largely upon the Malaysian experience of economic development since 1969 (Chang, 1998: 97-114). The heavy reliance of the Malaysian experience of economic development on FDI (perhaps far more so than other states in developing East and Southeast Asia – with the notable exception of the city states of Hong Kong and Singapore), therefore, makes it a useful case study in seeking to test ideas regarding the impact of FDI on local societies. If it can be shown that even in the country hailed as a model of successful economic growth based upon FDI, economic development is dependent upon the exploitation of gendered inequalities, then it is possible to raise questions regarding the extent to which mainstream development thought has failed to appreciate the interconnections between gender inequality and the models of economic growth that are prescribed by this neo-liberal approach to development (Seguino, 2000).

The main objectives of this book are twofold. Firstly, to analyse how the MNC contributes to the construction of gendered inequalities ("fashioning inequality"), highlighting the role of recruitment practices and, secondly through this analysis, to provide a critique of the notion of the "progressive firm" that has

ed liberal IPE. This will be done in several steps. Firstly through an
ᴉn of the contending liberal and feminist approaches to FDI. Secondly,
through the study of the role of the state in the economic development of Malaysia
looking at how economic development strategies based upon the attraction of FDI
were dependent upon the availability of low cost female labour. Finally, the case
study research itself highlights the significance of low cost female labour to the
functioning of the global garment industry, with the description and analysis of
company recruitment practices drawing attention to how the firm actually benefits
from its engagement with gendered inequalities and divisions through recruitment
practices.

The structure of the book

The first part of the book (chapters one and two) concerns the introduction and
analysis of the competing liberal and feminist approaches to the impact of FDI on
local societies. A critical introduction to the liberal IPE perspective is provided,
followed by an overview of the various feminist approaches relevant to the study of
gender and FDI. In chapter one, we see how Liberal writers such as John Dunning
have analysed the nature of FDI (Dunning, 1993, 2000) and although very little
literature exists specifically addressing the impact of FDI on gender relations in
host states, there are implicitly gendered assumptions made regarding the generally
beneficial nature of this FDI. UNCTAD's *World Investment Reports* are perhaps
the best example of how mainstream development thought has taken on these ideas
concerning the beneficial impact of FDI, and is one of the few liberal sources to
directly address issues of gender and FDI (Dunning, 1993, 2000; UNCTAD, 1994:
201-203; 1999: 273). The *World Investment Reports* and other more general texts
concerning women and global economic integration that have emerged from the
international financial institutions (IFIs) display a liberal commitment to ideas of
modernization and progress. In spite of efforts to 'mainstream' gender issues into
the thinking of the IFIs, these texts remain committed to the view that women's
greater incorporation into the global market economy (for example, as employees
of MNCs) undermines locally produced, unequal, patriarchal relations.

By contrast, chapter two, presents feminist perspectives on women's
employment in MNCs. These studies have highlighted the endurance of social
inequalities within the workforce, as women are stratified into the lowest paying
segments of the workforce and endure relatively poor working conditions (Elson &
Pearson, 1981: 22-23). Many of these studies acknowledge that women's
employment in 'world market factories' (MNCs or export-sector firms) may lead to
disruptions in local gender hierarchies. But these approaches differ from the liberal
approach associated with UNCTAD or the IFIs not least in that they show the firm
to be a gendered actor. Rather than conceptualising the firm as a gender-neutral
rational economic actor bringing rational globalized liberal values and working
practices to developing societies, the firm is shown to draw upon and benefit from
structures of inequality.

FDI may well upset certain sets of social relations, and one of the most important issues to bear in mind when looking at how gender relations impact upon the operations of the multinational is the fact that certain groups of women are affected quite differently by employment in the MNC. Post-colonial feminist scholarship is especially useful in enabling us to deconstruct how the differences between women are affected by global economic changes. A variety of different social inequalities intersect with gender divisions in post-colonial societies – for example divisions based upon ethnicity cross-cut with class (Anthias & Davies, 1983: 68; Brah, 1992; Liddle & Rai, 1993: 19). Because the research presented in this book was collected in Malaysia, a post-colonial, ethnically diverse state, questions and issues relating to differences between women are as important to this study as issues concerning how global economic restructuring affects women and men differently.

The discussion then moves away from these more theoretical issues and turns to look at the process of FDI itself from the perspective of both the host state (chapter three) and the firm itself (chapter four). These chapters look at the context within which FDI takes place. In chapter three, concern with the social divisions in a post-colonial society is at the forefront of a discussion of how the Malaysian state promoted a strategy of export led industrialization (EOI) based largely upon the attraction of FDI. It is suggested that this state-led model of economic development was influenced by ethnic politics whereby the Malay political elite sought to attract FDI as part of the wider restructuring of the economy away from Chinese ownership. But the process of EOI in Malaysia and the policies aimed at attracting foreign investors need to be viewed not only in terms of ethnicity but also in terms of a consideration of the gender dimensions to this process. Firstly, the EOI strategy was based upon labour intensive industries such as electronics and garment manufacturing; industries that sought out low wage female labour for employment in routine assembly line jobs. Secondly, the women employed in these jobs in the export industries were largely Malay women from rural areas seeking industrial employment for the first time. The chapter therefore raises questions concerning why these women were regarded as the most appropriate source of labour for the newly emerging export industries, and looks at the role of the Malaysian state in promoting a model of economic development based upon low waged female (Malay) labour.

Chapter four then turns to look at the case study firm's decision to shift production overseas to Malaysia. In order to provide this explanation, it is necessary to look at the context within which the firm made its decision to go offshore; the changing world-wide patterns of garment production and how this impacted on the UK-based industry. The decision made by the case study firm to locate and to expand production facilities in Malaysia from 1989 onwards, mirrors decisions taken by other garment firms in the sector, and helps to explain the collapse of UK employment in garment manufacture that has taken place during the 1980s and 1990s. The analysis of the firm's decision to move offshore then shifts to look at how the firm actually went about the process of FDI and how the firm manages offshore production.

The parent firm is shown to lay down certain minimum standards, including a commitment to equal opportunities. However, the firm is operating in a sector with a history of high levels of workforce stratification along the lines of gender and ethnicity which effectively confine women of certain ethnic and class groupings to low waged, low status employment. Chapter four, for example, introduces an analysis of the operation of gendered and racialized inequalities within the UK garment sector. A commitment to equal opportunity amounts to very little, therefore, in an industry in which gendered inequalities are so thoroughly institutionalized. As the discussion in chapter four turns to look at the day to day management of the investment process, we see that the parent firm takes virtually no responsibility for the recruitment process in the subsidiary firm, and yet, we see a replication of the gendered inequalities that characterize global employment in garment manufacturing. Thus there is an issue here about how the fashioning of gendered inequalities is taking place in a global social space. Most notably, there is an issue concerning how the gender-neutral discourse of the progressive firm (which draws upon notions such as efficiency and equal opportunity) actually serves to perpetuate a male biased model of economic development within which women's work is effectively devalued.

In the final two chapters, the focus turns to field research conducted within the firm's Malaysian operations. This part of the book explores and examines gendered patterns of employment in the case study firm and the way that company recruitment practices act to sustain this workforce segmentation. The case study research presented draws upon field-notes, semi-structured interviews, company reports and documents. The choice of an in-depth case study approach reflects certain concerns that I had relating to the lack of empirically grounded studies of the firm within IPE. Many of the key IPE texts relating to FDI are very general in nature, and therefore, largely fail to support their claims that MNCs have a progressive impact upon the states that they invest in. The case study approach also reflects an increased recognition, within more critical or "new" studies of IPE, of the importance of the local level of analysis in understanding the impacts of globalization on everyday processes (Kofman and Youngs, 1996, Murphy, 1996). But this concern with the local/the everyday also raises methodological issues and dilemmas that are more commonly found in the writings of sociologists or anthropologists. The development of a gendered political economy approach to the study of the firm needs, therefore, to recognize the centrality of questions of methodology. The discussion of methods that is presented at the start of chapter five, highlights the importance of feminist research methods when conducting research into discriminatory workplace practices.

The nature of gender divisions at UK-Apparel Ladieswear Malaysia (UKALM) is outlined in chapter five. The purpose of this discussion is to identify how recruitment practices act to confine women to low waged work. It is shown that women workers are deemed most suitable for those jobs (in particular sewing machine work) that require manual dexterity ("nimble fingers") and are also thought of as 'naturally' suited to the performance of repetitive tasks on factory production lines ('diligence' and 'docility'). Male workers, by contrast, are viewed as more technically minded, easily bored and unwilling to work for low wages.

Consequently male workers are recruited to work in the better-paid jobs, often with better employment prospects than those in the feminized sewing machinist jobs. The analysis of the link between recruitment and workplace division also indicates that jobs not only become associated with a particular gender, they also become associated with a worker's ethnicity. Clear ethnic divisions within the workforce are yet another indicator of the way that the firm has drawn upon pre-existing social divisions in order to maintain a stable and low cost workforce.

The final chapter extends this analysis of gender and ethnic workplace divisions in order to suggest that the firm actually benefits from the operation of these inequalities. The firm needs workers that are both low paid and easily controllable. Managers generally view local Malay women from the surrounding rural areas as constituting the prime source of such workers. The desire to keep wages as low as possible has also meant that the opportunities for career advancement and better pay for this group of workers are severely limited. Although early feminist writings on women and development in Malaysia (and in East and Southeast Asia more generally) stressed that export industries tended to recruit young unmarried women into assembly-line production, the case study firm has moved toward the recruitment of married women with children as younger, more economically mobile workers have sought employment in the better paying electronics sector or elsewhere in the economy. Thus, rather than acting to pull-up employment standards and undermine the gendered segmentation of the workforce, the MNC under consideration in this book actually acts to consolidate the connection between female labour and low paid work. This is a finding that fits well with more macro-level writings that have considered the way that the globalization of labour-intensive production has led to both a feminization of the global workforce (Ibrahim, 1989; Standing, 1989; 1999, Wood, 1991; Seguino, 2000) and an overall decline in employment standards in those countries that have selected this "low-road" model of economic development (rapid growth through the expansion of labour intensive industries based upon the availability of low cost labour) (Sen, 2001).

Chapter 1

Liberal IPE and the Idea of the Progressive Firm

What is the liberal IPE perspective?

Before turning to discuss the mainstream (liberal) approach to the MNC (the "progressive-firm" perspective), it is first necessary to understand the theoretical underpinnings of this perspective as well as the specific claims made in this literature regarding the impact of FDI on host states. The liberal tradition in IPE draws heavily upon classical liberal political economy whereby the institution of the free market is viewed as central to the organization of social life. Although there are huge variations within the liberal IPE tradition (ranging from popular globalization texts such as Kenneth Ohmae's *Borderless World* (Ohmae, 1990) to John Stopford and Susan Strange's account of the rise of multinational firms as new sources of power in the global economy (Stopford, Strange, and Henley, 1991)), it remains the case that all of these approaches share a basic commitment to the benefits of the "free market" in their understandings of the global political economy.

In classic liberal political economy, the market, which could be broadly defined as a meeting place for the exchange of commodities, is regarded as self-regulating, that is to say governed by the laws of supply and demand (Smith, 1970). Because this self regulating, or "free" market is directed by price considerations alone it is argued that markets will have a strong tendency towards equilibrium – thus free markets provide the most efficient (or "utility maximising") way of organising society.[1] Furthermore, the self regulating market is considered "free" because it is not controlled by political actors, rather it is viewed as emerging spontaneously, the result of human interaction between rationally motivated individuals. Thus liberals see a clear-cut distinction between the state and the market, or, more generally, between politics and economics. State

---

[1] In terms of discussing liberal perspectives in political economy, it is useful to note that more recent approaches in liberal economic analysis have often been termed neo-liberal, or neo-classical. This school of thought is often associated with a greater emphasis on the study of principles or (economic "laws") that relate to the optimal allocation of scarce resources (efficiency) and more "scientific" methodologies. However, it should be recognized that both classical liberalism and neo-liberalism rest upon the notion of the free, utility maximizing market, and therefore, the critique of economic liberalism provided in this book is equally valid for both approaches.

intervention in the market economy is regarded with suspicion (Balaam and Veseth, 1996: 43), with a clear preference for policies of *Laissez-faire* (keeping state intervention to a minimum).

But why is it important to look at these core economic liberal premises in this book? As suggested in the introductory section, liberal economic theories dominate discussions of FDI in IPE, and, more generally, mainstream ideas relating to economic development and globalization. The encouragement of an FDI-led strategy of EOI found in mainstream development thinking reflects a rigid adherence to economic liberal principles; in particular, the deep distrust of state intervention in the economy. Economic growth is the primary consideration of this development model, and it is the market, not the state that is best able to provide this development objective. Such a view is seen quite clearly in writings on the bargaining relationship between states and firms whereby the state is shown as "facilitating" foreign direct investment through active engagement with the global market economy (Stopford, Strange, and Henley, 1991). Hence states such as the High Performance Asian Economies (HPAEs) (as the World Bank referred to the rapid growing Asian economies of the 1980s and 1990s)[2] are often viewed in terms of performing this "facilitatory" role; attracting FDI into sectors oriented towards a global market. The export orientation of the HPAEs, that is, the way these economies linked themselves to a global "market" economy, is emphasized in most neo-liberal accounts of the Asian "miracle" (World Bank, 1991: 39), whilst high rates of FDI into Asia during the 1980s and early 1990s are seen as indicators of the region's assimilation into the global economy (UNCTC, 1992: 22).

This belief in the superiority of a global economic system organized around the principle of the free market, is further reflected in the liberal commitment to the idea of progress. That is to say, in a market system improvement in social life will occur because the individual has maximum freedom of choice (an argument, therefore, in favour of *Laissez-faire* individualism). Given that this chapter considers how liberal writers have understood the impact of FDI on developing countries, it is suggested that these writings reflect an approach associated with the "modernization" tradition in development theory whereby development is viewed in terms of a *natural* progression or "a route from poverty, barbarism, despotism and ignorance to riches, civilization democracy and rationality" (Shanin, 1997: 65 - see also Mehmet, 1999: 2). This view is particularly relevant when, later in this chapter, the discussion turns to consider how liberals have treated the impact of FDI on gender. In these writings patriarchal gender relations are often viewed as part of a pre-modern "backward" social order, and multinational firms (as agents of economic liberalism) act to undermine such social inequalities.

---

[2] According to the World Bank, the HPAEs consist of Japan, the four Asian "Tiger" economies of Singapore, Hong Kong, South Korea and Taiwan, and Indonesia, Malaysia and Thailand in Southeast Asia (World Bank 1993: 1).

The economic sociology critique of the idea of the free market

The central assumptions found in both classical economic thought and more recent neoliberal influenced development thinking have been heavily criticized by scholars, often working within more sociological traditions. Firstly, the liberal model is viewed as resting upon a view of the individual as rational acting economic man and thereby somehow detached (or "disembedded") from his or her social and political surroundings (Polanyi, 1957: 43; Swedberg and Granovetter, 1992). Secondly, critics have attacked the idea that states and markets can be viewed as analytically separate entities, and suggest that the economy should be viewed in much broader terms. Block, for example, rejects the way in which neo-classical economists separate economics from "exogenous factors" such as politics, culture and social forces (Block, 1990: 21-45). The concept of the "socially-embedded market" developed by Karl Polanyi (Polanyi, 1957: 41), and later emphasized in economic-sociology (Block and Sommors, 1984; Lie, 1991; Swedberg and Granovetter, 1992) is presented as an alternative to the liberal economic model. It is suggested that the methodological individualism of liberalism should be replaced by a more holistic methodology that places human behaviour within the context of social structures and institutions (Stansfield, 1980: 599; Swedberg, 1987). Importantly, given the focus of this book, the recognition that markets are embedded within a social context, allows us to appreciate how gendered inequalities are an integral feature of the global political economy (Swedberg, 1987: 65-104).

Another economic-sociology backed critique of the analytical separation of state and market stresses the role that the state plays in the process of transition towards a market economy. For Karl Polanyi, this theme is taken up in order to demonstrate the centrality of the British state in forging the evolution of an economic system based upon the free market (Polanyi 1957: 139-40) (thus casting doubt on the extent to which free markets can be assumed to arise spontaneously, a natural result of human interaction). This leads us on to the final criticism levelled at economic liberalism; that the idea of the self-regulating market is a socially constructed concept perpetuated through mainstream economic discourse which therefore serves an ideological purpose of presenting the self-regulating market as the "best" way in which to organize society. Thus, for example in Polanyi's account of *The Great Transformation*, he discusses how ideas of *Laissez-faire* served to perpetuate the idea that land, labour and capital could be treated as commodities to be bought and sold on the free market (Polanyi 1957: 72-3) (a critique that owes much to Marx's *Capital* (Block and Sommors 1984: 76)). Polanyi demonstrates, therefore, how the shift towards a market economy was connected to this emergence of this powerful and "convenient" ideology (Polanyi 1957: 139).

Economic liberalism needs to be viewed as a powerful ideological position – one in which the shift towards free markets in a globalized world is presented as overwhelmingly beneficial to the states concerned. The very positive understanding of the impact of FDI found in much of the liberal writings (see below), clearly reflects an ideological position. For example, in some of the writings from the early 1990s appearing in the UNCTAD sponsored journal *Transnational Corporations*, the beneficial impact of FDI is simply assumed (Brittan, 1995; McMillan, 1993; Ostry, 1992). Indeed, it is interesting to note that there has been a depoliticization of the discourses surrounding the nature of FDI. Writing in *Transnational Corporations,* the then vice president of the European Commission, Leon Brittan, claimed that in today's world, "The issue of foreign direct investment has been largely divested of the ideological overtones of the 1960s. Investment is recognized for what it is..." (Brittan, 1995: 1). But we need to recognize that the shift towards greater acceptance of FDI in countries' development strategies, also reflects an ideological shift toward *Laissez-faire* individualism. Statements such as Brittan's, do reflect an ideological position, that of entrenched neo-liberal values, although it is perhaps typical of the liberal approach not to recognize its ideological biases (Goodwin, 1997: 35).

The firm in liberal IPE: An outline of the key issues

Having outlined the liberal IPE perspective in general terms, the discussion now turns to look in more detail at how exactly this approach has sought to conceptualize the firm. The literature review provided here discusses some of the work within the liberal mainstream on the multinational firm. I am using this term "the liberal mainstream" to describe this approach to the firm because not all of the authors overviewed in this section would place themselves within the disciplinary boundaries of IPE. A discussion of these authors is, however, included in this section because their work has been drawn upon heavily by IPE scholars (Grunberg, 1996; Stopford, Strange, and Henley, 1991). Indeed, many of the IPE scholars working on the multinational firm depended directly upon the secondary accounts of foreign direct investment provided by economists and business specialists, rather than their own research into the impact of foreign direct investment on local states and societies.

Theories of Foreign Direct Investment

The literature on the MNC goes back to the 1960s, with writers such as Vernon charting the evolution of US corporations into internationally organized corporations operating in a variety of locations worldwide. Early theories of the MNC, such as Vernon's product cycle theory, maintained that a firm would expand offshore in order to maintain its market share in the face of domestic competition (Vernon, 1966). An understanding of what constitutes an MNC is generally defined in terms of the firm's ability to engage in FDI – that the firm is not only sourcing goods from overseas via systems of international trade, but actually investing capital offshore and establishing wholly or jointly owned subsidiary companies in these overseas locations. The process of FDI, therefore, is not simply a matter of international capital flows; it is a process whereby a firm in one country creates (or enlarges) a subsidiary operation in another country. One of the pioneers in the development of theoretical explanations of the MNC was Stephen Hymer

(1976) who sought to define FDI in terms of the transfer of capital (as well as other resources such as technology or managerial skills) overseas and, most importantly, argued that there is no transfer in the ownership of these resources. The process of FDI is, therefore, distinct from other forms of international capital flow (e.g. trade) in that it represents an expansion of the firm's control over offshore subsidiary operations (Krugman and Obstfeld, 2000: 171). Most theories of FDI refer to this process as the "internalization" of markets – the offshore relationships that firms might once have engaged in via external markets (e.g. networks of suppliers, licensing arrangements etc.) are replaced by transactions that take place internally within the organizational structures of the firm (Caves, 1997).

John Dunning (1977) built upon these theories of internalization in order to develop an "eclectic paradigm" approach to FDI that represents an attempt to combine the internalization approach associated with Hymer and others with theories regarding the particular dynamics of company organization. (It is important to consider Dunning's theories concerning why firm's become multinational, because he is one of the few scholars who has written comprehensively about the impact of FDI on host states).[3] Dunning claims that a firm will engage in FDI when certain conditions are present. Firstly, it must have market power that derives from ownership of some specialized knowledge or "intangible assets". These are labelled ownership specific advantages (or "O") and would include factors such as superior technologies compared to local competitors or greater access to global markets in a particular product. Secondly, it must consider the particular foreign location advantageous for new investments relative to alternative locations, including its home market. These are the location specific factors (or "L"). Thirdly, it perceives some sort of advantage in internalising its activities ("I") (Dunning, 1993b: 79-80).

What the eclectic, or OLI, paradigm does is to "offer the basis for a general explanation of international production" (Dunning, 1993b: 80) by spelling out the sorts of conditions that must be met if a firm is to engage in FDI. Thus different types of MNC are shown to engage in FDI for quite distinct reasons. For example, "resource seeking" firms are firms that invest offshore to gain access to resources that are either not available or more expensive at home. His second category, the "market seekers" are generally horizontally organized firms that invest offshore in order to gain access to markets for their products (usually due to the existence of trade barriers). The third category of firm is the "efficiency seeker" – a firm that engages in cross border specialization in order to take advantage of economies of scale and scope and also to spread the risk of foreign investment Finally, there are the "strategic asset seekers" – firms that engage in FDI through the acquisition of the assets of foreign corporations. For Dunning, it is these final two categories that are becoming increasingly important in today's global economy (Dunning, 2000: 29) either because they act to draw marginalized areas of the world into the global free market economy (efficiency seekers), or because they embody the more

---

[3] It is also evident that the work of Dunning has had significant influence other mainstream writings concerning the impact of FDI. Most notably the authors of UNCTAD's World Investment Reports (see, for example, UNCTAD 1993: 121-127, UNCTAD 2000: 8).

complex patterns of private ownership that contribute to greater world wide economic interdependency (strategic asset seekers). Thus Dunning comments

> the most marked organizational developments of the past 20 years have been the emergence of the truly global enterprize and the mushrooming of all forms of co-operative alliances (Dunning, 1993b: 129).

The concept of the efficiency-seeking firm demands particular attention in the context of this book, because it is generally this type of investment that is linked to ideas concerning the progressive impact of multinational investment upon developing societies. That is, they are linked to the neoliberal model of FDI based economic development. Furthermore, in terms of Dunning's definitions, the case study firm under consideration in this book would most likely be categorized as "efficiency seeking". These are the types of firms that are generally described as stretching the production process across national territorial space and consequently creating a new global division of labour, which acts to draw previously marginalized areas of the world into the global economy (UNCTAD, 1994: xxi). Technological changes are held as key to these developments – improvements in transport and communications in particular making this dispersal of production processes possible (Dicken, 1992: 103-110; Ostry, 1992; UNCTC, 1992: 102). The efficiency seeking MNC will therefore tend to locate the higher value added, more capital intensive aspects of the production process in the developed world whilst those activities that are more labour intensive, for example assembly line production, are located in developing countries where labour costs are significantly cheaper.

The firm as an agent of globalization

During the post-war period MNCs became major players in the world economy. It has been estimated that they control 75% of world trade and, significantly, over a third of this is intra-firm trade (Stopford 1994, cited in Chang 1998: 98), thus indicating the extent to which production lines have taken on a global character. In this sense, the transfer of goods and services across borders has become increasingly internalized by the MNCs, leading Dunning to suggest that:

> The powerful role of the MNE in the contemporary global economy reflects its capabilities and willingness to organize, for good or bad, cross-border production and transactions more effectively than any other alternative institutional mechanism (Dunning, 1993b: 133).

The significance of MNCs in the global economy is a trend strikingly revealed in table 1.1 where it is shown how growth in FDI (both in terms of FDI stocks and FDI flows) has, since 1986, outstripped growth in world trade (measured in terms of exports) suggesting that more and more countries are being drawn into the global economy. One study of the globalization of the world economy, for example, comments that such developments have led to a situation whereby:

In the 1990s few economies are outside the reach of MNC activity and global production networks... all regions of the globe, to a greater or lesser extent are both the home and the host to MNCs or their foreign affiliates (Held, McGrew, Goldblatt, and Perraton, 1999: 244).

One very significant feature of the patterns of FDI that have emerged during the late 1980s and 1990s is that the rise in FDI has been concentrated in the manufacturing sector. MNCs today account for almost all of the world's manufactured exports. This is a clear contrast to the early post-war years when MNCs were concentrated in the primary sector (Held et al. 1999: 254). The multinational firms engaged in manufacturing are often described in similar terms to Dunning's efficiency seeking firm – spreading their production processes worldwide in order to take advantage of lower production costs or particular competitive conditions of a national market. These trends are especially relevant given that states such as Malaysia have based their economic development strategies on the expansion of their export-manufacturing sector through incentives to foreign investors.

Table 1.1 Annual growth rates of FDI, 1960-1994

Years	FDI Stocks	FDI Flows	Gross World Product	Exports
1960-7	7.5	7.4	5.2	7.8
1967-73	11.1	14.3	10.4	18.0
1973-80	14.2	10.7	11.1	20.0
1980-5	5.3	7.3	5.6	-0.4
1986-94	15.0	19.4	8.0	10.7

Source: Held *et al.* (1999), *Global Transformations: Politics, Economics and Culture*, Cambridge, Polity Press, 242.

The importance of MNCs in the global economy emphasized in most contemporary accounts of globalization has led to much wider claims being made concerning the way in which these firms are becoming "transnational" or even "stateless" (Chang 1998). Higgott, Underhill and Bieler discuss, for example, the differences between multinational and transnational corporations (TNCs), with the former referring to the more traditional definition of the MNC as horizontally organized, replicating its activities within different regions of the global economy and the latter seeking to establish global operations based upon an international division of labour with little regard for national boundaries (Higgott, Underhill, and Bieler, 2000: 1-2).[4] This globalisation of corporate activity is a trend referred to as "complex integration" (UNCTAD, 1995), in a sense an inevitable characteristic of Dunning's efficiency seeking firm.

The firm is thus placed at the centre of the emergence of a global economy "one in which the stress is placed upon the erosion of national boundaries and the movement of economic activities across national boundaries" (Allen, 1995: 1995). This is an important point to consider because in much of liberal IPE, globalization is defined in terms of a process of economic integration, whereby national markets gradually converge into a global market economy. FDI is given a primary role in this economistic view of globalization (Barnet and Cavanagh, 1994; de la Torre, Doz, and Devinney, 2001: xi; Lairson and Skidmore, 1997; Reich, 1992: 77). For example, statistics showing the rapid rise in FDI over the course of the 1980s with, by the mid 1980s, the volume of international production exceeding the volume of international trade are usually presented as "evidence" of globalization (Graham and Krugman, 1993: 17). Hence FDI rather than trade becomes the major integrating force in the global economy and the more permanent nature of the FDI relationship forces ever closer integration around shared (liberal) market principles. Dunning, writing in the early 1990s, commented:

> There is every sign that FDI will be both a major engine of growth in the 1990s, and also an increasingly important fashioner of economic integration and world trade (Dunning, 1993a: 303).

Along the same lines, Julius writes:

> International investment is both multiplying and deepening the trade and production linkages among national markets; in the same way as that financial integration took place from the mid-1970s to the mid-1980s (Julius, 1990: 303).

Indeed, in many of the accounts of globalization that emerged in the 1990s, globalization was simply equated with the rapid rise in FDI that occurred during that period (Ostry, 1992: 7).

However, the assumption that increased levels of FDI are leading to an ever more integrated world economy needs to be qualified. The bulk of FDI flow occurs between the world's most developed economies, MNCs themselves remain confined to a very small group of countries (Held et al 1999: 258), and very few MNCs actually originate from the developing world. The share of developing countries in total FDI (presented in figure 1.1) is considerably lower than that of the developed countries. Figure 1.1 shows the rapid growth in FDI that has occurred during the 1990s, and how most of this growth has been concentrated in the developed world. Even in years when the share of the developing countries in

---

[4] In this book, I have used the term multinational corporation (MNC), rather than transnational corporation (TNC). The main reason for this, is that I regard the term TNC to relate much more to neo-liberal perspectives that present a clear relationship between FDI and progressive visions of globalisation.

world FDI was relatively high – for example in 1994 when it stood at 35.5%, when these figures are disaggregated, it is evident that 14.6% of this FDI went into China alone (UNCTAD, 1995: 391-396).   Furthermore, looking at how FDI shares were distributed world-wide over the same period, FDI flows into the developing world have mainly been concentrated in two areas (Latin America and the Caribbean, and South, East and Southeast Asia). This is shown in table 1.2, where it can be seen that by 1998 even though FDI inflows into South, East and Southeast Asia fell following the impact of the Asian financial crisis from US $87,835 million in 1997 to US$77,277 million, this figure was significantly higher than other regions of the developing world bar Latin America and the Caribbean where the level of FDI inflow in 1998 stood at US$71,652 million.   In Africa, for example, FDI inflows accounted for just US$7,931 million.

Figure 1.1   FDI inflows (millions of US$), developed and developing world, 1987-1998

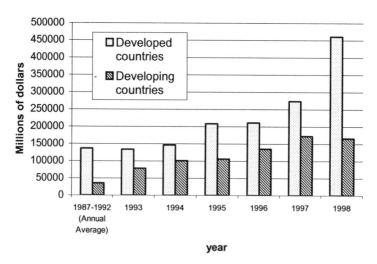

Source: UNCTAD (1999), *World Development Report 1999: Foreign Direct Investment and the Challenge of Development*, New York, United Nations, annex table B. 1, 477.

These patterns of FDI have led to the suggestion that liberal ideas concerning the globalizing effect of FDI are widely off the mark (Chang, 1998: 9-100; Hirst and Thompson, 1999: 366). But what of a country like Malaysia where levels of FDI investment have been considerable (see chapter three)?   Thus in the following section I turn to examine how the impact of FDI on local states and societies in the developing world has been treated in the mainstream literature. In this respect the central question is how do the "agents of globalization" described above impact upon the national economies that they invest into?

The impact of FDI: general overview

Some of the assertions that are made about the impact of FDI include the role of the firm in the transfer of technologies, skills and knowledge as well as products and finance capital to developing countries (Grunberg, 1996: 345). Given that this book is concerned with how recruitment practices sustain gendered employment practices within a MNC operating in Malaysia, the focus here is on the claims made in the mainstream literature regarding the impact of FDI on employment in general and on women workers in particular.

That MNCs have a developmental impact on host economies is a position that is set out in the work of Dunning and others (Economist, 2000; Dunning, 1993b; Spero, 1990). Dunning, for example, suggests that the role of FDI in economic development may be understood in terms of a number of "stages" (thus drawing clear parallels with the work of the earlier modernization scholar, Rostow (1959)). Countries in the early stages are thus characterized as having low levels of FDI largely confined to the extraction of raw materials. Countries may then experience a second stage of development in which "investment capital" in higher value activities becomes more important, before moving toward the more "innovation-led" and "information processing" forms of FDI found in more mature economies (Dunning, 1993b: 272-273). Significantly, the MNCs themselves are viewed as playing a potentially key role in the shift toward the later stages of this development model. For example commenting on the "investment capital" stage Dunning suggests that:

> By upgrading the capabilities and productivity of local resources and by stimulating competition, inward investment may play an important tutorial role in steering a country through this stage of development, particularly if it is pursuing an export-led strategy (Dunning, 1993b: 273).

Table 1.2 FDI inflows by host region and economy, 1987-1998 (millions of US dollars)

	1987-1992 (annual average)	1993	1994	1995	1996	1997	1998
Developed countries	136628	133850	146379	208372	211120	273276	460431
Developing countries	35326	78813	101196	106224	135343	172533	165936
Western Europe	75507	78684	84345	121522	115346	134915	237425
North America	52110	48283	53299	68031	85864	120729	209875
Other developed countries	9011	6884	8735	18819	9910	17632	13130
Africa	3010	3469	5313	4145	5907	7657	7931
Latin America and the Caribbean	12400	20009	31451	32921	46162	68255	71652
Developing Europe	82	274	417	470	1060	970	1297
West Asia	1019	3710	1562	-418	621	4638	4579
Central Asia	25	1327	897	1479	2017	3032	3023
South, East and Southeast Asia	18569	49798	61386	67065	79397	87835	77277
The Pacific	220	226	170	562	180	146	175
Central and Eastern Europe	1576	6757	5932	14266	12406	18532	17513

Source: UNCTAD (1999), *World Investment Report 1999: Foreign Direct Investment and the Challenge of Development*, New York, United Nations, annex table B.1, 477-481.

Like Dunning, many accounts of FDI characterize the MNC as an external force that pushes local economies towards greater market orientation by increasing competitive pressures in the local economy (McMillan, 1993). Such views are found in a whole range of liberal writings on the MNC. UNCTAD's *World Investment Reports*, and the World Bank's *East Asian Miracle*, for example, show a clear influence of the work of Dunning in their optimistic account of the impact of FDI (UNCTAD, 1995; World Bank, 1993: 318). MNCs are often regarded as possessing superiority *vis á vis* local firms in terms of their ability to produce goods efficiently. Crucial to this view is an assumption that MNCs will transfer superior technologies and working practices into the host economy (Casson, 1992). Furthermore, the multinational firms operating in export sectors are more likely to employ economies of scale commensurate with their desire to supply goods to a global market. Given that these firms will have access to foreign investors they are more likely to be able to raise the sort of capital needed to establish large and technologically more sophisticated operations in a developing economy (Estrin, Hughes, and Todd, 1997: 236). As noted above, significant emphasis is also placed on the spill-over effects of FDI for the local economy. Examples of these spill-over effects include linkages with local firms supplying components, materials and services to the multinational (Dunning, 1993b: 445-471).

The impact of these linkages may also lead to a diffusion of knowledge or managerial expertize that benefits the economy as a whole (World Bank 1993: 318). The 1994 *World Investment Report* suggests that MNCs can "play a leadership role in promoting high standards of corporate social responsibility" (UNCTAD, 1994: 338). In effect then, the MNCs take on the position of "role model", promoting superior practices in terms of financial accountability, environmental and employment standards (Ellis, 2001: 15-20; UNCTAD, 1994: 338-339). Furthermore MNCs are also credited with introducing greater levels of competition into the domestic economy (Dunning, 1993a: 462-468). Local firms may be forced to become more efficient in order that their products can compete with the multinational rivals (Grunberg, 1996: 346) and because multinational firms are generally viewed as having better working practices and labour standards, competition for skilled workers may lead to a rise in labour standards overall (Dunning, 1993b: 358-359).

The impact of FDI on employment

An emphasis on the importance of the export sector in generating employment is found in most mainstream interpretations of economic development (World Bank, 1990: 16-18; 1995: 17). The World Bank's interpretation of economic development in East Asia, *The East Asian Miracle* (World Bank 1993), considers how export-led growth generated employment opportunities and wider economic benefits that were spread across society ("growth with equity"). States are thus encouraged to adopt export-led growth through policies such as the establishment of free trade zones (FTZs). Such zones seek to attract multinational firms by offering incentives to export sector firms, further enabling MNCs to take advantage of the opportunities afforded by the new international division of labour. Table 1.3,

its figures concerning the numbers employed in MNCs in the developed and
veloping world. What can be seen from this table is the relative shift in
employment to the developing world as the numbers employed in MNCs grew
throughout the late 1980s and 1990s.

Table 1.3 Employment in TNCs (millions of employees)

	1985	1990	1992	1995	1998
Total estimated employment in TNCs	65	70	73	78	86
Employment in parent companies at home	43	44	44	n.a.	n.a.
Employment in foreign affiliates	22	26	29	n.a.	n.a.
Of which:					
Developed countries	15	17	17	15	17
Developing countries	7	9	12	15	19
China	n.a.	3	6	n.a.	n.a.

Sources: UNCTAD (1994), *World Investment Report 1994: Transnational Corporations,
Employment and the Workplace*, New York: United Nations, table IX.2, 265.
UNCTAD (1999), *World Development Report 1999: Foreign Direct Investment
and the Challenge of Development*, New York: United Nations, table IV.3, 175.

But claims regarding the benefits of FDI go beyond simple statistics concerning the
numbers employed in MNCs and point to the impact of MNC employment on
workers in host countries. Although the growth of MNCs operating in the
developing world is generally characterized by a growth in low-wage labour
intensive production processes, liberals suggest that the jobs created by MNCs
generally pay better and that these firms will implement better working conditions
compared to their local competitors. Returning to Dunning's OLI paradigm,
Dunning has suggested that crucial "O" advantages of MNCs exist in their ability
to attract local labour and also to train and, therefore, upgrade this labour
(Dunning, 1993b: 372). UNCTAD's *World Investment Reports*, make similar
claims, suggesting that, overall, multinationals pay better, have better working
conditions and better training programmes than local firms in the same sector
(UNCTAD, 1994: 338). Furthermore, the impact of these practices by
multinational firms may well have the effect of stimulating improvements in
employment practices across the host economy as competitors seek to attract a
skilled and stable workforce (UNCTAD, 1994: 199). The higher rates of pay are

often a reflection of the way in which multinational firms are viewed as transmitters of superior technologies and working practices to developing countries. In developing economies, foreign firms are generally larger, more technologically advanced, and employ more sophisticated working practices. Thus higher wages reflect the higher levels of labour productivity that are achievable in the foreign firms (UNCTAD, 1994: 198-199).

Dunning is keen to reject the view that multinational investment associated with export processing creates only low paid, low skilled work. Within MNCs there is considerable opportunity for "upgrading" the workforce's skills. Firstly, the tight production schedules and high quality standards demanded of the foreign affiliates of vertically integrated (or even complexly integrated) MNC may lead to firm's implementing so-called "best practice" policies towards their workforce. Consequently, it is suggested that multinational firms have greater experience in developing and implementing training programmes and are more fully aware of the benefits of such training programmes (Dunning, 1993b: 372-373). Secondly, the suggestion is made that investment by MNCs operating in the export sector is not confined to the lowest skill, most labour intensive sections of the production process. Rather there will be an inevitable shift toward more capital-intensive production and a consequent rise in the demand for skilled labour in these industries (Dunning, 1993b: 358).

The potentially progressive role of the multinational firm is given even greater emphasis in the various UNCTAD *World Investment Reports* (UNCTAD 1994, 1995, 1999, 2000). Here the argument that MNCs generally pay better and have better working conditions is taken even further with suggestions that MNCs act as role-models for local firms. Although Dunning acknowledges that the competition for workers may lead to better working conditions in domestic firms (Dunning 1993b: 359), the *World Investment Reports* suggest that improvements in labour standards may be the result of multinational firms behaving in a more "ethical", or "socially responsible" manner towards their employees. The 1994 report, for example, claims that foreign firms that operate codes of conduct (i.e. sets of minimum standards that are applied across their subsidiary operations and along their supply chains) in employment practices may force their local suppliers to comply with these standards thus raising labour standards across the economy as a whole (UNCTAD, 1994: 201 – see also Luinstra, 2001).

Impact of FDI on women

There are some similarities between those writings that deal with the impact of FDI on employment in the host economy and those that look at gender impacts – for example, the notion that firms act as role models to local firms in the introduction of equal opportunity practices (UNCTAD, 1994: 202-203). But in general, the consideration given to gender issues is limited to simple assertions regarding the sheer numbers of women employed in export sector MNCs, and the position of women employees in multinational firms is something that is generally overlooked in the mainstream approaches to FDI. The lack of a gender analysis reflects a more general problem with the liberal literature on FDI; that these authors are more concerned with pointing out the general beneficial impact of FDI on host economies in the developing world than analysing the differential impact of FDI on different sections of the population. In other words, there is no attempt made to ask exactly who benefits from foreign direct investment and consequently an analysis that charts the gender, ethnic or class divisions within multinational firms is considered irrelevant.

The way in which feminist scholars have exposed the gendered nature of FDI is a debate that will be discussed in more detail in chapter two, but it is worth pointing out that there has been some, limited, acknowledgement of the importance of gender to studies of FDI, and trade liberalization more generally within the liberal mainstream. These studies have mainly come from international organizations (in particular UNCTAD and the World Bank), and consequently they tend to be largely prescriptive – pointing to FDI as a means through which greater numbers of women can be incorporated into the global market economy, rather than looking at the gender hierarchies and inequalities that characterize these global transformations. The acknowledgement of gender issues in relation to trade liberalization and FDI reflects the movement by multilateral agencies towards "mainstreaming" gender into its activities by integrating gender analysis into all of its projects rather than devising women-only projects (Corner, 1999).[5] This shift in international policy circles to a concern with the relationship between gender and trade reflects recent events. The impact of the Beijing Platform of Action ratified at the 4th World Conference on Women has seen multilateral institutions (in particular the World Bank and the United Nations) make efforts to try and develop more gender sensitive policies (Grown, Elson, and Catatay, 2000: 1146). More recently, the impact of the Asian crisis and the increases in poverty associated with the crisis have led to an incorporation of social policy concerns into the more traditional macroeconomic interest in economic growth – a policy change that some commentators have characterized as the end of the Washington consensus (Grown, Elson, and Catatay, 2000: 1146). However, the extent to which any real shift in thinking has occurred is debatable. The writings on gender and trade, for example that have emanated from the major international institutions rest upon implicit assumptions concerning how economic growth based upon an FDI-led economic growth model is generally beneficial to women (Razavi, 1999: 656).

UNCTAD's *World Investment Reports* are the most notable example of attempts from within the liberal mainstream to incorporate gender analysis into the understanding of the impact of FDI. It is evident that many of these reports (in particular those from 1994 and 1999) draw upon some of the feminist scholarship discussed in chapter two. But it is suggested here that despite the acknowledgement of the gender inequalities that often accompany FDI, the approach laid out in these studies remains firmly within a liberal tradition which views market actors (such as firms) as gender neutral agents of progressive change for backward developing societies. Consequently, this approach falls easily within the modernization traditions in development studies noted earlier.

---

[5] For discussions of gender mainstreaming relating directly to the World Bank, see Murphy (1997).

The impact of multinational employment on women is first dis
1994 *World Investment Report*. Here it is suggested that there are ı
benefits that multinational employment brings for women. In partɨ
MNCs operating in the export sector tend to favour young wome
open up opportunities for a group that is traditionally discriminateᴅ agaᴜ…
wages paid in the MNCs are generally much higher than the traditional or informal
sector forms of employment open to women in the developing world and the
greater availability of employment opportunities for women has also had the effect
of raising women's educational standards (UNCTAD, 1994: 202). But the authors
of the report do acknowledge that women employed in multinational firms face
problems – they may be working in hazardous working conditions and be expected
to work long stressful hours that may negatively affect their health. The authors
also acknowledge that women workers may be recruited to work in the export
sector factories because they are viewed as easier to control. However, in general
the Report concludes:

> It is important to note that the negative experiences of female workers in TNCs as well
> as other enterprizes are often related to broader cultural phenomena, such as rural-urban
> migration, gender subordination in society and other cultural factors. At the same time,
> it should be underlined that for many women in developing countries or backward
> regions, factory work in TNCs is a step upwards towards economic well being and
> independence (UNCTAD, 1994: 203).

Wage inequalities, or the segmentation of women into the low-skill assembly-line
jobs in MNCs are viewed as the result of pre-existing local social inequalities, not
the result of company recruitment and employment practices. For example,
although the 1994 report does not discuss wage inequalities between male and
female workers in MNCs, the 1995 report suggests that with economic
development the wage differentials between men and women tend to decline
(UNCTAD, 1995: 4). UNCTAD reports convey an analysis of the firm itself in
very gender neutral terms (i.e. there is no recognition of how gender inequalities
may actually be a fundamental feature of FDI). MNCs are transmitters of a
progressive commitment to equal opportunities and, as gender neutral rational
actors, can challenge the "irrational", sexist attitudes found in local firms where a
localized culture of discrimination prevails. It is notable, for example, that almost
all company codes of conduct that have been introduced by MNCs contain a
commitment to non-discrimination and equal opportunity (Uriminsky: 2001) not
only within their own overseas subsidiary firms but often also in the firms of local
suppliers. MNCs are, therefore, perceived to be much more gender-neutral, and
thus, progressive in there outlook compared to local firms. More generally, gender
discrimination is perceived to be at odds with the efficiency-seeking nature of
modern progressive MNCs.

The conceptualization of FDI as having the potential to undermine local
gender inequalities is a theme that is seen more widely in some of the liberal
writings on the impact of economic globalization on women. Most importantly the
stress on expanding employment opportunities for women in the export sector

**LIVERPOOL JOHN MOORES UNIVERSITY
LEARNING SERVICES**

industries that make extensive use of labour is often viewed as key to undermining poverty in developing countries. In order to enlarge these employment opportunities for women, the intensified opening of the national economy to global market forces – in particular FDI – is emphasized (World Bank, 1995: 43-44, DFID, 2000: ch. 5). And again we see that the policy prescriptions that result from such claims conclude that women's best interests are served by facilitating export-oriented growth and FDI, rather than direct labour market interventions aimed at improving women's economic status (Razavi, 1999: 656).

For example, in World Bank writings such as the 1994 *Policy Paper on Gender and Development* and the 1995 *World Development Report* the argument is put forward that by incorporating women more fully into the global economy they will receive a greater share of the benefits of economic growth and development (World Bank, 1994; 1995: 43-44). The 1995 Report echoes liberal ideas of progress and modernization in its claim that, in a global market economy, gender divisions of labour that tend to confine women to low and unpaid work in the domestic sphere or the informal sector are "inefficient". The proposition is put forward, that as the impact of economic development has seen family size fall and technological changes have placed higher premium on the "skill" rather than the physical strength of the worker, "traditional" gender divisions are likely to dissolve. Again, gender inequality is portrayed as external to the functioning of the market, and the Bank suggests that the persistence of gender inequalities in most national economies is due to the resilience of traditional cultural beliefs about the role and position of women.

This overtly neo-liberal view has been modified somewhat in the more recent World Bank publication on gender and development; *Engendering Development: Through Gender Equality in Rights, Resources and Voice* (World Bank, 2001). In this report, social institutions (including markets) are shown to often shore-up discriminatory practices that prevent women from having access to equal resources, "well-being" and "voice" compared to men (World Bank, 2001: 13). Furthermore, the report accepts that states may have a role to play in (re)turning the market into a gender-neutral space (a position that reflects the influence of more neo-insitutionalist thinking in mainstream development circles – see chapter three).

However, despite these institutionalist interventions into the World Bank's understanding of gender inequalities, the Bank remains committed to the view that a well functioning (i.e. "free") market economy is an essentially gender neutral space and that economic development will, in general, lead to a lowering of gender inequalities. Gender inequalities themselves are presented as a barrier to economic development, i.e. as something that prevents the market-economy from operating freely and efficiently. For example, at one point the report claims that:

> Gender inequalities impose costs on productivity, efficiency and economic progress. By hindering the accumulation of human capital in the home and the labor market, and by systematically excluding women or men from access to resources, public services or productive activities, gender discrimination diminishes an economy's capacity to grow and to raise living standards (World Bank, 2001: 10).

Gender inequality is viewed as antithetical to economic development, because it prevents, markets from operating freely. By contrast, the argument put forward in this book, suggests that the gender inequalities and divisions that are apparent in the operations of the market are a fundamental feature of the model of export-led economic development sanctioned by the international financial institutions.

Chapter 2

Feminist IPE and the Political Economy of Foreign Direct Investment

Introduction

A feminist informed approach to the study of the multinational firm provides an alternative framework within which to study the impact of FDI, one that recognizes the way that FDI is a *gendered* process. This chapter discusses the various feminist contributions to debates concerning the impact of FDI and the role of women in export manufacturing in the developing world. A number of issues pertinent to the construction of a feminist informed framework for understanding the impact of FDI are considered.

Initially, the focus is on the more theoretical aspects of the topic; focusing on how a feminist perspective differs theoretically and methodologically from the kinds of neo-liberal assumptions regarding FDI found in chapter one. Debates regarding women, multinational firms and export-led growth in the developing world are then introduced, the aim being to outline some of the key feminist writings in this field. These debates are subdivided into three main categories. Firstly, I discuss those authors who deal directly with the issue of the impact of MNCs on women workers often with reference to theories of a new international division of labour (NIDL). Secondly, those more general, macro-economic, writings concerning gender and export-expansion in the developing world are explored. Finally, I cover writings that have emphasized women's experience of industrial employment in the global economy. This final collection of writings is particularly useful because it represents the sort of approach that has traditionally been ignored by the liberal mainstream of IPE, representing as it does a perspective that takes into consideration people's everyday experiences of global processes such as FDI. Gills (2002), for example, has commented that in spite of this large body of feminist literature that deals with globalization and women's work in the developing world "to date, serious discussion of the issue of women's labour in the mainstream globalization debate has been minimal" (Gills, 2002: 1).

The writings on female factory workers in export manufacturing raise issues such as the conditions of work, the age/class/educational profile of these women and their attempts at resisting the structures of factory employment. Most significantly, much of this literature has stressed the importance of looking at the household context within which female factory work takes place, thus bringing out the interconnections between patriarchal social relations, state development policies and the "market" for women's labour. In recognising how these overlapping relationships are played out when multinationals invest in countries such as Malaysia, it is possible to move away from the liberal commitment to the progressive firm.

To return to the Polanyian concept of socially-embedded markets introduced in chapter one, therefore, a feminist informed perspective on FDI, can enable one to take into consideration the social context that women workers are embedded in (i.e. the embedded, and thereby gendered, nature of labour "markets"). It will also be argued here that the notion of social embeddedness is useful in unpacking the way in which gender identities are embedded within global market actors such as firms. By recognizing an interplay between the local and global dynamics at work in the construction of these socially embedded gendered market places, it is possible to take a more holistic approach to the study of FDI, one that takes into account the intersection between global capitalism, state policy making and a local society. Consequently, one is forced to move away from the idea that MNCs are a progressive, "westernising" external force for change on local societies and to look, rather, at how local inequalities are both reproduced in the workforce of the MNC and sustained by global business practice.

Feminist IPE

How might a gendered approach to the study of IPE (what Cook, Roberts and Waylen (2000) have called a "gendered political economy"), provide an alternative to the liberal conceptualization of the impact of FDI? As already stated in the previous chapter, FDI is regarded in most IPE texts on globalization as playing a key role in the restructuring of the global economy and the process of global economic interdependence. It is suggested here that a gendered, or feminist, IPE, provides critical insight not simply into how the impact of FDI upon those women employed in multinational firms is understood, but more generally into the way in which gender inequalities are central to the functioning of the global political economy.

This is not to suggest, however, that there is a single feminist position that can be taken on the issue of gender and FDI. Indeed, many liberal feminist writers would not dispute the argument that the impact of greater incorporation into the formal market economy is seen in the undermining of traditional, discriminatory social structures that disadvantage women (Lim, 1991).[1]

Gendering economic development and economic discourse

The terms "gendered political economy" and "feminist IPE" are being used in this book to refer to those approaches that recognize the significance of gender inequality in the functioning of the global political economy. In other words, both "states" and "markets" are regarded as inherently gendered, thereby rejecting the

---

[1] This theme is discussed in more detail below in terms of the distinction between liberal feminist and "gendered" approaches to the study of IPE.

notion that there is such a thing as "gender neutrality" in the construction of the
categories of analysis that are used in IPE (Pettman, 1996). In this sense, we need
to recognize the distinction made by Cook and Roberts between those scholars that
see gender as a "basic tool" of analysis in how an understanding of IPE is framed
(Cook, Roberts, and Waylen, 2000) (what Peterson and Runyan (1993: 21) have
referred to as applying the "lens of gender") and those that simply regard gender
inequality as an important area of study, but one that can be approached using
essentially the same methodologies and categories of analysis found in more
mainstream approaches (Cook et al. 2000: 3). The latter approach is often
characterized as that of "adding-on"(Elson, 1996: 1), and is generally associated
with the liberal influenced Women in Development (WID) perspective (Boserup,
1970; Tinker, 1976).

For many WID scholars and practitioners, gender inequalities are the result of
the marginalization of women from the development process caused largely by the
irrational (sexist) attitudes of the development planners. WID does not challenge
the commitment to the free market typical of liberal-modernization approaches,
and puts forward the view that women's subordination can be overcome through
greater incorporation into the market and the public sphere.[2]   Mainstream
approaches to dealing with gender inequality are usually articulated through the
discourse of "equal opportunities" (this was seen in the previous chapter, for
example, in relation to company codes of conduct in MNCs). The discussion of
gender inequality in multinational firms found in the *World Investment Reports,* is
typical of this approach because it regards women's incorporation into factory
employment in MNCs (and thereby the global economy) as a modernising process,
undermining gender subordination, whilst ignoring the way in which the operations
of the firms themselves (and the market more generally) are inherently gendered.

WID can be contrasted with alternative feminist perspectives on
development, generally referred to as Gender and Development (GAD), which
emphasize the role of gender relations (i.e. the social relations between men and
women) both inside and outside of the market economy. The GAD perspective
surfaced in the 1980s, building upon the well-established structuralist/dependency-
influenced critique of WID,[3] and incorporating influences from post-structuralist
and socialist-feminist thinking in its analysis (Visvanathan, 1997: 18-19, 23-24).
In terms of the emergence of feminist IPE, GAD writings have been particularly
influential not least because development concerns remain central to the agenda of
a feminist IPE (Enloe, 1989; Pettman, 1996). Waylen has also drawn attention to
the theoretical contributions made by feminist economics in the emergence of
feminist IPE scholarship claiming that both GAD writings and feminist economics
provide important starting points for the development of a gendered political
economy perspective (Waylen, 1997). Indeed, given that mainstream IPE scholars
have adopted wholeheartedly the methodologies and language of orthodox
economics, it is no surprise that feminist IPE scholars have drawn upon this

---

[2] For a critique of the WID perspective see Beneria and Sen (1981) and Kabeer (1994).

[3] For a review of some of these structuralist writings, in particular the New International
Division of Labour (NIDL), see below pages 36-38.

alternative, feminist, critique of orthodox economic thinking that directs attention to the gender biases implicit within the mainstream of economic thinking. It is suggested that the discipline of economics is constructed in terms of masculine and feminine sides; making central the masculine whilst ignoring the feminine; or rather, relegating the "feminine" to a place outside of economics (Strober, 1994: 143-147). For example, feminist economists have criticized the liberal economic mainstream's failure to take account of the way that the operation of "markets" is in fact based upon a sexual division of labour between the "masculinized" formal productive economy and a "feminized" household realm (Donath, 2000; Ferber and Nelson, 1993). Feminist economists, therefore, have pointed to the way in which both the subject matter of economics, as well as the positivist methodologies employed and the ontological premises (for example rational acting economic-man (Ferber and Nelson, 1993: 146)) found in economic thinking are shown to reflect masculinist biases and assumptions.

Jennings (1999) has commented that the downgrading of a private household sphere in contrast to the public sphere of the market exposed in feminist critiques of mainstream economic discourse owes much to the feminist critique of scientific method (see for example Harding, 1986). The construction of economic life around the public-private, work-household dichotomy is shown to reflect Cartesian dualistic modes of knowledge construction. These dualisms include the distinctions between mind and body, objectivity and subjectivity, reason and emotion and the universal over the particular; with greater value given to modes of enquiry that embody an objective, reasoned, universally applicable method (i.e. the modernist position that science can be free from subjectivity). However, Jennings argues that "[b]ecause modernist values are (falsely) universalized, both their partiality and their social history are obscured; they are 'normalized', while 'other' values are tainted with abnormality" (Jennings, 1999; 145). Indeed, feminist scholarship exposes the gender assumptions built into such dualistic thinking, with emphasis being placed on the way in which the production of "scientific" knowledge reflects gendered power relations. Hence, "while 'man' is a universalized category, 'woman' has been particularized, restricted and disqualified from full participation in the social production of privileges – and thus potentially authoritarian – knowledge" (Jennings, 1999; 145). The use of dichotomous thinking, as Hooper argues, "is a way of trying to fix the gender order in a way that keeps masculinity both naturalized and privileged" (Hooper, 2001; 44). Thus the feminist critique of economic discourse goes further than simply exposing the gendered assumptions that are built into the discipline, but actually highlights the way in which the construction of gendered dualisms within economic thought impacts upon social realities.

The contribution of feminist IR scholarship

Like these feminist critics of orthodox economic theory and practice, many feminist IR scholars also pick up on the feminist critique of positivist method. Feminist IR has pointed, for example, to how dominant theories in IR such as realism construct states as essentially masculine actors (Tickner, 1991). The embedding of masculinist biases and assumptions in IR and IPE,[4] are shown to reflect not only the way in which knowledge claims are constructed so as to implicitly rank the "masculine" over the "feminine" (Peterson and Runyan, 1993) but also the dominance of male scholars within IR and IPE. Thus the point is made that IR is "one of the most masculinist of disciplines" (Marchand, 1996; Peterson, 1996; Pettman, 1996: vii; Whitworth, 1997: 1).

The feminist IR theorist, Christine Sylvester (1994), has highlighted the value of feminist deconstructions of core concepts in IR theory such as rationality, criticising the way in which positivist theories (such as those found in liberal political economy) draw boundaries in order to construct parsimonious "scientific" concepts free from gender, race or class. The same is clearly also true of mainstream economic discourse and Sylvester argues that "we have to explore the privileges and biases built into boundary drawing" (Sylvester, 1994: 115). This practice of "boundary drawing" can be recognized in how the separation between the public and the private sphere at the heart of liberal theory informs political practice in prioritising the activities of the "rational" male actors that make up states and markets over women's activities in the private sphere of the household and the family (Sylvester 1994: 114 – See also Tickner, 1991). If markets and market actors are to be viewed as gendered, this is an explicit rejection of the liberal claim that the market is a gender neutral space regulated purely by the "scientific" laws of supply and demand. More generally, feminist IR scholarship has focussed on disciplinary boundaries, looking at how certain subject matters defined as "international" or "global" are regarded as "appropriate" for the study of IR whilst subject matters that are more concerned with issues such as gender relations, ethnicity or identity are deemed to be outside of the disciplinary boundaries of IR. "The international" therefore, comes to be regarded as a gender neutral realm in which the particular is subsumed within universalized categories of rational actors such as states or firms.

But the critique of IR theory moves beyond claims that the discipline is rooted in implicit gendered assumptions and moves to look at the relationship between the theory and the practice of IR. Charlotte Hooper's work is especially useful in this context because she has sought to expose how masculinist practices within the international arena are shaped by gendered discourses of rationality and competition that are generally privileged in mainstream IR theory. She argues that the global sphere cannot be regarded as a gender-neutral arena, but rather, becomes a site for the production of gender identity. Part of the reason for this is the hegemonic position of certain groups of men; "if international relations are deemed to be about the very public world of high office at state, interstate and

---

[4] It is worth pointing out that most feminist scholarship in this area does not make a clear distinction between a feminist IR and a feminist IPE (or gendered political economy). It is generally accepted in feminist IR texts that gender issues in global politics cannot be understood without reference to a broader understanding of a gendered political economy (Enloe, 1989; Whitworth, 1997) or gendered new international division of labour (Pettman, 1996: 157-208). These writings all point to the relevance of the material basis of gender inequality in reconstructing a feminist understanding of IR.

multinational business level, they have reflected the interests and activities of men" (Hooper 2001; 13). But male dominance within what we define as "the international" is not the only reason for thinking about a gendered global arena, we also need to look at the impact of these masculinist assumptions embodied in the scientific positivism that pervades the dominant discourses relating to IR, IPE and globalisation more generally. For example, within international business practice, one can observe values of individualism and competition that are pervasive to modern globalisation discourse. Similar themes are explored by Ling in her study of how media images in Asia play a role in producing a masculinized vision of globalisation (Ling, 1999). Hence "competitive masculine imagery is mobilized in the construction of "globalization" as a masculine space" (Hooper, 2001: 15). Furthermore, the promotion of globalization as a masculinist arena, is above all, a reflection of the interests of a certain type of masculinity which she terms "hegemonic masculinity", one which reflects the values and interests of an Ango-American elite.

Hooper provides an analysis of the *Economist* newspaper as an example of how mainstream media has internalized the idea of value-free neutrality in its written style (Hooper, 2001; 117-218) and consequently reproduced a hegemonic masculinist view of the world. I suggest that it is equally useful to look at how masculinist assumptions lie behind the discourse of the progressive firm. Most notably the emergence of writings that stress how firms have become "actors" in global politics tend to emphasise an image of the firm as a unitary rational actor, in the same way that the state is viewed in realist IR thinking (Amoore, 2000). The internalization of markets charted by Hymer (1976) and Dunning (1993b) provides the basis for powerful and competitive economic units who are cast as agents of globalization spreading their knowledge and expertise world wide. Dunning's models of MNCs are characterized as "seekers" (i.e. market seekers, efficiency seekers etc), pursuing economically rational ends by moving overseas in order to gain some kind of competitive advantage (Dunning 1993b: 80). Firms come to be conceptualized as supremely rational actors – largely because they are viewed as agents of a rational economistic vision of globalization and in performing this task, they are characterized as powerful, efficient and more effective than any other "institutional set of arrangements" (Dunning 1993b: 133). We can also look at how some of the more specific claims made about women and employment in MNCs found in mainstream writings reflect gendered notions such as equality of opportunity, which fail to appreciate the constraints (cultural, household-economic etc.) placed upon women as workers compared to men. The progressive firm thesis suggests that merely by incorporating women into the sphere of the rational progressive market economy, firms serve to undermine gender inequality. However, in the later sections of this book it will be revealed that the notion of equal opportunities does little to change the deeply embedded structures of inequality within the firm. "Equal opportunity" in many ways serves as a masculinist smokescreen for the preservation of an unequal gender order.

Hooper's work also draws attention to how mainstream texts have conceptualized the process of FDI in terms of masculinized (rational, economically-driven) actors investing in feminized (backward, low cost) societies.

She notes at one point, for example, how "metaphors of aggressive (hetero)sexual conquest and rape" (Hooper, 2001: 139-140) were used by the *Economist* in relation to an article on foreign investment in Myanmar. Headlined "Rich for Rape" the article demonstrated how the language of FDI itself has become a site for the assertion of hegemonic masculinities. Thus, feminist thought forces us to consider the gendered assumptions relating to rational economic action that are implicit within the discourse of the progressive firm.

By exposing the neo-liberal assumptions at the heart of the discourse of the progressive firm (see chapter one), and then moving to look at how these assumptions reflect masculinist assumptions, we can then move to look at the role of the firm itself as a site for the production of a global gender culture. Since mainstream globalization discourse regards the firm as a agent of neo-liberal globalization, the firm itself becomes a site for the globalized production of ideas relating to gender roles. International business practice has come to reflect certain hegemonic masculinist ideals and these will inform its practice (an argument that will be expanded in the later chapters of this book).

However, the way in which firms have become global sites for the production of gender inequality is a process that is in constant negotiation with localized masculinities, or patriarchies, embedded in the political economies of host states. Accordingly, (given the emphasis on the political construction of markets in the economic-sociology writings of Polanyi and others) one must also recognize the role of the state in the development of gendered market-places. Writers such as Ling (1999) have sought to demonstrate how states in East Asia have promoted a particular vision of economic development which is overtly gendered in that it involves authoritarian, patriarchal-Confucian states pursuing economic development strategies within societies conceived as essentially feminized. Ling utilizes the notion of hypermasuclinity (first utilized by Ashis Nandy (1988) in relation to British colonial power relations) to convey the glorification of aggression, competition, accumulation and power that are a hallmark of these states. Rather than talking of a hegemonic form of masculinity (as Hooper does) Ling prefers the notion of hypermasculinity because it is viewed as a particularly aggressive form of masculinity that is articulated in specific circumstances when masculinities are felt to be under threat (Agathangelou and Ling, 2001: 5). Asian states are viewed as pursuing hypermasculine developmentalism as a reaction to an aggressive, competitive form of globalization and thus "[e]conomic development, in particular, is the site of this enactment of hypermasculinity" (Ling 1999: 280). Within this context, Ling argues, that women come to appear as the most exploited group as "the most feminized of feminized subjects" (Ling, 1997: 10).

The model of hypermasculine developmentalism is a useful way of thinking about how global and local forces play out in the reconstitution of gender relations in specific national contexts. This is a theme also addressed by Troung (1999), for example, who has discussed the interaction between local patriarchal states and global capitalism in the construction of the East Asian developmental state. The theme of the state as a gendered actor, is taken up in more detail in chapter three of this book. But an introduction to the significance of both the state and the firm as masculinized rather than rational actors is essential to explaining how feminist reconstructions of IPE highlight the gendered power relations implicit within the operations of both "states" and "markets". A feminist IPE moves beyond the artificial dichotomy between the public and the private sphere demonstrating how the operation of a market-economy remains deeply embedded in patriarchal social relations, in this sense, building upon the critique of liberalism from an economic-sociology perspective as outlined in chapter one.

The distinction between liberal feminism that adds on women to existing accounts and a feminism based on a political economy of gender is not to suggest that "gender" is a more appropriate category of analysis in IPE than the category of "woman" (Zalewski, 1998). Indeed, a political economy of gender is one that asks (as Enloe did in her work *Beaches Bananas and Bases*) "where are the women [in IPE]?" (Enloe, 1989: 4). By identifying the positions and roles that women occupy in the global economy feminists have opened up new areas of study previously considered to be outside of the "boundaries" of IPE (Murphy, 1996). The "lens of gender" allows us to reformulate the way in which we perceive the "globality" in a way that re-prioritizes the position of the particular, the local, the feminine, the "other". The feminist perspective thus creates space for approaches in IPE that assert the importance of the local level of analysis (Youngs, 1996), and people's "everyday" experiences of global processes. Thus in the discussion presented below, a more general discussion of the gendered nature of trade liberalization and the rise of the export-led Newly Industrializing Countries (NICs) is linked to writings on women's experiences of employment in multinational export sector firms. Bringing the experiences of ordinary women (and men) into their analysis of the global economy, has created methodological challenges for mainstream IR, forcing scholars to engage with the perspectives of the disadvantaged (Murphy, 1996).

Differences between women in the global political economy

This leads us onto the wider issue of difference and diversity between women. This is a point that has been made by a number of Black feminist and post-colonial scholars, who have suggested that categories like "patriarchy" that characterize (White) Western radical feminism fail to take into account the very different experiences of women of different ethnicities, races and nationalities (Anthias and Davies, 1983: 68; Brah, 1992; Liddle and Rai, 1993: 19). These writings are relevant to this book because it will be shown in later chapters that the gender inequalities that the firm engages with through its recruitment practices are cross-cut with other forms of social divisions (in particular ethnicity). Thus feminist IPE must recognize that gender relations never exist separately from other power relations, they intersect with other socially constructed power relations of class, race, nationality and age. The role of these power relationships within the workings of the capitalist market economy is a theme that has been developed by Mies *et al.* (1988) in their work *Women the Last Colony*, in which the authors make the comment that:

> We cannot simply add the hitherto neglected areas – women and the colonies – onto existing theories; to tack on women and the colonies cannot make an incomplete theory whole. The inclusion of these neglected spheres transforms previous social theories root and branch by placing new contradictions and relationships centre stage. For example the relationship of wage labour and capital once regarded as *the* central relationship – is now increasingly seen simply as one part of a much more comprehensive contradiction between human labour in general (including non-wage labour) and capital, with an additional contradiction between waged and non-wage labour (Mies, Bennholdt-Thomsen, and Welfhof, 1988: 3).

Although many recent feminist scholars have criticized Mies for taking too overtly a structuralist perspective in her work (suggesting that Mies tends to treat women as the victims of global capitalism combined with the forces of colonialism (Kabeer, 1994: 50-55)), the above quotation does suggest that Mies recognizes how an engagement with the perspectives of the disadvantaged raises questions about the theory and methods of mainstream development thinking. This is a theme that will be developed in later chapters where the focus on how company recruitment practices intersect with local social inequalities reveals problems in the mainstream's understanding of the role of firms in the global economy. A feminist IPE therefore not only points to the gender divisions and hierarchies that are inherent in a global process such as FDI, but also creates a space for looking at how gender divisions are cross-cut with other divisions in society (including how multiple forms of masculinity as well as femininity are constructed within the global political economy (Hooper, 2001)). Thus in the final chapter of the book the discussion turns to consider how different groups of women in Malaysian society (in particular women of different ethnic groups) are affected differently by incorporation into factory employment.

Post-colonial feminism not only highlights the multi-layered nature of gender identities and gender relations, it also raises questions of the way in which western feminist has created universalizing concepts – in particular, that of patriarchy – which tends to lock all women into a position of victimhood. Rai (2002), for example, warns of the latent problems of universalizing concepts such as "hypermasculinity". Thus although this is a concept that "makes a contribution towards opening up the debate on gendered regimes of market access as well as market operations", it also "seems to set up binaries" whereby "[t]he feminine/feminized is characterized as powerless" (Rai, 2002: 98). An understanding of women's role in export manufacturing therefore, needs to recognize how female employment may deliver certain benefits to these women workers, a theme that is developed in the literature on women's experiences of export sector employment reviewed in the final section of this paper.

Women workers in the global economy

Writings on women workers in MNCs in the developing world have generally taken as a starting point the rise in female employment in the light manufacturing-for-export sector industries. As has already been shown, in chapter one, much of the growth that occurred in levels of FDI into developing countries during the 1970s and 1980s was related to the rise of export manufacturing as firms sought to shift labour intensive production into economies where labour costs were considerably lower. However, this kind of FDI was confined to a select number of developing countries (most notably in East and Southeast Asia) in which the state had played an active role in encouraging FDI as part of its broader strategy of export-led economic development through policies such as the establishment of FTZs (Lim, 1991: 105).

The discussion presented here, considers how feminist scholars have sought to highlight how this form of FDI and the process of export-led development more generally, are gendered processes. The focus is on how global shifts in the manufacture of certain products has been dependent on the incorporation of low cost female labour into the (formal) waged economy. This issue is considered from two different angles. Firstly, to examine those writings that focus specifically on the role of the multinational firm in seeking to benefit from women's inferior position compared to men within the NIDL. Secondly, to look more generally at how quantitative shifts in the employment of women in the developing world can be linked more generally to strategies of export-led development and the globalization of economic activity. In understanding the impact of MNCs on gender relations, it is necessary to bear in mind that patterns of high female employment within MNCs in the developing world are essentially confined to those firms operating in the labour-intensive export manufacturing sectors. This is a point that is raised by Lim in her 1985 study of female employment in MNCs in which it is shown that most employment in MNCs in the developing world is male dominated (overall women make up only a very small proportion of multinational industrial workers). Furthermore, although female employment has been consistently high in multinational firms involved in export manufacturing, these firms account for a small share of all female industrial workers in the developing world (Joekes and Weston, 1994; Lim, 1985; Pearson, 1992).

However, despite these general world-wide trends in female employment, we can identify certain countries in which export-led development strategies have been dependent on considerably high levels of FDI. Both Malaysia and Singapore would fit into this particular model (Lim, 1991: 105), and this goes some way to explaining why FDI into Malaysia has been selected as a suitable context for the case study evidence presented in this book. An examination of how the process of FDI into the export-sector of certain developing countries is dependent upon gender inequalities not only suggests that the idea that MNCs can exert a "progressive" impact on local societies is rooted in certain gendered assumptions, but also sets up an important discussion concerning how the models of economic development are themselves dependent on gender inequalities.

Women's employment in MNCs and the New International Division of Labour

A recognition of the gendered nature of these export-led growth strategies emerged in a number of key works from the late 1970s and early 1980s. In particular, these writings noted the role of MNCs in establishing patterns of female labour force participation (FLFP) whereby large numbers of young, unmarried women migrated from rural areas to work in the expanding export sector industries (Fernandez Kelly, 1981; Nash, 1983). These authors sought to discuss the growth of women's employment in light manufacturing for export within the context of the emergence of a New International Division of Labour (NIDL) whereby manufacturing firms involved in labour intensive production (in particular in the garment and electronics sectors) sought to reduce their production costs by re-locating their assembly line operations to developing economies where labour costs were considerably cheaper (Safa, 1981). There are three main reasons given for the NIDL. Firstly, the expansion of Western trade that occurred in the post-war period leading to increased competition between firms based in the industrialized countries forcing them to seek new ways of keeping (labour) costs low. Consequently, these industries were often dubbed "runaway" or "footloose" capital (Safa, 1981). Secondly, technological developments such as improved transportation and communications made such shifts possible (Heyzer, 1989: 1116-1117). Finally, the emergence of a group of countries engaged in export-led development strategies often involved incentives to foreign firms to locate their production there through the establishment of FTZs and other incentives (Lim, 1985). The rise in female employment in the developing world was therefore linked directly to the decline in women's employment in these industries in industrialized countries (Mitter, 1986: 2).

This feminist literature provides an alternative to the liberal view-point that multinational firms have a beneficial impact upon the role and position of women in the societies that they invest in. The NIDL writers portray women's employment in export sector manufacturing as low wage, monotonous assembly line work in jobs structured in such a way that career progression is very limited and consequently women's employment is confined to low wage employment in a limited range of industries. Thus despite access to formal waged employment, women remain peripheral to the process of economic development.

The attitudes that employers have toward their female labour force is an important element of this model of women's MNC employment in the export-sector. Women are regarded as secondary workers in the labour market, their incomes merely supplementing that of a male "breadwinner". At the same time, other perceptions of the female worker as "diligent, dextrous and nimble fingered" also mean that employers see women as an ideal source of workers for routine assembly line work (Elson and Pearson, 1981). In chapters five and six of this book, it will be shown how these perceptions about the woman worker have remained, and actually contribute to the low waged nature of these jobs because the skills that women utilize on the factory floor are viewed as natural/innate rather than developed in the workplace. Furthermore, the preference for female workers in assembly line work also stems from the way that women workers are perceived as less likely to be involved in union activities that might force up wage costs.

For authors such as Mitter, however, the lack of unionization in the FTZs is not so much a reflection of women's natural "docility", but a consequence of the way that the state in many developing countries has sought to maintain a low wage female labour force through the suppression of union activities. She notes, for example, the success with which "militarized" or authoritarian states have been able to attract FDI (Mitter, 1986: 69-70).[5] Through the curtailing of labour activism in the export sector, these authoritarian states thus provide the institutional support for economic development policies based largely upon the exploitation of low wage labour. Mitter's analysis draws heavily upon the NIDL work associated with Fröbel and others (Fröbel, Heinrichs, and Kreye, 1980; Jenkins, 1987), which, in turn drew upon the structuralist traditions of the dependency writers. An alliance of interests between the state and multinational capital thus locks these states into a position of "dependent development", something that Mitter has suggested is not a sustainable route towards economic development: "the only benefit seems to be the creation of employment of a rather vulnerable and unbalanced nature" (Mitter, 1986: 69). Integral to this process is the construction of women as low wage earners, a process mediated by both international capital and the state. Maria Mies' work is notable here (Mies, 1982, 1986; Mies, Bennholdt-Thomsen, and Welfhof, 1988). Mies introduces the concept of "housewifization" (a concept developed in her earlier work *The Lacemakers of Narsapur* (Mies, 1982)), in order to explain how the construction of women as secondary, low wage, income earners is supported by a collusion of interests between the state and international capital. Thus the notion of the woman as housewife takes on a form of political and ideological control over women (Mies, 1986: 116).

This more structuralist approach to women's employment in a NIDL has been heavily criticized on a number of grounds. It is suggested that it places far too much importance on the role of multinational firms in the development of new sources of female employment in the global economy, and that it fails to recognize the relatively better working conditions found in MNCs compared to local firms in the same sector (Lim, 1991). Furthermore, it could be suggested that this is an approach that simply casts women as "victims" of global capitalism and fails to recognize the many benefits that waged employment may bring to women. However, it is argued here that although works such as Mitter's *Common Fate Common Bond: Women in the Global Economy* (1986) do tend to oversimplify the relationship between FDI and the nature of women's employment, the NIDL approach remains useful in that it recognizes firstly, how gendered inequalities are key in multinational firm's decisions to invest overseas and secondly, the way in which the state acts to shore up this gender inequality through anti-unionism in the female dominated export sectors. But it is worth noting that although these writings do emphasize the role of the multinational firm, they recognize the broader context within which these developments are taking place. The growth in

---

[5] See also, Enloe (1983), pp. 407-425.

multinational firms employing female labour in the export sector in a small number of developing countries reflects the broader trend of increased female labour force participation in a number of states in the developing world that have implemented policies of export-led growth.

Recent feminist writings on the MNC

Despite the fact that the emphasis on the MNC found in the feminist NIDL perspective, has been criticized by writers such as Lim (1991), the MNC remains an important subject of study for feminist political economists. Writers such as Elson and Pearson (1989) have suggested that although the MNCs may not constitute the major employers of female workers in the export sector (as Lim (1991) has emphasized), they are worth focussing on because they possess a "transformatory capacity" that could bring about real changes to the role and position of women in the workforce.

> We should expect multinationals to be in the forefront of improving women's work opportunities… most multinationals have devoted much more effort to restructuring the international organization of their activities than to restructuring the sexual division of labour in manufacturing so as to improve women's opportunities (Elson and Pearson, 1989: 1).

The extent to which MNCs actually perform a "role model" function is thus cast into doubt. Although there is a general consensus that MNCs may well offer better rates of pay and working conditions compared to local firms (Lim, 1991), this is not always the case, and the evidence suggests that MNCs are just as likely as local firms to crowd women workers into the lowest paid work (Elson and Pearson, 1989: 2). Recent work from Mexico has suggested that rather than comparing the conditions of employment for women workers in multinational firms with local firms in the same sector, a more useful comparison is to look at the alternative forms of employment available to women especially in the clerical and service sectors. Many female workers no longer regard employment in the *maquiladora* industries as a desirable option (Pearson, 1995: 161) and consequently these export-industries have sought to draw upon new sources of low cost labour; women with children and relatively uneducated women who constitute a sector of the labour force with few other employment options (Fussell, 2000: 63, 69-72). It has been suggested that such a situation, rather than revealing the ability of MNCs to transform employment practices, instead represents "a race to the bottom in manufacturing wages resulting from the globalization of production" (Fussell, 2000: 77).

An alternative line of argument has suggested that the negative dimension of employment in an export-oriented MNC is not so much to do with the rates of pay available to women working in MNCs but with the conditions of work. The needs of the parent firm, may therefore, lead to an intensification of the production process, with workers expected to achieve high targets and work long hours. Elson and Pearson have suggested that this is often because MNCs are not only concerned with keeping labour costs as low as possible, but also with maintaining the levels of productivity and flexibility that are necessary for production on a global scale (Elson and Pearson, 1989: 3). Women are thus preferred as employees because they can be easily controlled, are regarded as more diligent workers and are consequentially seen as the preferable employees in globally organized systems of production that are based around fast response times and short-run orders. A process that has been labelled by Fussell as "making labour flexible" (Fussell, 2000).

What is common, then, to both the NIDL writers and the more recent work by scholars such as Fussell is the view that the firm takes an active role in the creation of gendered divisions within the workforce. It is very difficult to suggest that the firm can actually perform as a "role model" to local employers in the way that the liberal mainstream has suggested, given that its recruitment practices are largely based upon securing low cost labour and draw women from the least advantaged local social groups in order to maintain the low cost of labour. In this sense, the firm benefits from gender (and ethnic) workplace divisions; it is suggested in this book that these divisions are an integral feature of the process of FDI rather than external to it.

Export-led growth as female-led

The literature that focuses specifically on women's employment in MNCs is rather limited. Thus it is useful to place the studies outlined above within the context of broader studies of the role of women in export-led economic development. The expansion of employment opportunities for women that accompanied the shift to export led development is well documented. For example, Heyzer (1989: 1117) notes that in Malaysia in the ten years following the adoption of export-oriented industrialization women's employment rate in the formal (waged) sector doubled. This reflects the more general trend linking export orientation to rapid growth of female waged employment with virtually all countries with established FTZs experiencing faster employment growth among women than for men. Many authors conclude that the economic growth experienced in the Asian "miracle" economies was as much "female-led" as "export-led" (Greenhalgh, 1985). Table 2.1 indicates that female employment increased at a much more rapid rate compared to male employment during the 1970s in a range of East and Southeast Asian countries that embarked on export orientation strategies either during the 1960s (Taiwan and Singapore) or the 1970s (Malaysia and Thailand). Indeed, it has been suggested that these "second wave" Southeast Asian newly industrializing countries replicated the East Asian model of export-led growth that depended heavily on the absorption of low cost female labour into the formal waged economy (Joekes and Weston, 1994). Such findings, therefore, suggest something of a causal link between export orientation and high levels of female employment.

**Table 2.1 Relative growth of male and female employment in manufacturing,
       1970s**

Average annual employment growth

Country	Male	Female
Taiwan (1970-1980)	9.9	16.2
Singapore (1979-1980)	6.1	11.4
Malaysia (1970-9)	11.0	16.6
Thailand (1970-6)	10.9	16.0

Source: Lim (1993), 'The Feminization of Labour in the Asia-Pacific Rim Countries: From
       Contributing to Economic Dynamism to Bearing the Brunt of Structural
       Adjustments' in N. Ogawa, G.W. Jones, and Jeffrey G. Williamson (eds.), *Human
       Resources in Development along the Asia-Pacific Rim*, Singapore: Oxford
       University Press, 178.

The discussion of global trends in female employment and the emergence of an
export-manufacturing sector in a number of developing countries is one that has
warranted particular attention from a number of economists writing in journals
such as *World Development*. These authors have sought to test statistically the idea
that there is a general model of female employment whereby export-orientation
leads to increases in low wage female employment (Joekes, 1987).   These
observations that export oriented development strategies lead to increases in the
share of women employed in the industrial sector has been investigated in a
statistical study by Wood (1991). Using data concerning women's formal sector
employment in manufacturing, Wood notes the strong tendency for increased
export orientation to lead to increased employment of women in manufacturing.

In explaining the high levels of female employment in export-oriented
economies, it is important to note the general patterns of female employment that
occur within these economies.   It is notable that female employment is
concentrated in specific sectors of the economy, particularly those more inclined
towards exports. It is shown in figures 2.1 and 2.2, that the female employment
share in key export industries such as garments and electronics is considerable.
These are light manufacturing industries with labour intensive assembly line
production and consequently a requirement for low wage labour. Figures 2.1 and
2.2 indicate the high levels of female employment in the clothing and the
electronics sectors in countries that have, since at least the 1970s, adopted export-
led growth strategies centred on these kinds of industries (Seguino, 2000). But it
has also been noted that high levels of female employment have been found in

certain newly emerging export sector industries in the Asian "tiger" economies, for example in finance and services (Joekes and Weston, 1994: 53).

Figure 2.1   Women's share of jobs in the clothing industry (%), selected countries, 1977-1990

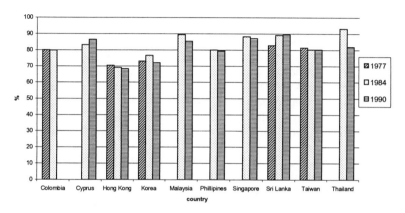

Source: Seguino, S. (2000), 'Gender Inequality and Economic Growth: A Cross Country Analysis', *World Development*, Vol. 28(7), pp. 1211-1230.

Figure 2.2   Women's share of jobs in the electronics industry (%), selected countries, 1977-1990

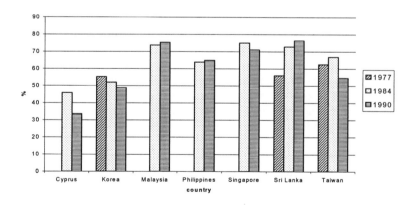

Source: Seguino, S. (2000), 'Gender Inequality and Economic Growth: A Cross Country Analysis', *World Development*, Vol. 28(7), pp. 1211-1230.

Standing (1989, 2000) has linked these developments to a deregulation of labour markets that has accompanied the global shift towards a more liberal market economy. Labelling this process "Global Feminization through Flexible labour", Standing's work suggests that policies of EOI as well as structural adjustment are symptomatic of this shift to a more liberal global market economy and leads to the emergence of "feminized" jobs such as assembly line work in which there is little to no protection of the worker. Although it is difficult to draw conclusive arguments from such a general study of global employment trends, the idea of a feminization of employment does offer an interesting insight into how one might deal with the liberal claims presented in the first section of this chapter that MNC employment can significantly raise the status of women in a local economy because of the better terms and conditions of work available in these firms. The discrimination, low wages and lack of career prospects found in jobs traditionally associated with female employment are unlikely to alter since these traits are built into the construction of available jobs. Thus Ibrahim (1989) has suggested that there are limited opportunities for women to move into better paid occupations:

> This so-called feminization of labour is problematic for those who champion greater access to formal sector jobs for women. Of particular concern, replacement by women does not reflect women's advances in education, training or skills, but is instead related directly to a degradation process affecting the jobs that they move into (Ibrahim, 1989: 198).

A number of studies have sought to address these issues – particularly those relating to rates of pay that women receive within the export sector. Mehra and Gammage, for example, have suggested that the male-female wage differentials are greatest in countries where the female share of employment is increasing rapidly and the manufacturing sector has grown most rapidly (Mehra and Gammage, 1999: 534), a finding that fits with the general model of female-led export oriented industrialization. Of course, findings concerning low levels of pay and wage inequality are to a certain extent challenged by those authors who argue that women employed in MNCs face better pay and working conditions compared to women employed in local firms (Joekes, 1987). However, despite the relative differences between rates of pay in MNCs and local firms, the absolute picture in states pursuing EOI is one of extreme gender inequality. Recent studies have suggested that there is an important link between gender inequality (in terms of rates of pay) and the model of export-led economic development practised in much of East and Southeast Asia.

Seguino's recent work on gender inequality and economic development in Asia has found that gender inequality in Asia is amongst the highest in the world, and argues that this inequality was itself fundamental to the making of the so-called "economic miracle". The Asian "miracle" is usually characterized in terms of rapid economic growth, whilst at the same time levels of inequality remained relatively low (Seguino, 2000). However, such studies were based largely on household data that failed to take gender into account. What Seguino's work, therefore contributes to the debates surrounding EOI and women's employment is to bring the statistical support to earlier claims such as those made by Greenhalgh that the crowding of women into low wage, low status employment represented "the other side of growth with equity" (Greenhalgh, 1985). Given that the model of EOI often involves incentives to multinational investors, it would appear to be the case that the feminization of the labour force in semi-industrialized economies acts as a stimulus to FDI.

What such findings show is that a male-biased (or, as Ling (1999) would put it, "hypermasculine") model of economic growth systematically disadvantages women. Multinational investment into export-oriented East and Southeast Asian economies depends upon women workers as a source of low cost labour and, consequently, women are stratified into the lower segments of the industrial workforce. These macro-economic studies provide a general picture of women's subordinate position within the labour market in developing countries undertaking EOI strategies. What these studies fail to do, however, is to consider how gender becomes such an important component in the making of this model of economic development. Indeed, this is hardly surprising given that most of these studies utilize traditional tools of economic analysis such as the theory of comparative advantage in understandings of gender inequality. Gender inequality, therefore becomes largely a debate about rates of pay with little to no analysis of why women's rates of pay are so considerably lower than men's in the first place (Tzannos, 1999: 558). Consideration, therefore, needs to be given to those writings that actually deal with the social context that women workers operate within. What is needed is an appreciation of the gendered nature of the labour "market" (Elson, 1999: 611-627; Razavi, 1999a: 678). Rather than viewing gender inequality as a result of global capitalism's search for cheap labour or in terms of the dependence of a particular economic development model on low cost female labour, it is necessary to consider how these factors interact with a labour market embedded within local social structures. The firm that constitutes the case study in this book is viewed as drawing upon well established patterns of gender inequality, thus it is useful to look at the work of those scholars who have considered the social context within which women's formal labour force participation takes place within the export-sector.

Women's experience of employment in world market factories

There is a very large literature that examines women's experience of employment in MNCs, FTZs and the export sector in general. It is not the intention here to overview all of this literature, but rather to highlight some of its main themes, drawing mainly upon studies of women workers in the export sector from East and Southeast Asia. The three main themes that emerge from these studies are, firstly, the emphasis on the household context of women's formal labour force participation. Secondly, the work suggests the importance of differences between different groups of women – in other words looking at how gender inequalities intersect with other forms of inequality such as class, race, ethnicity and rural-urban divides as well as divisions based upon age and educational status within a specific social context. Finally, there are those writings that have emphasized how women have sought to resist some of the forms of inequality that they face in export sector factories, or specifically in the MNCs. This literature, which is usually found within sociology and anthropology, thus provides the other-side to the macro-economic perspectives on gender and EOI outlined above. These in-depth studies are of considerable use in explaining why women work and how they have experienced employment in the export-sector.

Many feminist studies suggest that the pattern of female employment in the export sector whereby women are grouped into low paid work stems from the patriarchal nature of society and, in particular, the role and position of women within the family. Gallin for example has claimed that:

> This traditional ideology effectively shapes them [women] into the kind of labour force required – that is one that is docile, minimally trained, tractable and willing to accept low pay, lacklustre jobs, and irregular work depending on the exigencies of the economy (Gallin, 1990: 185).

Such statements are typical of much of the early studies of women's experience of employment in the NICs. It was suggested that the shared Confucian traditions of these societies served to lock women into inferior positions within the household, which fed into the gender inequality within the workplace. Writers such as Arrigo (1980), Salaff (1981), Greenhalgh (1985) and Gallin (1990) have described a model of the Confucian household whereby parents have complete control over the earnings of daughters and given that daughters effectively leave the household on marriage, there was considerable pressure on young women to engage in the new factory jobs that were emerging in the NICs during the 1960s and 1970s. The usefulness of such studies is that they highlight the interplay between capitalism and patriarchal social relations as women enter the formal labour market. Clearly export sector firms benefit from the subordinate position that women occupy in the labour market, a position that reflects her own role and position within society.

However, such studies do tend to over simplify the relationship between women's employment in the global market economy and their subordinate role in society. There is very little analysis of how women's ability to earn income might impact positively upon their role and position within the family. Looking at women's employment in a very different social context, studies from Southeast Asia have drawn attention to the way in which women's ability to earn in the export sector factories may actually contribute to a rise in their status within the household.[6] Furthermore, it is also clear that the model of female export-sector employment established in the NICs and replicated in countries such as Malaysia is itself changing. Most notable is the rise in numbers of married women employed in the export industry, so whereas earlier accounts of female factory work usually described them as young unmarried women who would either be sacked or cease to work on marriage, this is no longer the case (Pyle, 1994: 143).

---

[6] In particular the work of Diane Wolf (1992) on factory women in Java.

Interestingly, the rise in married women's employment in the export sector has often reflected government policies aimed at increasing married women's labour force participation in order to deal with problems of labour shortages that were perceived as undermining export competitiveness (i.e. labour costs). Indeed, it is important to recognize the role of government policy-making in the development of a low cost female labour force (a theme that is developed in chapter three). Studies of women's employment in MNCs need to recognize, therefore, that the nature of gender inequalities vary across states and reflects an interplay between government development policies, local social values and institutions and the demands of multinational capital for low cost labour. Fundamental to this kind of "holistic" approach to gender and FDI, is a recognition not only of how FDI is a process that benefits from the existence of gendered divisions and hierarchies, but also to consider how other forms of social division or inequality intersect with these patterns.

The writings on women's experience of employment in MNCs from feminist scholars have placed a certain amount of emphasis on the ability of women to try and resist some of the worst aspects of factory employment. These studies have often focussed attention on women organising in trade unions. However, given the point raised earlier in this section that the state in many Asian export-led economies has systematically acted against the formation of unions in the export sector, many writers have sought to look for examples of women's resistance to global capitalism in terms of everyday acts of rebellion (Ong, 1987).

The usefulness of these studies is that they bring women's experiences into the analysis of a global process such as FDI. This represents a shift away from the generalized assertions about the beneficial impact of FDI found in the mainstream literature. It presents case-study evidence concerning the impact of FDI on female workers and brings in important issues relating to women's agency and globalization, moving away from perspectives that cast women as "victims" of global capitalism (Razavi, 1999b). From this "experiences" literature, we can see that the process of FDI is not universally beneficial to women, yet at the same time can offer women some opportunities for changes to their role and position within society (Elson and Pearson, 1981: 31-33).

This book, however, moves away from a concern simply with women's experience of employment, and look instead at the issue of recruitment – investigating how the recruitment process operates to confine many women to low paid assembly line work. The aim is to utilize the case study methodology found in the "experiences" literature and apply it to a study of how a MNC impacts upon gender relations in a local society. Thus the use of detailed case study research in this book will help to develop a clearer understanding of how notions of the "progressive firm" need to be replaced in favour of a gendered political economy perspective on the MNC.

Chapter 3

FDI and the Political Economy of Malaysian Development

Introduction: The state and economic development

In the previous chapter, it was established that the process of Foreign Direct Investment (FDI) in the export-manufacturing sector is gendered; drawing women into employment in multinational corporations (MNCs) seeking low wage employment in offshore locations. This chapter turns to consider the role played by the state in the promotion of this model of FDI-led development directed toward the export sector, focusing on the experience of Malaysia. What this discussion shows is that the construction of Malaysia as an appropriate site for FDI, is closely tied to the emergence of a low paid, unorganized female workforce. Such a discussion, therefore, confirms the argument put forward in the previous chapter concerning the importance of taking a gender perspective when looking at the issue of export-led economic development. A consideration of Malaysia's experience of export oriented industrialization (EOI), shows how the gender divisions that were so crucial to the formation of a low waged labour force were cross-cut with other social cleavages, most importantly those relating to ethnicity. Indeed, the suggestion is made that whilst the direction of economic development strategies in Malaysia since the 1970s was overtly shaped by the politics of ethnicity, implicit to these strategies were assumptions regarding the role of low cost female labour in export-oriented development.

"Statist" economic development in East and Southeast Asia

In attempting to explain how the state sought to construct Malaysia as an appropriate site for FDI (and thereby, according to liberal models of economic development, become more fully integrated into the global market system) it is relevant to refer back to the work of Polanyi. It was shown in chapter one that Polanyi utilizes a historical argument, based upon evidence from Britain's industrial revolution to argue that the market economy was politically constructed in its origins (Polanyi 1957: 139-40). Parallels, therefore, might be drawn between Polanyi's argument that 19th century economic liberals called for state intervention in order to establish and maintain the market system (Polanyi 1957: 149), and recent debates on the nature of state interventionism in East and Southeast Asia.

A "statist" position concerning economic development in East and Southeast Asia, has re-established the importance of looking at the transformatory potential of the "developmental state" in the economic development process (Amsden, 1989; Rodan, 1989; Wade, 1990). This is a theme that characterized the earlier development thinking of scholars such as Myrdal who linked state development strategies to understandings of the need to develop effective state institutions which could guard against the control of state apparatus and bureaucracy by powerful elite groups in society (Myrdal, 1968). Chalmers Johnson's study of the Japanese State drew upon these themes in his analysis of the "Capitalist Developmental State". Key features of this type of state are its technocratic bureaucracy insulated from direct political influence, clear demarcation between the state and the private sector and a preference for market-oriented interventions based on the price mechanism. These are all part of what Johnson terms the "plan-rational" approach to economic development (Johnson, 1982) which, he argued, shared many similarities with the role of the state in the development process in many of the NICs (Johnson, 1987). The influence of these statist perspectives has recently crept into World Bank development thinking. The characterization of the state found in the World Bank's publication *The East Asian Miracle* (1993), for example, draws upon ideas from new institutionalist economics (North, 1990; Stiglitz, 1989) in order to conceptualize state interventionism largely in terms of adherence to market principles ("getting the fundamentals [i.e. the policies] right") (World Bank 1993: 23-26, 352-354).

An embedded state?

It is important not to regard the institutional basis of economic development in Asia purely in terms of an ideal model of economic development that all states are able to replicate. The significance attached to ethnic politics or gender relations in shaping Malaysia's industrial policy-making procedures is an interpretation of Malaysian economic development which has often been overlooked by scholars pre-occupied with the identification of regional patterns and economic "models" of Asian development (World Bank, 1993). Thus a number of writers have approached the study of economic development in Southeast Asia by looking in detail at the way in which market based systems have emerged as the product of social and political interest and conflict. A more historically grounded approach to economic development in East and Southeast Asia is emphasized in certain more "radical"[1] writings. Rasiah (1997), for example, writes that although the new institutionalist interventions into the developmental state debates have served a useful purpose, these accounts focus too much on policy-makers *per se* and fail to appreciate the intricate web of social relationships that underpin these specific institutional set-ups.

---

[1] The use of the term "radical" here refers to the usage of the term by Rasiah Rajah who describes his approach to the study of Malaysian economic development as stemming from a "radical political economy" perspective. Rasiah Rajah (1997: 121). The term is used very broadly to include a number of scholars working from Marxist, pluralist and social constructivist perspectives (see Robison, Rodan, and Hewison (1997: 13-15)).

Many writings on the developmental state which simply stress the adherence of the state to basic market-principles could be regarded in terms of these under-socialized accounts of actor (in this case state) behaviour. It is therefore interesting to apply Polanyi's holistic methodology and notion of social embeddedness to an understanding of the state (Rai, 1998). A conceptualization of the state as "embedded" enables us to build into our understanding of the developmental role of the state issues such as the unique nature of the transition from colonialism, or the specific form that gender and ethnic divisions take within society. Writing on the experience of economic development in Malaysia, Rasiah (1997: 121) notes that "the explanation for the transformation must trace a complex set of historical factors and tensions derived from Malaysia's colonial legacy that have been addressed through economic policy since independence". This is a reference to "competing class interests" and how they are "enmeshed with an ethnic politics that has deep roots in the colonial experience" (Rasiah, 1997: 122).

This "embedding" of the state opens up a space for looking at how gender relations (cross-cut with class and ethnic relations) are themselves concealed within liberal conceptualizations of a gender-neutral state, and how these gender relations are at the same time formed by the state (Waylen, 1998: 1-17), thus "gender practices become institutionalized in historically specific state forms" (Pringle and Watson, 1998). More importantly, a re-evaluation of the concept of the developmental state from a feminist perspective, reveals, the role of the (Malaysian) state in the construction of women as a source of low cost labour in order to compete for FDI. Thus it is argued in this chapter that the Malaysian state promoted a model of economic development that not only relied upon the availability of low cost female labour, but the state took steps in order to secure low labour costs. Examples of this process can be seen later in this chapter, where it is shown how the state acted to restrict trade union activities in the FTZs or, in the final section of this chapter, where there is discussion of the state's role in perpetuating the idea that women's primary role is within the home (thus legitimating the view that women are simply "secondary" workers). Indeed, the discussion presented in the final section of this chapter, raises the view that the role of the state in the creation of gendered subjects in Malaysia demonstrates how the state itself legitimates and reproduces the sorts of gendered social hierarchies that the MNCs sought to perpetuate by actively seeking out low cost female labour. Hence, it is the meeting of implicitly gendered state EOI strategies with the requirements of MNCs for low cost labour that form the backdrop to this study.

The development of export-led industrialization policy in Malaysia

The years since independence in Malaysia have witnessed a rapid transformation of the state's industrial and economic structure. In 1957, the year of Malaysia's independence from British colonial rule, the Malaysian economy was characterized by a peasant agricultural sector, on the one hand, and a foreign owned sector concentrated on primary production activities such as tin mining and plantation agriculture on the other. These primary sector industries accounted for 70% of export earnings in 1957. By 1990, one year after the case study firm's arrival in Malaysia, rubber and tin only accounted for 4.9% of total export earnings. Manufacturing was the big export earner by 1990, the result of export-oriented development policies that sought to expand the country's manufacturing base. This rapid industrial transformation relied heavily on FDI, and therefore it is necessary to look at the various different incentives that were offered to multinational investors as part of this industrialization strategy. However, questions also need to be raised regarding *why* the Malaysian State felt compelled to pursue a model of export-led development, which was heavily reliant on foreign investors. It is argued here that the Malaysian experience of export-led development cannot be understood without reference to the unique nature of ethnic relations/politics in Malaysia. Foreign capital came to play a very important role not simply in terms of the overall economic development of the country, but the government also saw foreign capital as essential to securing some sort of social restructuring along ethnic lines in what was known as the New Economic Policy (NEP).

Economic and political developments prior to 1969

To understand what could be described as the political economy of ethnicity in Malaysia, some discussion of the history of these ethnic cleavages is necessary. The dualistic nature of the Malaysian economy at independence (peasant agriculture and primary export industries) also reflected ethnic divisions in economic activities that were a product of British colonial rule. British rule in what was then Malaya had seen the large scale importation of labour from China and the Indian sub-continent to work as waged labourers in the mining and plantation sectors, whilst the original, mainly Malay, population remained confined to peasant agriculture. Such an ethnic division of labour was reflected spatially as cities became dominated by a newly emerging Chinese urban proletariat and business class. Despite the rapid growth of the Chinese business class (mainly in the retail and service sectors), political power was concentrated in the hands of the Malays, a consequence of British colonial political structures through which the Malays were positioned as the "natural rulers" of the country. The British founded their authority upon the idea that they were protecting Malay traditions (although the British also saw themselves as in the best position to define what these traditions actually were). The granting of land rights, governance through traditional (Malay) rulers, and attempts to incorporate aspects of *adat* (traditional) law were all based upon this myth of Malay privilege (Khan, 1997: 55).

In independent Malaysia, the post-colonial state remained a bastion of Malay political power (and also Malay employment). The post independence constitution enshrined a number of symbols of Malay political dominance such as Islam as an official religion and Malay as the official language and also allowed for a gerrymandering of the political system to ensure the dominance of Malay political parties (Crouch, 1993: 151). The formation of the Alliance party in the 1950s, an inter-ethnic party comprising the United Malay National Organization (UMNO), the Malaysian Chinese Congress (MCA) and the Malaysian Indian Congress

(MIC), was backed by the British and the dominance of UMNO within the Alliance shored up this Malay political hegemony (Milne and Mauzy, 1999: 16).

Surprisingly, given the political ascendancy of the Malays, economic policy up until the 1970s did not attempt to deal with the ethnic imbalance of the country's economy. Policies of industrialization based upon import substitution were introduced during the late 1950s, but this industrialization strategy tended to shore up the colonial legacies of ethnic divisions of labour. Khan notes that in the early independence period a newly emerging (albeit small) Malay middle class made up of government employees, businessmen and low-ranking party officials was especially vocal in their criticism of the way that independence continued to favour Chinese business interests and the Malay political elite (Khan, 1997: 56). Two *Bumiputera*[2] Congresses were held in 1965 and 1968, which provided a forum for these Malay nationalists to call for a restructuring of the economy in favour of the Malays. Furthermore, the import substituting industrialising phase of economic development from the 1950s until the late 1960s was characterized by economic growth yet rising inequality. There was a worsening distribution of income amongst all groups and rising unemployment (Jomo and Todd, 1994: 128). These ethnic imbalances contributed to political frustrations that spilled over in the racial riots of May 1969. The government attributed the riots largely to Malay frustrations at the economic success of the Chinese during the early years of independence (Crouch, 1993: 151).

The New Economic Policy

Following the events of 1969, the Malay dominated government acted to try and restructure state and society in an attempt to reassert the role and position of the Malays. The introduction of the NEP in 1970 came alongside the Second Malaysia Plan. The NEP ostensibly claimed to be a blueprint for socio-economic change which would both (a) decrease the incidence of poverty among all Malaysians and (b) eliminate ethnic inequalities in the economic structure of the nation (Malaysia, 1971: 1) (the latter claim usually referred to simply as "restructuring"). What this effectively meant was a radical shake-up of economic policymaking and state structures with the establishment of an array of quotas and institutions aimed at improving the representation of the Malay population in the modern corporate world. For example, it was claimed that within a single generation Malay corporate ownership and management would rise from just 1.9% of overall corporate ownership and management to 30% (Jomo, 1990: 155). This was a target that was not met, with Malay ownership of corporate assets standing at 20.3% in 1990. Although the National Development Policy (which replaced the NEP in 1990) maintained the target of 30%, unlike the NEP, it did not set a date for when

---

[2] The term Bumiputera means literally "sons" or "princes of the soil" and refers to all ethnic groups that comprise the "indigenous" population of Malaysia. However, although the term is a category that is supposed to represent a variety of ethnic groups, it is predominately Malay people (the dominant ethnic and political group in Malaysia) that the term usually refers to.

this goal would be realized (Leifer, 1995: 186). It is notable that these kinds of policies and social goals reflected many of the suggestions that had been put forward in the *Bumiputera* Congresses of the 1960s (Gomez, 1990: 51; Khan, 1997; Khoo Jy Jin, 1992).

Economic planning was viewed as central to the development policy shift. The then deputy Prime Minister, Tun Razak, effectively voiced many of the Malay criticisms that had emerged around 1969, recognising the challenge posed for subsequent governments when he claimed:

> The Government will take the initiative in industrialization and, if necessary, will participate in the establishment of industries either by itself or in joint venture with the private sector both local or foreign.[3]

What such a statement revealed was the extent to which economic planning for industrial development had become a government priority. From the 1970s onwards, the capacity of the state would be utilized to transform the ethnically based structure of the Malaysian economy, signifying a shift away from the more *Laissez-faire* state that had existed since independence (Jesudason, 1990: 76). The shift was reflected in the strengthening of the Economic Planning Unit (EPU), attached to the Prime Minister's Department, which occurred alongside the promotion of politically loyal, mainly Malay, staff within the Unit (Jesudason 1990: 78). Government policy relating to the development of a Malay-owned corporate sector was pursued through the expansion of state agencies and state owned enterprizes. These included; public enterprizes taking up share capital "in trust" for the *Bumiputera* (at least until they were in a position to purchase them); the establishment of agencies that would promote Malay businesses; and the establishment of public corporations and regional development corporations (either wholly or jointly-owned by the government) (Jomo, 1990: 155).

Post-NEP political developments: the securing of Malay political hegemony

The NEP can also be seen as a crucial aspect in the consolidation of Malay political power. The May 13 riots were a contributing factor to the fall in the Alliance vote by around 10% (although the party remained in political power, polling 48% of the vote and securing 66% of the seats in parliament) (Milne and Mauzy, 1999: 21). Following these events, Razak and his closest allies within government and the civil service undertook a series of political measures including the remodelling of the party system, co-opting opposition parties into a broader coalition party; the *Barisan Nasional* (BN) or National Front. During 1972, the non-Malay *Gerakan Ra'ayat Malaysia* party and, more significantly, the principle Malay opposition party *Parti Islam Se-Malaysia* (PAS) were brought into coalition governments at both the state and federal levels. The development of the BN was,

---

[3] Tun Abdul Razak, *New Economic Development Policy in a New Industrial Development Strategy* (Kuala Lumpur: Federal Industrial Development Authority, 1969), p. 2, cited in Cho (1990: 59).

LIVERPOOL
JOHN MOORES UNIVERSITY
AVRIL ROBARTS LRC
TEL. 0151 231 4022

therefore, a strategy whereby the dominance of UNMO was further consolidated through an effective neutralising of political opposition. It remained the pre-eminent political party in the Malaysian political system even after PAS left the BN in 1976. Furthermore, by actively promoting the interests of the majority Malay, or more generally *Bumiputera,* population, through the NEP, UMNO secured its power base as the "natural" party of government, protecting the interests of the "indigenous" population.

The policies of the NEP were always much more concerned with the position of the Malay population than other sections of the population. Gomez and Jomo have noted the growth of ethnically based patronage networks as the state machinery became much more closely associated with UMNO (Gomez and Jomo, 1997: 25). The expanded state was seen by many within the UMNO elite as a means through which Malay support could be guaranteed, for example through state subsidies, and lead to the development of a class of politically influential and economically powerful Malays (Gomez and Jomo, 1997: 26). The creation of this class, often through "money-politics" or "cronyism" has led certain scholars to suggest that the NEP was always much more about restructuring than about poverty reduction (in particular in building up a "new rich" Malay middle class) (Khan, 1997: 68). For example, there were little to no policies aimed at addressing rural poverty among Chinese and Indian groups. The Malaysian Indian Congress (MIC), part of the ruling BN, was especially vocal in its criticism that NEP policies had actually led to a deterioration in the position of the Indian population in Malaysian society (Gomez and Jomo, 1997: 40). However, it should be remembered that in 1970, the mainly rural Malay population did, on average, have much lower levels of household income compared to the Indian and Chinese population. In this year, the mean household income in Malay households was 44% of the mean income for Chinese households, and 57% of the mean income for Indian households (Shari, 2000: 118).

Between 1970 and 1990 Malaysia's economic growth was accompanied by a reduction in absolute poverty and income inequality. The major cause in the decline of absolute poverty is attributed to export-led industrialization, which had the effect of transferring many Malays from the rural (often peasant-based) agricultural sector into industrial employment (Shari, 2000: 199). If we look at figures on occupational categories in Malaysia in the post-NEP era, it is evident that there have been huge shifts in Malay employment in the industrial sector. For example, in 1970, 34.2% of production workers were classified as *Bumiputera*, 55.9% were Chinese and 9.6% Indian. By 1995, these statistics had changed considerably; 44.8% of production workers were classified as *Bumiputera*, Chinese made up 35% and Indians 10.3% (Malaysia, 1981; 1996: 82-82).

The impact of this industrialization programme is also witnessed in the rapid growth of the urban population that has occurred since 1970. The overall urban population rose from 1,666,969 in 1957 to 4,073,100 by 1980 (Sha'ban Muftah Isma'il, 1997). Rates of urbanization among Malays contributed significantly to the overall rate of urbanization. In 1957, 21% of the urban population were Malay, a figure that had risen to 37.9% by 1980. More significantly, the percentage of Malays living in urban areas rose from 11.2% to 25.2% over the same period.

Table 3.1 presents these figures in more detail, showing how these rates of growth among the Malay population were considerably higher than those for other ethnic groups.

Table 3.1 Ethnic composition of urban areas, percentage of each ethnic group living in urban areas and average annual growth rate of urban populations, 1957-1980, Peninsular Malaysia

Census year	Malays	Chinese	Indians
	Ethnic composition of urban areas (%)		
1957	21.0	62.6	12.8
1970	27.6	58.4	12.7
1980	37.9	50.3	11.0
	Percentage of each ethnic group living in urban areas		
1957	11.2	44.7	30.7
1970	14.9	47.4	34.7
1980	25.2	56.1	41.0
	Average annual growth of urban populations (%)		
1957	5.3	0.4	0.9
1970	7.9	1.8	1.8

Source: Sha'ban Muftah Isma'il (1997), *Women, Economic Growth and Development in Malaysia*, Petailing Jaya, Malaysia, IBS Buku, table 5.1, 10.

But the reduction in income inequality that occurred in the 1970s and 1980s was, argues Shari (2000), also a result of the state's interventionist employment restructuring strategies. These were not centred on the foreign dominated export sector, rather, the enlarged public sector provided large-scale opportunities for Malay employment, especially among educated Malays. The export-sector, by comparison provided mainly low paid production work for rural female Malays. The recruitment of Malay women into industrial employment will be considered in more detail later on in this chapter, but it is worth bearing in mind that for the bulk of rural Malays drawn into the industrial sector, job opportunities were often confined to production work with limited opportunities for career advancement (Shari, 2000). It is also worth noting that although the opportunities for employment in the export sector did contribute to a decline in levels of poverty and ethnic inequalities, the Malay population continued to constitute the bulk of the rural poor and, overall, the Chinese population of Malaysia has remained concentrated in urban areas (see table 3.1) and, is also considerably wealthier than the other ethnic groups (Shari 2000: 119). Managerial and Professional occupational categories remain Chinese dominated. In 1995, Chinese made up 27.3% of the total population of Malaysia and yet accounted for 54.7% of this occupational category (by contrast Malays made up 61.7% of the total population but just 36.1% of this occupational category) (Malaysia 1996: 82-83).

FDI and export-led development

The ambitious targets of the NEP (as set out in the Second Malaysia Plan) to reduce poverty and ethnic based inequality were predicated on economic growth. EOI based upon the attraction of FDI came to play a central role in the achievement of these objectives. The Investment Incentives Act of 1968 officially began the period of EOI, but it was only with the Free Trade Zone Act of 1971, which offered tariff free bases and tax exemptions to export oriented enterprizes, that the flow of FDI into Malaysia rose rapidly. Domestic capital (mainly Chinese entrepreneurs) was not generally attracted to these export-oriented industries mainly because these were industries that required access to international markets and high levels of capital and technology (Gomez and Jomo, 1997: 40; Jomo and Edwards, 1993: 6-7).

Incentives on offer to foreign investors took the form of partial or total relief from payment of income tax in specific sectors. The sectors that were pinpointed for increased levels of foreign investment were generally those involved in the manufacture of goods for export – particularly in the labour intensive light manufacturing sectors such as electronic assembly and garment production. Firms in the FTZs used mainly imported machinery and equipment, and the FTZ system encouraged in transnational corporations who were globally relocating sections of the production process offshore (Jomo, 1990: 114). The rapid increase in export processing from 1972 onwards was sustained by multinational firms who were eager to find tax-free bases in low cost countries such as Malaysia. The rise of export manufacturing enabled Malaysia to increase its manufacturing sector sizeably since, it is generally agreed in most of the literature on industrialization in Malaysia that, by the late 1960s, the domestic producing import substitution industries were limited by the low levels of domestic demand (Jomo and Edwards, 1993: 18-28). The rapidly rising importance of manufacturing industry to the Malaysian economy since the implementation of the EOI development policies is revealed in table 3.2 and indicates a quite significant rise in the importance of the manufacturing sector in terms of both output and employment.

What the figures in table 3.2 do not reveal is the contribution of multinational investment to the rise in employment and output in the manufacturing sector. The share of foreign ownership in manufacturing has actually declined since the 1960s, but in certain key export sectors such as textiles and garments and electrical/electronic equipment, foreign investment has risen significantly. In 1970 the foreign ownership share in textiles and garments stood at 39%, yet had risen to 61% by 1990. For the electronics and electrical products sector these figures were 67% and 89% respectively (Rasiah, 1997). The significance of foreign investment in these two sectors of the Malaysian economy is especially relevant given that these are the two sectors where female employment is highest.

Table 3.2 Manufacturing industry's contribution to GDP and employment in Malaysia, 1947-1997

Year	Manufacturing Value Added as a % of total GDP	Manufacturing Employment ('000s)	Manufacturing Employment as a % of total Employment
1947a	5.7	126	6.7
1957a	6.3	136	6.4
1960a	8.7	n.a.	n.a.
1965a	10.4	217	8.4
1970	13.1	448	11.4
1975	16.4	n.a.	n.a.
1980	19.6	755	15.8
1985	19.7	836	15.1
1986	20.9	818	14.7
1987	22.5	921	15.7
1988	24.4	1,013	16.6
1989	25.5	1,171	18.4
1990	26.9	1,290	19.4
1991	28.2	1,374	20.1
1992	28.9	1,639	22.9
1993	30.1	1,742	23.6
1994		1,892.1	24.8
1995		2051.6	25.9
1996		2177.8	26.7
1997		2,316.9	27.7

(a)   Peninsular Malaysia only

Sources: Jomo, K.S. and Edwards, C. (1993), 'Malaysian Industrialization in Historical Perspective' in K.S. Jomo (ed.), *Industrialising Malaysia: Policy Performance Profits*, London: Routledge. Malaysia, Department of Statistics (1998), *Social Statistics Bulletin: Malaysia 1998*, Kuala Lumpur: Department of Statistics.

Multinational investment was encouraged into Malaysia as a means through which the state sought to secure economic growth and NEP objectives. State planners aimed to attract FDI into the sorts of industries that were likely to create high levels of employment. The Malaysian Industrial Development Authority (MIDA), operating a number of offices worldwide, as well as at state and federal level, took on the role of the main body through which Malaysia was promoted to overseas investors and to which applications were made. The types of firms that invested in Malaysia's export manufacturing sector were generally involved in light assembly and/or labour intensive manufacturing. Electronics, in particular, established a huge export presence in Malaysia, although the textiles and garment sector was also targeted as the sort of industry that would rapidly absorb the rural Malay pool of (low cost female) labour largely involved in peasant agriculture.

The role of FDI in Malaysian economic development invariably reflected ethnic considerations. Jesudason suggests that such was the government's priority to restructure the control of industry away from the Chinese elite, that it was willing to increase Malaysia's dependence on foreign capital (Jesudason, 1990: 167). Indeed, whilst the (expanding) public sector as well as domestic sector industries faced, under the NEP, a number of quotas regarding the employment of *Bumiputera*, firms in the export sector were generally not subject to these controls. An increased level of foreign ownership was viewed as preferable to an expansion of the Chinese economic power base and foreign capital became central to the government's economic plans as well as their wider commitment to the policy of restructuring.

State policy and foreign investment in the 1980s

Having outlined the background to Malaysia's export-led development policies and the desire to bring in foreign investment, it is now necessary to look more specifically at what the investment climate was like in Malaysia at the time of the arrival of the case study firm in 1989. The early 1970s had seen a surge of foreign investment into the export sector in line with the government's commitment to export-led industrialization concentrated on labour intensive light manufacturing-for-export. During the period 1971-1975, the yearly growth of manufacturing exports had averaged 27.5% (Jomo and Edwards, 1993: 15). By the late 1970s, however, government industrial policy makers attempted to shift the focus of industrial planning towards heavier state-run industries such as automobiles and steel. This shift to heavy industrialization policies was again motivated by the demands for ethnic restructuring. The NEP had made claims about the development of a Malay business class, yet was predicated upon policies that involved a strong reliance on foreign multinational investment. From the early 1980s onwards, the government of Mahatir Mohammed sought to sponsor the development of this Malay business class with this government-led inroad into heavy industrialization.

However, a period of world economic recession in the early to mid 1980s, which hit the export sector exceptionally hard, and the overall failure of much of the heavy industrialization projects produced a situation in which the government sought to attract foreign investment with a renewed enthusiasm. Foreign capital was granted a range of generous investment incentives with the enactment of the Promotion of Investment Act (PIA) in 1986. This act came after the launching of the Industrial Master Plan, an economic report that had levelled criticisms at the Government's attempts to develop heavy industries. What is more, many policies associated with the NEP had worried foreign investors. The Industrial Co-ordination Act (ICA) of 1975, for example, was presented as a piece of legislation that would ensure the orderly growth of the industrial sector, yet sent worries throughout non *Bumiputra* investors (including foreign investors). The act was perceived as an attempt to extend *Bumiputera* involvement in terms of equity ownership in the country's manufacturing sector – thus for example, foreign equity ownership was limited, outside of the FTZs, to 30%. Following the ICA, *Bumiputera* participation in government approved manufacturing projects had risen massively. Alongside the PIA measures of the 1980s, therefore, the government also introduced changes to the ICA restrictions on equity ownership. Foreign equity ownership was permitted up to 80% for high exporters, and even firms that exported 20-51% of their production were allowed 51% foreign-owned stock. Consequently, over the period 1985-1989, foreign equity participation in manufacturing projects approved by state agencies rose from 17.8% to 73.9% (Nobuyaki, 1991: 340-1). A UNIDO study of industrialization in Malaysia from 1990, provides very interesting evidence of the nature of foreign investment in Malaysia at the time of the case study firm's investment. For example, the report notes a "special offer" during 1989/90 allowing firms to have 100% foreign ownership (a policy that even in the export sector would have seemed something of a reversal of NEP policy priorities) (UNIDO, 1991: 59).

FDI in the garment sector

Given that this book is dealing with a garment sector MNC, it is worth focussing on the nature of FDI into this sector. The textile and garment industry was, up until the end of the 1980s/early 1990s, a favoured industrial sector.[4] It was viewed by government officials as capable of generating the levels of employment and investment necessary for export-led growth and economic and social restructuring (Rasiah, 1993: 5-6). Foreign investment in the textile and clothing sector in Malaysia has been relatively high, especially when one considers how garment production is not especially reliant on expensive technological imports of machinery. Therefore it is an industry that could easily have been established by local entrepreneurs. Although the number of locally owned textile and garment manufacturing operations did grow throughout the 1970s and 1980s, by 1988 foreign firms still owned over 50% of fixed assets (O'Brien, 1993: 14). This level of foreign investment is all the more surprising when we look at the structure of the textile and garment industry in Malaysia and see that it is skewed in favour of lower technology processes, in particular garment assembly. The garment industry in Malaysia has itself been dominated by the simplest aspects of the production of clothing – namely Cut Make and Trim (CMT) production techniques typical of low-technology low-wage clothing manufacture (Beaudat, 1993: 150).

Crinis (2002: 155-156) notes that Malaysia's embarkment on EOI led to a rapid influx of textile and clothing (T&C) producing MNCs which "quickly

---

[4] Interview with Financial Director of UK-Apparel Ladieswear Malaysia (UKALM), 11th March 1999.

overshadowed" local industries in this sector. So how do we explain the dominance of foreign investment in Malaysia's garment sector? There are a number of factors to consider here. One significant factor is that of quotas under the Multi-Fibre Agreement (MFA). Thus firms from Hong Kong, South Korea and Taiwan, the "big three" textile and garment exporters expanded into Southeast Asia in order to take advantage of spare quota provision in the region (Beaudat, 1993: 85-86). Under the MFA, newly emerging producers of garments and textiles were granted quotas in order to regulate their export of textile products into the European and North American markets. Because Malaysia did not develop a sizeable textile and garment sector until the 1970s, its quota provisions have remained relatively low, yet at the same time there has been a large amount of spare quota provision. This attracted many investors from Northeast Asia, who were witnessing the restriction of their export-oriented textile and garment sector industries under the terms of the MFA. Most of these firms were manufacturers engaged in sub-contracted production chains. In my interview with the president of the Malaysian Textile Manufacturers Association (the manufacturers trade association), I was informed of the role that Malaysia played as a manufacturer of sub-contracted garments:

> The whole world is sub-contracting. These firms from Dior to Adidas are very unlikely to have their own factories because the marketing of clothing is separate from the manufacture. Malaysia has become a site for the manufacture of quality garment products. We make many international brand names; Nike, Gap, Levis etc. So we become known as a very good quality manufacturer.[5]

This reputation that Malaysia had (and indeed continues to have) as a manufacturer of good quality clothing was in itself a factor that attracted foreign firms (the case study firm discussed in this book included) to establish factories there. One can also observe how government policy sought to market this reputation as a quality clothing manufacturer to attract further foreign investors. Thus another important factor concerning the level of foreign investment in the textile and clothing sector in Malaysia is the way in which government policy up until the late 1980s targeted the garment industry as a key sector that could benefit from foreign investment. As a globalizing, labour intensive industry, that sought to benefit from the existence of low-cost manufacturing bases in many developing countries, the garment sector was viewed as a good potential source of FDI. The rapid growth that the sector experienced during the late 1980s must, therefore, be set within the broader context of the revival of state support for foreign investors during the late 1980s following the PIA. Thus O'Conner notes how the Malaysian T&C industry really took off in the mid 1980s (O'Conner, 1993: 235-237). The value of T&C exports more than doubled during the period 1985 to 1988 and the industry became the second largest export earner. However, the significance of T&C is perhaps more important in terms of its ability to generate high levels of employment. Table

---

[5] Interview with President of the Malaysian Textile Manufacturers Association, 1st March 1999.

3.3 (below) presents data on the numbers employed in the wearing apparel sector between the years 1973 and 1988. What these figures reveal is the rapid growth in employment in this sector from 10,370 employees in 1973, to 27,580 by 1983 and standing at 46,200 by 1988.

Table 3.3 Employment in the Malaysian garment industry, 1973-1988

Year	Employment in the wearing apparel sector (excluding footwear)
1973	10370
1974	11030
1975	10930
1976	11900
1977	--
1978	14910
1979	16130
1980	--
1981	24730
1982	--
1983	27580
1984	30850
1985	31100
1986	34100
1987	39300
1988	46200

Sources: ILO (1983), *Yearbook of Labour Statistics*, table 5B, 351. ILO (1987), *Yearbook of Labour Statistics*, table 5B, 497. ILO (1992), *Yearbook of Labour Statistics*, table 5B, 535.

Given the highly labour intensive nature of garment manufacture, by the early 1990s (not long after the arrival of the case study firm in Malaysia) the textiles and clothing industry began to face severe labour shortages and rising labour costs which, due to the limited scope for technological upgrading in the industry, could not be offset by gains in productivity associated with moving into higher value-added production. Whereas the electronics sector has experienced a quite significant shift away from simple assembly line production work into more technologically challenging and innovative production (Maznah and Ng, 1996: 5), the garment industry has remained largely reliant on labour intensive production techniques. Furthermore, the high levels of foreign ownership in the garment sector, contributed to the highly labour intensive nature of the industry because the higher value added, more capital intensive aspects of the garment commodity chain (for example marketing and design capabilities) remained located in the parent states or with the garment retailer (O'Conner, 1993: 239) (generally located in the developed world – see chapter four). Thus by the mid 1990s, garment firms were finding that they were no longer favoured in government policy making.[6]

Foreign investors and state-labour relations in Malaysia

The focus of the discussion presented in this chapter now shifts away from issues relating to economic planning and policy making in Malaysia, and turns to the role that the Malaysian state played in the formation of a system of labour relations that sought to keep wages low and suppress industrial unrest (thereby further enhancing the attraction of Malaysia to foreign investors). Initially the discussion focuses on the labour relations regime in Malaysia and the extent to which multinational investors influenced state policy in this area. A repressive system of labour relations fed into government attempts to suppress or co-opt oppositional social forces, thereby creating the foundations for a stable semi-authoritarian political regime. The issue of political stability is itself an important element in the attractiveness of a country as a site for FDI (and is something that came across in my case study interviews – see chapter three), hence it is important to look at the ways in which this political stability has been achieved in Malaysia.

Origins and development of patterns of state-labour relations

From the discussion presented so far in this book, it should be clear that any analysis of Malaysia as a site for FDI cannot ignore the role of labour costs. The reliance of the Malaysian government on a form of industrialization based upon low-wage labour intensive manufacturing placed the maintenance of low-wage rates at the forefront of economic development planning. Consequently, state-labour relations were characterized by the desire to keep wages as low as possible. It would be very difficult to prove the impact of trade union activity on wage rates. What matters however, is that there was the general perception in government and bureaucratic circles that unions would lead to high wages, a view that was also supported by many multinational investors.

Thus the way that government policies courted foreign investors ought not simply to be viewed in terms of tax incentives; the Malaysian state also sought to promote itself to foreign investors by drawing attention to its "harmonious" system of labour relations. For example, the Malaysian International Development Authority (MIDA) includes comments on the nature of labour relations in Malaysia in its investment brochure:

> The Labour Market in Malaysia is Free and Competitive and the employer-employee relationship is cordial and harmonious. Labour costs are low in comparison to the industrialized countries while labour productivity remains high (Malaysian Industrial Development Authority, 1999).

---

[6] Interview with Financial Director of UKALM (Site A, 11th March 1999).

This marketing of Malaysia as a site for FDI is interesting not only in terms of the way it highlights Malaysia's lack of serious industrial unrest, but the way in which it follows up this comment with statements on the cost of labour. Via this juxtapositioning, MIDA evidently wanted to convey the linkage between labour costs and industrial unrest (in both Malaysia and the industrialized countries) in its promotional activities. But what do statements concerning industrial harmony such as this actually mean? If we are to unpack this notion of "harmonious" labour relations, one can observe how the government's desire to attract foreign investors is closely tied to severe restrictions on trade union activities.

Looking firstly at the initial period of export-led growth, policies restricting organized labour were deemed to be a necessary component of the export-led development drive. Jomo and Todd's detailed overview of the history of state-labour relations in Malaysia makes a clear case for the way in which the shift towards export-led growth was accompanied by the evolution of a more repressive system of industrial relations, suggesting that:

> To attract labour intensive industries, such as electronics assembly and textile manufacturing, a cheap and docile labour force was deemed necessary. Trade Unions which might be capable of agitating for higher wages levels were to be shut out as far as possible (Jomo and Todd, 1994: 129).

Although the trade unions act of 1959 (which consolidated earlier colonial legislation on unions into a single piece of legislation (Arudsothy and Littler, 1993: 110-111)) granted the right to form trade unions, and there were, during the 1960s, some tripartite structures established, Jomo and Todd see this as little more than a "hollow corporatism" (Jomo and Todd, 1994). The post-independence state continued in the traditions of the British colonial regime's approach to state-labour relations, viewing labour legislation as a means through which the state could exert control over the union movement as a potential source of political opposition. The Trade Union Ordinance of 1946 (which was initially adopted in 1940 but could not be implemented due to the Japanese occupation) used the devise of compulsory registration in order to supervize and control unions by distinguishing between legal and illegal unions (Arudsothy and Littler, 1993: 111). This system of control over union activities was consolidated in the post-independence period. For example, the freedom of association that appears, at first glance, to be granted in the Trade Union Act is a severely limited freedom. Trade Unions may only be established in a particular trade or place of work if one does not already exist. A state body, the registrar of trade unions (RTU),[7] specifies whether an application to form a trade union can be permitted under these rules and the RTU has come to

---

[7] Although it should be noted here that the establishment of the RTU was not part of the 1959 Trade Union Act. It was, in fact, a body that was established under Colonial rule in the 1940s. But the 1959 Act did allow for a strengthening of the power of the RTU. See O'Brien (1988: 147,157).

play a significant role in obstructing worker's attempts to organize – especially in the export manufacturing industries (O'Brien, 1988: 157).

Since the adoption of export-led growth in the late 1960s, the state has progressively moved to further restrict the rights of trade unions in pursuit of a cheap and flexible workforce. Moves have included restrictions on the right to strike and restrictions specifying the issues unions were able to bargain on. A state of emergency that was announced following the 1969 racial riots provided the government with the opportunity to introduce the sorts of anti-labour policies that it believed would benefit the new policies of export oriented growth and attract in foreign capital. By the end of the state of emergency in the 1970s, strikes had become virtually insignificant. Hence Tun Razak, is quoted by Jomo and Todd claiming that this new labour legislation would

> maintain a manageable labour force, attract new investments, create employment opportunities and... make possible a more rapid pace of industrialization (Jomo and Todd, 1994: 125).

State-labour relations in the 1980s: The 'Look East'

Government policy-making in sustaining this "harmonious" industrial relations set-up, is closely tied to the policies introduced to attract foreign investors. When the state sought to increase the level of FDI in the mid-1980s with the introduction of the PIA, it also introduced a round of more repressive labour legislation (Jomo, 1990: 218-220; Jomo and Todd, 1994: 146-149). This anti-union stance reflected government concerns that union activity could lead to the wage increases that were viewed as an anathema to an industrialization strategy based upon attracting foreign investors into labour-intensive manufacturing.

One of the initiatives that the government attempted to utilize in order to defuse any potential union power, especially in the export sectors where unionization rates were especially low, was the encouragement of enterprize-based, or in-house, unions. Such a policy was presented as part of the government's (under Mahatir Mohammed) "Look East" strategy (Jomo and Wad, 1994). A policy that incorporated attempts to emulate aspects of the Japanese industrial system (including enterprize unions), encourage Japanese investment at a time of massive Japanese industrial expansion in Southeast Asia, and even provide justification for the more repressive and anti-labour aspects of Mahatir's administration. The anti-unionism implicit within the Look East strategy was further espoused in the rhetoric of "Asian Values" whereby Mahatir (along with Lee Kuan Yew in Singapore and Suharto in Indonesia) sought to justify repressive measures against those who displayed opposition to their authoritarian regimes (see for example Mauzy, 1997).

The logic behind the preference for in-house union structures was that it was felt that they would improve company loyalty, as well as improve work ethics and industrial harmony (Grace, 1990; Jomo and Wad, 1994; Wad, 1997: 12). What is more, there was an element of ethnic policy-making in the decision, since the government argued that the new Malay workforce would be better suited to these types of unions – since it had little experience of industrial life (Wad, 1997: 12). Linked to official preference for in-house union structures, therefore, were moves by the government to allow Islamic organizations into factories, especially export-sector factories in which Malay females dominated employment (see below). In my interviews with an official of the Malaysian Trade Union Congress (MTUC), the umbrella organization for private sector trade unions, the nature of government union policies during the 1980s and 1990s was explained as:

> The government policy with regards to unions since the 1980s clearly regards unions within a human resource management perspective. They believe, that unions do, perhaps have a role, but only limited to assisting the company in managing human resources and industrial harmony. Therefore, they advocate unions to be somewhat, placid, not to take any action that could be seen as aggressive. Their role is simply that of dialogue and negotiation with management.[8]

This "human resource management perspective" on unions was described in greater detail to me by a labour activist who heads a NGO that works to help improve the bargaining position of specific trade unions. He commented that these in-house unions were often a means through which employers could exert greater control over their workforce:

> When we talk about in-house unions we should also be aware that a lot of them are not unions at all. In-house unions can be registered by the personnel officers to ensure that the workers don't join a national union. They pick whoever they want to be the leaders of the union and send it to the Registrar for registration... So, they will get an in-house union that way and then they [the workforce] are not allowed to join a union. It is one of the techniques the firms use to prevent what they see as outsider intervention in the factories.[9]

Such a policy towards trade unions was revealed in interviews at the case study firm. The HR director expressed a clear preference for in-house over nationally organized (or, in the case of the garment sector, state-level unions). Although he felt that unions played a "constructive role in the workplace", he went on to suggest:

> If a company is smart they will take the lead in forming a union. That way the management are seen to be fair. You don't want management to respond just because they are forced to. Then employees only see them [management] to be doing it because they have to. I say, lets be proactive on this issue... this is in the best interests of the company.[10]

---

[8] Interview with Research Officer Malaysian Trade Union Congress (MTUC), 18th February 1999.
[9] Interview with official from the Labour Resources Centre (LRC), 12th March 1999.
[10] Interview with HR Director UKALM, Malacca, 18th August 1999.

Table 3.4 Employment, Trade Union Membership and Trade Union Density, total figures and figures for manufacturing, 1992-1996

	1992	1993	1994	1995	1996
Employment					
Total (thousands)	7,096,000	7,396,200	7,603,000	7,915,400	8,180,800
In manufacturing (thousands)	1,639,000	1,576,700	1,892,100	2,051,600	2,209,000
% of total workforce in manufacturing	23.1	23.6	24.6	25.9	27.0
Trade union membership					
Total	680,007	693,581	699,373	706,253	728,246
In manufacturing	149,569	147,487	147,359	141,021	144,814
% of total trade union membership in manufacturing	22.0	21.3	21.1	20.0	19.9
Trade Union Density (Trade Union membership as a percentage of total workforce)					
Across all sectors	9.6%	9.4%	9.2%	8.9%	8.9%
In manufacturing	8.4%	8.5%	7.9%	6.9%	6.6%

Source: Malaysia, Ministry of Human Resources (1997), *Malaysia: Labour and Human Resources Statistics 1992-1996*, Kuala Lumpur: Ministry of Human Resources, tables A.8 and C2.12, pp. 14, 142.

The 1980s witnessed a significant decline in the power of the trade unions. A situation that was worsened by the fact that the 1980s also saw an increased reliance on foreign migrant labour in certain sectors and government and firms ensured that this workforce remained largely unorganized (Jomo, 1990: 219). Jomo claims that Union membership declined during the 1980s, despite an overall fall in unemployment and increases in the number of workers in waged employment (Jomo, 1990: 218). This is a trend that has continued into the 1990s as can be seen in table 3.4. Although total trade union membership rose between the years 1992 and 1996, from 680,007 to 728,146, trade union density (trade union membership as a percentage of the total workforce) actually fell from 9.6% to 8.9% during that period. In manufacturing, these trends are even more pronounced, with trade union density falling from 8.4% to 6.6% between 1992 and 1996. This fall in trade union density in manufacturing is further reflected in the fall in the percentage of total trade union membership in manufacturing from 22% in 1992 to 19.9% in 1996.

Foreign capital and state-labour relations

These enterprize unions (as well as the increase in foreign workers) can be viewed as a dimension of the government's low wage policies aimed at attracting FDI. It is, therefore, important to look at the role of foreign capital in state-labour relations. To ask, to what extent have the anti-union policies of the Malaysian government been shaped and influenced by foreign capital? Such an issue is pertinent given that many foreign investors in Malaysia, in particular American multinational electronics corporations, have had explicitly anti-union policies for their subsidiary operations (Chandran, 1997). Bhopal and Todd, for example, characterize many MNCs as operating either "non-unionism" or "anti-unionism" policies, with the former referring to a paternalistic human-resource-management approach to labour relations and the latter involving the dismissal, intimidation and harassment of union activists (Bhopal and Todd, 2000: 200-204). My interviews with trade union officials in Malaysia suggest that these strategies tend to go hand-in-hand.

One of the best examples of the influence of foreign MNCs on government industrial relations policy-making is the electronics sector where government policy and all relevant state institutions have acted to prevent the formation of unions (Grace, 1990). The electronics MNCs had been given special assurances that there would be no union formation in their industry. In this female dominated sector, a bar on union activities remained in place up until the late 1980s. Even today, no electronics unions have been able to successfully register themselves and therefore gain state or company recognition (Bhopal and Todd, 2000; Grace, 1990). Unsurprisingly, therefore, in my interview with a representative from the Harris Trade Union where much of the fight for trade union recognition in the electronics sector has been based (Bhopal and Todd, 2000: 203), the suggestion was made that foreign capital has a strong influence over the government. He commented:

LIVERPOOL JOHN MOORES UNIVERSITY
LEARNING SERVICES

The electronics industry and the government are in collaboration – no secret is made of this... these companies don't pay tax, and the government thinks that this is fine because they bring in jobs, and the government lays on all the infrastructure for them. So our taxes pay for it and what do we gain in the end?[11]

Others whom I interviewed in the Malaysian trade union movement felt that the relationship between foreign capital and government anti-unionism was less overt than this. Most interviewees felt that MNCs themselves had little direct influence over policy-making. Rather anti-unionism was regarded more as a device that the government used to attract foreign investors.[12]

Compared to electronics, in the textiles sector, the situation is somewhat different. However, the influence of the MNCs on the activities of unions is just as significant. The textile and garment sector has no national union level organization, rather, the sector was organized at the level of local states. However, membership of these local state level unions is very limited. The two textile and garment sector state-level unions that I was able to meet with (Penang and Selangor states), only organized a handful of factories, and these tended to be textile rather than garment assembly firms.[13] Many firms have encouraged workers to form enterprize unions in order to keep the state level union out (therefore using the 1959 Trade Union Act which restricts union membership in a single enterprize to a single union) (Bhopal and Todd, 2000: 204-206). Although in many firms unions simply do not exist at all.[14] An increased reliance on foreign migrant workers in garment production has further impacted upon the level of trade union membership in this sector because it is a condition of these workers' contracts that they can not join unions (Crinis, 2002: 161).

The state, labour and political stability

Many of the pieces of legislation that were used to suppress union activities were developed around the time of independence, and reflected the desires of both the Colonial state and the post-independence state to secure a form of political stability. Thus one labour activist told me that the techniques and legislation that the Malaysian government uses to suppress unions are as much to do with controlling and limiting potential sources of opposition to the regime as to do with attracting foreign investors:

---

[11] Interview with Harris Trade Union Representative, 5th March 1999.

[12] Interview with Industrial Relations Officer, Electrical Industry Workers Union, Prai, Penang (17th March 1999). Interview with General Secretary, Textile Workers Union of Penang, Prai, Penang, 17th March 1999.

[13] Interviews with General Secretary Textile Workers Union of Penang, Prai, Penang, 17th March 1999 and Executive Secretary of Selangor and Federal Territory Textile and Garment Industries Employees Union, 27th March 1999.

[14] Interviews with General Secretary Textile Workers Union of Penang, Prai, Penang, 17th March 1999.

Labour control has a more important function which is to provide political stability. This invariably helps convince MNCs that it is good to invest. But more importantly, labour control is about keeping the elite in power.[15]

This is a view that is supported by writers such as Frederic Deyo in his study of labour relations in the Asian NICs (Singapore, Hong Kong, Taiwan and South Korea). In these states (which were the first to engage in the export-led development policies later emulated in Malaysia) tight labour controls were imposed *prior* to embarking on industrialization programmes. Consequently, labour has had little role to play in influencing government policy making. Deyo therefore characterizes these states as operating "exclusionary labour regimes" (Deyo, 1989: 9).

The political exclusion of labour was deemed to be necessary in ensuring "political stability" and the political continuity of the regime. The reason why such a discussion is brought in here is because issues of political stability influence the way that foreign investors think about the "risk" involved in investing offshore. It will be shown, for example, in chapter four that the influence of issues pertaining to political stability was an important factor in the case study firm's decision to invest in Malaysia. In part, this preoccupation with political stability is to do with the rule of law (e.g. will contracts be honoured? Might profits be seized?). But it is also to do with whether it is possible to do business in a state beset by constant political destabilising factors such as riots and industrial unrest. A discussion of Malaysia as a site for FDI, therefore, needs to look beyond the overt policies that were introduced to attract investors, and look to the importance of the broader political context of the investment process.

The Malaysian government has always regarded with suspicion the organization of opposition along class lines. The repressive nature of state-labour relations in Malaysia was in many ways a continuation of British colonial policy towards the labour movement which was viewed as a source of potential leftist and/or communist opposition. Atlas, for example, has shown how labour militancy in British Malaya was almost totally destroyed (Atlas, 1997: 73). Under the State of Emergency that was declared by the British in 1948 and lasted for 12 years, the activities of labour unions were massively restricted. Most notably, the Communist organized Pan Malaysian Federation of Trade Unions (PMFTU) and the Communist Party of Malaya (CPM) were banned under the state of emergency. The years 1948-1950 saw militant trade unionism effectively wiped out by the colonial state (Jomo and Todd, 1994: 84-85). Industrial unrest that had occurred during the 1940s was not only a response to the harsh conditions that the (mainly Chinese and Indian) workers employed in industry and commercial agriculture faced, but also reflected the organization of anti-colonial forces by the Chinese dominated CPM. Inevitably, the government reacted by seeking to eliminate the PMFTU, effectively bringing to an end the chances of organizing a mass class-based anti-colonial movement (Atlas, 1997: 77). After 1950, the relationship between the state and trade unions is viewed as much tamer, and it has been

---

[15] Interview with official from the LRC, 12th March 1999.

suggested that those unions that survived the 1948-1950 period probably only managed to survive due to collaboration with the colonial authorities (Jomo and Todd, 1994: 86). Thus Hua comments; "although the workers' struggles from the 1960s onwards have been less intense than those of the previous three decades, this is largely a reflection of ruthless state repression and its infiltration of the labour movement" (Hua, 1983: 150).

Labour and political opposition in the post-independence period

In the post-NEP era, the government has been equally worried about the formation of class-based organizations. But the NEP itself has acted to shore up support for the regime along the lines of ethnicity rather than class. Yet although the years since 1969 have seen a huge increase in a Malay industrial working class, this has not provided the basis for class-based oppositional movements. Part of the reason for this lies in the NEP, which has been central in the way that the government has been able to mobilize its support along ethnic lines and maintain the political hegemony of UMNO. The trade union movement failed to keep up with the rapid growth of the labour force and, in particular, the rise in Malay industrial employment as the Malay population moved out of agricultural and into industrial employment during the NEP era. Non-*bumiputera* workers increasingly felt disadvantaged by government policies aimed at improving the economic position of the Malays, heightening tensions between ethnic groups (Jomo and Todd, 1994: 129-130). The lack of political opposition movements with the capability of providing an effective alternative to the BN (and UMNO in particular) plus the widespread support amongst the Malay community for the NEP, allowed for a level of toleration to the sometimes authoritarian actions of the state.

But to what extent does political stability depend upon authoritarianism? This is an issue that has divided scholars of Malaysian politics. Hua (1983) regards the state as highly authoritarian, claiming that "continued repression through communalism is the cardinal mechanism by which the Malaysian ruling class can maintain the loyalty of the Malay masses" (Hua, 1983: 193) and has pointed to the use of legislation such as the Internal Security Act (ISA) and the Sedition Act by the state to effectively crush opposition (especially left wing) movements. But this is disputed by writers such as Atalas (1997), who take the view that the UMNO-controlled state is something more like a benign oligarchy. In between these two writers is Crouch who has talked about the way in which the Malaysian State embodies aspects of both democracy and authoritarianism (Crouch, 1993: 133-158).

It is suggested here that authoritarian rule is closely linked to perceptions about political stability. Foreign investors feel comfortable with investing in a state which has reasonably secure and transparent processes regarding investment and the appearance of democratic institutions whilst, at the same time pursuing a level of repression that controls opposition to the regime (especially from labour-based organizations) which may directly impact on a firm's profitability. Given that recent debates regarding the ethics of FDI have criticized firms that invest into highly authoritarian regimes with poor records on human rights (see for example

Amis, 2003; OECD, 2002), many MNCs are keen to appear to be investing in states that are "politically appropriate",[16] thus the semblance of democracy and the role of law emphasized by writers such as Crouch matters.

Gender and economic development in Malaysia

This chapter has already shown how state policies played a role in suppressing union activities in order to keep wages low, but it is also important to look at how state-led policies of export-led growth were as much predicated on the exploitation of pre-existing social divisions as they were upon the suppression of emerging class-based divisions. Thus the discussion now turns to look at the gendered nature of economic development in Malaysia. This gendering of the economic development process was witnessed in employment trends as well as in government policy-making. However, given the emphasis placed upon the role of a political economy of ethnicity in Malaysia's economic development, it is shown that gender divisions cross-cut with ethnic divisions played a key role in sustaining this economic transformation.

Gendering employment in export manufacturing

A look at the broader picture of women's employment in Malaysia when the case study firm arrived in Malaysia in 1989, confirms the view that there were already entrenched patterns of gendered employment in both multinational and locally owned firms in the export sector. Reiterating the more general argument put forward in chapter two, it is suggested here that the mobilization of a young female workforce in these industries was a fundamental component of export-led industrialization in Malaysia. The state in Malaysia, therefore, sought to integrate female labour into industrial employment, a trend typical of states that have undergone the shift toward EOI based development concentrated in labour intensive manufacturing (Phongpaichit, 1990: 151-153).

Such an argument is supported by the available statistical data on the increase in female employment in manufacturing that accompanied export-led development. Table 3.5 (below) reveals how the rise in manufacturing employment was mirrored by a decline in agricultural employment The table shows how female employment has grown dramatically in the manufacturing sector, relative to both other sectors and to male employment in manufacturing. The percentage of women employed in manufacturing rose from 3.7% in 1957/60 to 20.2% by 1987 and the percentage of female workers in manufacturing rose from 16.4% of the workforce to 46.1% over the same period.

---

[16] This point is discussed in more detail in chapter four in relation to why the case study firm decided to invest in Malaysia.

Table 3.5 Employment distribution of women and percentage of workers who are female by industry, Malaysia, 1957-1990

Industry	1957-60	1970	1980	1987	1990
Employment distribution of women by industry (%)					
Agriculture	80.4	61.6	44.4	30.8	25.6
Mining	1.4	0.7	0.3	0.2	0.2
Manufacturing	3.7	7.3	14.7	20.2	26.6
Utilities	0.1	0.1	0.0	0.1	0.2
Construction	0.8	0.5	0.9	0.8	0.8
Commerce	3.1	5.2	11.5	19.7	19.2
Transport	0.3	0.5	0.6	1.2	1.6
Services	9.8	14.7	17.6	27.1	26.1
Activities not adequately defined	0.5	9.5	10.0	0.0	0.0
Total	100.0	100.0	100.0	100.0	100.0
% of workers who are female					
Agriculture	34.0	38.0	39.0	35.3	34.5
Mining	15.6	12.5	10.4	11.2	11.4
Manufacturing	16.4	28.1	40.1	46.1	47.7
Utilities	7.5	6.8	7.1	2.8	9.4
Construction	3.4	5.4	7.0	4.7	4.6
Commerce	9.7	18.2	29.3	38.2	37.5
Transport	2.1	4.3	6.3	9.9	11.5
Services	19.5	28.9	29.4	39.3	39.0
Activities not adequately defined	17.2	53.3	44.5	40.0	0.0
Total	26.4	32.1	33.6	35.4	35.5

Source: Ariffin, Horton, and Sedlacek (1995), 'Women in the Labour Market in Malaysia' in S. Horton (ed.), *Women and Industrialization in Asia*, London: Routledge, table 6.4, 319; ILO, 1992, table 3b, 407.

But where the data on female manufacturing employment gets especially interesting is when we look at the breakdown of this data by industry. Here we see that female employment in manufacturing is concentrated in specific sectors. Figures 3.1 and 3.2 present data from 1987, revealing the way in which female employment was concentrated in those industrial sectors most associated with export-manufacturing: garments and electronics. Especially relevant, given the choice of case study, is the significance of garment manufacturing for female employment. The workforce in the garment industry is overwhelmingly female (78.1%) and 21% of all women employed in the manufacturing sector work in the garment industry. It can be concluded, therefore, that increases in the female manufacturing labour force were brought about by the rapid expansion of these export sector industries during the 1970s and 1980s.

Figure 3.1 Top five manufacturing industries with the highest percentage of female workers

	Industry	% of workers who are female within an industrial sector
1	Garments	78.1
2	Electrical Machinery	72.4
3	Professional and Scientific	64.6
4	Footwear	62.9
5	Textiles	58.0

Source: Ariffin, Horton, and Sedlacek (1995), 'Women in the Labour Market in Malaysia' in S. Horton (ed.), *Women and Industrialization in Asia*, London: Routledge, table 6.4, p. 319.

Figure 3.2 Top five employers of women in the industrial manufacturing sector

	Industry	Distribution of women employed in a particular sector (as a % of total female manufacturing employment)
1	Garments	21.0
2	Electrical Machinery	20.4
3	Food	13.1
4	Wood and cork	7.6
5	Textiles	5.6

Source: Ariffin, Horton, and Sedlacek (1995), 'Women in the Labour Market in Malaysia' in S. Horton (ed.), *Women and Industrialization in Asia*, London: Routledge, table 6.4, p. 319.

There are a number of factors that need to be considered in explaining how the gendered division of labour has operated in the Malaysia. What comes out from a reading of the secondary sources on women and industrialization in Malaysia is that women's employment in the export sector is the result of many different factors including; state industrialization strategies that depended on there being a supply of low cost labour to work in a multinational dominated export sector, the demands of employers for the low cost, relatively well educated workers suited to assembly line production, and also the woman's own position within Malaysian society and the way in which gender divisions have operated in the context of the household. This linkage between state industrialization policy, multinational capital's demands for a type of worker and the position of women in Malaysian society is neatly summed up in the frequently cited Malaysian investment brochure which marketed Malaysia to multinational investors by promoting female worker's nimble fingered suitability to assembly line work:

> The manual dexterity of the oriental female is famous the world over. Her hands are small and she works with fast and extreme care. Who, therefore, could be better qualified by nature and inheritance to contribute to the efficiency of bench assembly production than the oriental girl?[17]

These views also came across in the interviews. For example, the head of one textile union joked "these companies came to Malaysia because they were told that the women here had such beautiful hands".[18]

Given statements such as these it was inevitable that women workers were concentrated in jobs at the lower end of the occupational hierarchy, in the sorts of assembly line operations that required a level of manual dexterity. Women in the manufacturing sector were employed overwhelmingly as production workers. For production workers, the percentage of workers who are female rose from 17.4% in 1970 to 27.0% by 1987 (ILO, 1974: table 2A, 94; 1990: table 2B, 152). More significantly, if we look at the major employers of female labour in the export manufacturing sector (garments and electronics) there were distinct gender divisions of labour in which women were concentrated in production work (as opposed to supervisory, managerial or technical roles).

Government planning and women's role in economic development

Women have been the main recipients of employment in the expanding light manufacturing export sector in which FDI is concentrated. Yet beyond the above quotation taken from the Malaysian investment brochure, there is little other evidence, prior to the 1990s, of the state outwardly acknowledging the importance of women in its industrial development strategy. This was mainly because state development planners did not recognize the extent to which EOI development strategies would be based upon an expansion of female labour force participation. The assumption was that it would be men who would be the potential new recruits in the foreign owned multinationals (Chin 1998: 171; Lim, 1980). The investment brochure reflected, therefore, the belated recognition by the Malaysian state of the importance of female workers in multinational systems of production (Chin, 1998: 171). This is a very important point in terms of the research presented in this book,

---

[17] For example, this brochure is cited by Hua (1983: 188) and Chin (1998: 171).

[18] Interview with Secretary General, Penang Textile and Garment Workers Union, 17th March 1999.

because it indicates that the emergence of women as a low cost source of labour was less of a deliberate strategy by the Malaysian state (at least initially) and reflected more the requirements of the MNCs. In this sense, I am returning to an argument articulated in chapter two, that the firm needs to be conceptualized as an actor that is actively involved in the construction of gendered identities. This is not to suggest, however, that the state development policies are unimportant to the study of how women workers emerge as a low cost source of labour. As the discussion presented so far in this chapter should have indicated, the state actively sought to attract FDI on the basis of low cost labour, and curtailed the rights of workers to organize within the key export sectors. Because of the dominance of women workers in these sectors, state policies towards labour emerge as a gendered set of practices. In what follows, I trace the way in which the recognition of women's role in export-oriented economic development emerged in official development discourse in Malaysia.

Up until the late 1980s, what is most notable from official statements on women and development is that women were viewed primarily in terms of their domestic role, a discourse that was seen most clearly in the pro-natalist population policies that emerged in the 1980s. The launching of the New Population Policy in 1984 which set the target of 70 million Malaysians by 2100 (the population in 1984 was 12.6 million) (Leete, 1996: 58-9) can very much be seen in terms of an official restatement of the importance of women in terms of their responsibility to produce the next generation of Malaysians.

"Women specific" government policies that emerged during the 1970s and 1980s were concerned largely with women's domestic role as mothers and domestic workers (including workers in informal sector home based production (Ng and Maznah, 1990: 77)) rather than her role in industrialization and factory employment. For example the Malaysian Handicraft Development Corporation within the Small-scale industries division of the Ministry of Rural Development was established to promote the income generating activities of rural women within the home. The setting up in 1961 of a Community Development Division (KEMAS) within the Ministry of National and Rural Development was another example of this type of policy running educational and "family development" programmes (Ariffin, 1994b: 20-21). Even though such programmes did focus on raising women's employment potential, their focus remained on placing women within a firmly domestic context and they generally viewed women as a group that needs to be targeted by government poverty alleviation programmes rather than as active participants in the development process.

It was not until the sixth Malaysia plan (1991-1995) that the role of women in the industrial sector was more widely recognized, devoting an entire chapter to the topic of Women in Development (WID) (Malaysia, 1991: 413- 427). This was the first plan to include any mention of WID, although it was keenly pointed out that "[t]he Government has long acknowledged the significant contribution by women to overall national development" (Malaysia, 1991: 413). The incorporation of WID into government economic planning was largely the result of the National Policy for Women (NPW) launched in 1989 which emphasized women's active contribution to EOI based economic development strategies (Ariffin, 1994b: 21).

The NPW was formulated by the two key state bodies with responsibility for women's issues; the National Advisory Council on the Integration of Women in Development (NACIWID) attached to the Prime Minister's department and the Secretariat for Women's Affairs (HAWA), as well as women's NGO groups.

The Sixth Malaysia Plan is interesting in that it not only acknowledges the contribution of women to export-led development, but it also recognizes many of the difficulties that women face as waged employees in the formal economy such as wage inequalities, poor working conditions and the lack of adequate career advancement for women in labour intensive manufacturing. Yet in spite of this, women's role in economic development as waged workers is overshadowed by the emphasis of the report on women's domestic role. A reading of the WID chapter from the sixth plan subtly conveys the message that women are, first and foremost, reproducers and homemakers:

> Women play an important role in national development. As wives and mothers, they are the primary force behind the development of future generations of caring and progressive Malaysians. Outside the home, they are an important economic resource (Malaysia, 1991: 422).

What statements such as these reveal, in addition to earlier women specific policies and fertility policy, is that, within government development planning, women are perceived in terms of their dual roles as both reproducers and producers. But there is also a class story in operation here, with middle class women in particular being targeted as reproducers of the next generation of Malaysians. Chin (1998) notes, for example, how the government rhetoric that accompanied the launching of the NPP was focussed almost exclusively on groups of upper-middle and middle-class women. The policy therefore represented an attempt to "redomesticate Malaysian women from specific social classes" (Chin, 1998: 167). The launching of the NPP reflected concerns about labour shortages (and therefore rising employment costs) in an export-oriented economy dependent on attracting FDI to Malaysia as a low cost operating base. Thus whilst working class and rural women could be relied upon to provide the low cost workforces for the export sector firms, middle class women were conceptualized as, first and foremost, homemakers. Chin's work, thus conveys the impression that the discourse of domesticity is applied much more rigorously to middle-class women.

However, by the 1990s, the time of the sixth Malaysia plan, the Malaysian economy had begun to rely on foreign migrant work and women from all social classes actively engaging in the formal labour market. This is not to suggest that conceptions of the household as the appropriate sphere for respectable middle-class women has declined in importance. Chin's research into middle-class women and the employment of foreign domestic labour notes, for example, the lack of childcare facilities available to mothers working outside of the home which stems from a culture of Asian patriarchy which constructs women as essentially homemakers. The employment of foreign domestic maids by middle-class households, therefore, is indicative of the way that "women negotiate this constraint by transferring the responsibility of domestic labor (sic) to Filipina and Indonesian women who work under their supervision" (Chin, 1998: 167).

Issues of the double burden of family and work outside of the home are of course, more pressing for many of the working-class women employed in export sector factories. As has already been discussed in chapter two, for many authors writing on women and industrialization in Asia, there were certain advantages in perceiving women as only able to work in the export sector factories for a limited period prior to marriage. This led to a constant turnover of staff, which benefited many labour-intensive light-manufacturing firms because it enabled them to keep wages as low as possible.

It is also worth noting that the above quotation from the Sixth Malaysia Plan reveals ideas about the symbolic significance of women within nationalistic discourse, as the reproducers of the nation's next generation, imbuing notions of femininity and appropriate feminine roles with a moral and political (as well as religious) significance (Rai, 1996: 10-11; Yuval-Davis and Anthias, 1989: 6-12). Thus the accession of large numbers of women into formal sector employment, and suggestions that even greater levels of female labour force participation are needed to sustain Malaysia's industrialization momentum, has created tensions within national development discourses concerning the appropriate role and position of women; tensions that were heightened during the 1980s period of Islamic revivalism in state and society. Indeed, it has been suggested that the prevailing official discourse of women as reproducers rather than producers reflects concerns raised by Islamic groups over the impact of employment in export sector factories (and the migration to cities that this often necessitated) on the morality of women (Chin, 1998: 172; Ong, 1987: 183).

The interface of gender and ethnicity in the multinational firm

Many studies of women workers executed in the 1970s and 1980s reveal the nature of factory employment in the newly emerging export manufacturing sector. One of the most notable findings of these studies is that they highlight the link between women's work and low pay (Ariffin, 1994a; Lim, 1980), findings that fit with the more general studies of female employment under EOI in Asia mentioned in chapter two.

How might we account for these trends and patterns in the role and position of women workers in Malaysian manufacturing? We have already considered the way that the state sought to pursue economic development strategies that came to require the rapid absorption of women into export-sector employment. But to more adequately understand the patterns of female employment in Malaysia, we need to look at both employer attitudes towards women workers (i.e. the way that women workers were viewed as especially suited to routine assembly type work) and the position of women in Malaysian society more generally. In particular, studies of women's factory employment in Malaysia needs to take into consideration the role of ethnicity in understanding the overall patterns of female labour force participation.

Research undertaken by scholars such as Ackerman and Ong has provided a considerable amount of qualitative ethnographic detail concerning the type of workers that entered manufacturing employment in the 1970s and 1980s, the sort of social background that these workers came from and also the way in which these workers regarded employment. These two studies therefore add valuable case study material relating to female employment that allows us to look beyond the overall statistics and patterns of female employment and to consider the socially specific context of women's employment in Malaysia prior to the 1990s. Ackerman's study suggests that young women were attracted to the "clean light work" available in export factories viewing it as a means of escaping the confines of domestic life and gaining some form of autonomy. Ong's study goes even further than this, stressing the importance of the specifically Malay social context within which female workers in Malaysia are embedded. It is to this discussion of how ethnicity combines with gender in creating patterns of employment in the manufacturing sector we now turn.

It is not the intention of this section to look in detail at the way in which patterns of labour force participation in terms of ethnicity have been borne out in Malaysia over recent decades. Rather, what is argued here is that in the context of Malaysia, a focus on the characteristics of the workforce in MNCs in terms of gender is not enough. Since this book makes a case for the economic-sociology approach to the study of the labour market, one cannot ignore the role of ethnicity in the Malaysian workforce and the way that firms have benefited from ethnic as well as gender inequality in their recruitment practices (and, as will be argued in the later chapters of this book, play a role in the shaping of these inequalities in the first place).

Figures that take into account both the gender and ethnic breakdown of the Malaysian workforce suggest that the rapid rise in the number of skilled Malays in industrial employment is largely attributable to increases in the employment of Malay women (Shamsulbahriah Ku Ahmad, 1999: appendix two). The growth of the electronics sector in particular has been most responsible for these increases in Malay female employment. This urban-rural shift is noted in other studies, often drawing attention to the expansion of female employment opportunities in the export sector that emerged during the 1980s and the accompanying process of urbanization (often characterized by very poor quality living conditions) (Ariffin, 1994a).

Malay women were attracted by the employment opportunities in sectors such as electronics, and many young women moved from the rural states of Eastern Peninsular Malaysia to the centres of industrial employment in Penang and Selangor on the West coast. The companies in light manufacturing for export industries were keen to attract these workers for labour intensive employment since they constituted a plentiful source of low cost labour. As a group of workers from the largely rural areas, these women's alternative employment options were largely confined to agricultural or home-based production. The electronics sector in particular was viewed as a good source of employment by young Malay women migrating from the rural areas.

If we focus in on the garment sector and look at how ethnicity operates in this industry, somewhat different trends are revealed largely because this sector has faced difficulties in attracting the kinds of rural migrants employed by the electronics industry. In this sector there is also a high level of female Chinese employed as production workers. A survey of Penang-based garment firms shows that Chinese women made up 71% of skilled sewing machinists (Rasiah, 1993). However, these findings are quite different to the situation at the case study firm utilized in this book where Malays dominate production and sewing machine jobs. In chapter five there is an analysis of why sewing work at the case study factory is so Malay dominated, but it is worth noting some of the reasons that Rasiah gives for the high levels of Chinese employment in the garment industry such as the preference for Chinese employees in Hong Kong and Taiwanese firms (and therefore suggests a level of ethnic-based employment networking) (Rasiah, 1993). This was something that I also came across during my field research on a visit to a Hong Kong-owned garment factory on the island of Penang (a northern state of peninsular Malaysia). Here Chinese workers dominated the workforce.[19] It is important to point out, however, that the ethnic characteristics of Rasiah's study reflect the nature of the sample, since his survey is confined to Penang based firms and, demographically, the Chinese population of Penang is much higher than other states in Peninsular Malaysia. In 1991, Chinese made up the largest single ethnic group in Penang (550,600 compared to the Malay population of 422,000) whilst in Malacca (the state where the case study firm used in this study is located) the Chinese population stood at just 176,000 compared to a Malay population of 301,800 (Leete, 1996: 23-24).

Crinis (2002: 157) has also noted the high levels of Chinese employment in garment manufacturing. However, she makes the point that these firms tend to be confined to urban areas (such as Penang), and notes how there has been a shift towards establishing factories in more Malay dominated rural areas in which wages are considerably lower. She found that these rurally based factories tended to be foreign owned and employ an almost totally Malay workforce. Clearly then, the case study firm discussed in the rest of the book would fit into this category.

The most useful contribution to an analysis of the intersection between gender and ethnicity in Malaysian industrialization comes from the already mentioned study by Aiwah Ong (1987). The study focuses on the contradictory processes at work as young rural Malay Muslim women were brought into the factory environment, drawing attention to the way in which the interface and interplay between gender and ethnicity in the Malaysian workforce is a complicated process administered via cultural, capitalistic, political and household institutions and practices. Ong is particularly interested in the study of female Malay workers' everyday experiences in and out of the workplace. Malay workers are subject to multiple forms of pressure and power (from capitalist discipline to Islamic revivalism) as they engage in factory working and Ong describes the way that women have reacted to these pressure through forms of resistance which include

---

[19] Interviews with a personnel manager of the company Penn Apparel Sdn. Bhd., and factory tour with a company personnel officer, Penang, 18th March 1999.

spirit possession attacks and mass hysteria. Ong's work is especially useful to the argument developed in this book because she stresses the interplay between local states and international capitalism in the generation of gendered workplace roles that are transformed by the existence of other forms of social inequality. Hence; "transnational institutions are locally mediated by pre-existing cultural constructions of inequality" (Ong, 1987: 155). In this sense, MNCs investing in Malaysia may have had specific requirements for a female labour force, but the emergence of specific groups of women as factory workers reflects locally embedded and gendered norms and practices.

> The subjugation of labor to capital in modern factories does not proceed according to a pre-determined logic. The organization of capitalist production is embedded in and transformed through cultural discourse/practices. Furthermore, relations of production cannot be self determining when played out through multiple forms of power (Ong, 1987: 155).

The idea of the firm working with embedded structures of gender and ethnic inequality is a theme that will be developed in the final two chapters of this book. But what this discussion has shown is how women, especially Malay women, have both a symbolic and a material role in this process of state-led economic development.

Chapter 4

Moving Offshore: The Case Study Firm in the Context of the UK Garment Sector

Introduction

Why does a study of a (British) multinational garment sector firm provide a suitable case study for an analysis of the impact of FDI from the perspective of gender relations? The discussion presented in this chapter introduces the case study firm and looks generally at why this firm decided to engage in a process of FDI. The nature of garment manufacture has changed massively since the 1960s with the emergence of low-wage competition from the NIC economies of Taiwan, Singapore, South Korea and Taiwan which began the shift away from the role of the developing countries as producers of raw materials towards that of manufacturers of garments. Today's garment industry is highly globalized operating across complex networks of producers. These options for offshore production strategies have been described as bringing to the industry "flexibility at low-cost" (Scheffer, 1994: 11). However, un-packing this language of "flexibility" reveals the extent to which these developments have been reliant on the availability of cheap female labour.

This chapter provides background information on the firm and how it is located within the British garment sector, followed by an examination of its decision to invest offshore. The analysis of the firm's offshore investment strategy is undertaken from two different perspectives. Firstly, within the broader context of the restructuring and decline of the British garment sector and secondly, in relation to the firm's internal decision-making procedures, concerning why Malaysia was chosen as a site for FDI. The focus on the context of the British garment sector, does more than simply provide the necessary background information for this case study firm, it also considers how firms in this sector have faced up to the challenge of competition from low-wage countries, highlighting the role of low-cost female labour (both at home and abroad) in the process of economic restructuring. What we can see is that the structure of the UK garment industry has undergone massive changes over the past twenty years. The rise of foreign competition has forced the industry into decline, and the industry has responded through an increased reliance on subcontracted production practices and offshore investment.

Why focus on the garment sector?

The decision to focus on the garment industry reflects a number of issues pertinent to this study. For example, in the last chapter, we saw how the expansion of garment production was central to EOI in Malaysia. Across the developing world, the garment industry has been particularly important to export development strategies (Dickerson, 1999: 4-5; Green, 1998) from the Mexican *Maquiladoras* established in the 1970s to the younger garment industries in states such as Sri Lanka (Kelegama and Foley, 1999), Bangladesh (Rhee, 1990; Rock, 2001), Morocco (Caroli, 1999) and China (Leung, 1996) to the growth of export manufacturing in central, eastern and southern Europe (Smith, 2003). For these states, the development of garment production as an export industry is an attractive proposition because its low technology and labour intensive nature enables them to exploit their position as a low-cost production base whilst not requiring investment in expensive technological production processes. The spread of garment production world-wide on the back of these export-led growth strategies has seen the industry develop into a highly fragmented global industry operating through subcontracted networks of manufacturers, producing garments mainly for developed world markets (Christerson, 1995: 60; Dicken, 1992: 239-244).

The global spread of the EOI model of economic development is one of the reasons behind the rapid globalization of the industry that has occurred. But the discussion in this chapter will also show how it is also a reflection of the way in which firms and retailers sought to keep costs down by shifting production overseas. Like many industries, the globalization of garment manufacture was aided by the spread of instant communication technologies and improvements in global transportation links. In fact, the high levels of FDI, subcontracting and the emergence of the complex production networks that characterize the industry make it one of the most globalized industries in the world. Dicken for example, has commented that "[t]he textile and clothing industries were perhaps the first industries to take on a global dimension" (Dicken, 1992: 233), and this occurred in spite of the high levels of trade protectionism that characterize this sector (Underhill, 1998). Thus taking a gendered perspective on the process of FDI by a garment sector MNC enables a wider discussion of the gendered nature of (economic) globalization itself.

Further reasons for selecting a garment sector firm relate to the role of gendered workplace relations within the operation of garment sector employment and the gendered notions of skill that are deeply embedded in this global industry. Thus it is not enough to say that the garment industry, because of its labour intensity) is reliant upon low wage labour, it is necessary to highlight how low wage labour has been constructed as feminized. Specific groups of women in particular are deemed most appropriate for garment sector production. As will be shown in this chapter, the exploitation of ethnic minority women in sweatshop production has become a hallmark of garment production within industrialized countries (Phizacklea, 1990) and across the world some of the marginalized groups of women workers are confined to homeworking systems of production. Focussing on the garment industry (and more specifically on a single garment industry firm) therefore, takes us beyond the broad brush macro-level studies of feminized employment in the global economy, and highlights the fine grain detail of how a particular industrial sector (and case study firm) has sought to utilize low wage female labour (Hale and Shaw, 2001: 510).

The garment industry is also an interesting case study because of the way that it has been targeted by NGO campaigns concerning labour and human rights standards. "Anti-sweatshop" campaigns, in particular, have focussed on the globalized garment industry and are often closely associated with the wider "anti-globalisation" movement.[1] The sportswear company Nike and the clothing brand Levis have both faced considerable negative publicity surrounding the issue of labour standards in supplier factories, which led these firms to introduce codes of conduct in order to head off negative publicity (Frenkel and Scott, 2002). In chapter one it was shown that the idea that firms can improve labour standards (and even alleviate sexual discrimination in the workplace) through performing a role model function, was explicitly linked to the emergence of codes of conduct in MNCs. Codes of conduct are especially prevalent in the garment sector, demonstrating the relevance of the selection of a garment sector firm in developing a critique of the progressive firm thesis.

The case study firm in the context of the British garment industry

The firm used as a case study in this book will be referred to throughout by the name UK-Apparel PLC. UK-Apparel is a supplier to the firm Marks and Spencer (M&S) a company that has dominated British clothing retailing since the Second World War. Around 85% of UK-Apparel's sales are to M&S,[2] and the firm has become M&S's largest supplier, with the retailer sourcing approximately a quarter, or 26% of its clothing requirements from UK-Apparel in 2000.[3] Indeed, the UK-Apparel factories that I visited in both Malaysia and Britain were solely engaged in the production of M&S product lines. The firm is therefore, typical of some of the larger firms found within the British garment industry that have depended heavily upon contracts with M&S. The growth of the largest British garment firms took place largely on the back of their ability to secure contracts with M&S and in the post-war period, the retailer developed a network of UK-based suppliers, which

---

[1] These NGO campaigns concerning labour conditions can also be linked to a wider NGO movement that has sought to tackle the issue of rising corporate power in a globalizing world – most notably, the campaign to abolish the OECD's Multilateral Agreement on Investment (MAI), which would have granted MNCs an effective status under international law that was akin to that held by states. See Richter (2001).

[2] UK-Apparel, "A Brief History of UK-Apparel", Company information leaflet provided by the Personnel Director, 11th November 1998. See also, UK-Apparel company reports. UK-Apparel PLC, *Annual Report 1999*, pp. 5-6. UK-Apparel PLC, *Annual Report 1998*, pp. 5-6.

[3] Interview with the head of womenswear procurement, M&S Baker Street HQ, London, 8th June 2000.

included large integrated textile and garment firms such as Courtaulds and Coats Viyella.

Retailers and suppliers

In order to understand something of how the case study firm operates, it is necessary to consider in more detail its relationship with the retailer. M&S is not involved in the actual design and development of products. This is a function performed by the suppliers themselves, and therefore many firms (UK-Apparel included) sought to consolidate their relationship with M&S through the establishment of London offices close to M&S's Baker Street headquarters, which act as design showrooms and spaces for the design and development of garment lines. The major suppliers compete for M&S contracts on the basis of the product lines developed in these showrooms. In a store such as M&S, there are a number of standardized clothing lines. Examples of these product lines might include men's underwear and men's non-crease shirts or jeans. Since these product lines require very little in the way of design changes, they command long, stable production runs, and have consequently become the mainstay of much of the UK garment industry. There is fierce competition within the industry over the contracts to produce these lines.[4] Many manufacturers were willing to commit themselves to these retailers (despite exposing themselves to dependence on a single supplier) because large orders of standardized products gave the manufacturers the opportunity to rapidly expand their output through economies of scale.

Often these firms moved out of the major "rag-trade" cities and onto greenfield sites in order to establish large factories. These larger sites were suitable for the operation of mass production techniques that incorporated technological developments and Taylorist production lines which were based upon a high level of control over the labour process through industrial engineering based scientific measurement techniques (Cockburn, 1985: 45). Cockburn has also noted how these firms employed a largely female workforce, and tended to view these women as working to supplement the family income (rather than as breadwinners in their own right). The case study firm in this book, for example, operated these kinds of manufacturing sites in Cheshire, the Northeast and South Wales.

The development of large-scale greenfield production is not unique to M&S suppliers since large retailers (commanding many standardized product lines) dominate the UK garment industry. A large-scale separation between manufacturing and retailing occurred from the interwar years onwards. This development is discussed by Rannie who claims that it laid the foundations for the structure of the modern UK clothing sector (Rannie, 1984: 146-147). In the post war years the emergence of large multiple chain clothing retailers with nation-wide branches and standardized product lines provided UK clothing manufacturers with

---

[4] Interviews with Quality Director for the Light Sewing Division, UK-Apparel, Cheshire (27th September 1999). Interview with the head of womenswear procurement, M&S Baker Street HQ, London (8th June 2000).

reliable markets for their products. UK clothing retailing has been overwhelmingly concentrated on a few large multiples, with M&S in the dominant position. Rannie cites for example the figure that by 1976, large retailers accounted for 50% of all UK clothing and footwear sales (Rannie, 1984). The highly concentrated nature of UK retailing has endured to the present day. The UK has by far more large retail groups and, correspondingly, less independent clothing retailers compared to other western European states. This is a situation that has given the major retailers considerable power over their suppliers. Furthermore, up until the mid-1990s, M&S was unique among British clothing retailers in operating a policy of "buy British" (i.e. only sourcing clothing produced in the UK) and remained committed to its traditional suppliers such as UK-Apparel (Ostrovsky, 1998). Production supply-chains in the garment sector are often described as "buyer-driven". In other words, the power of the retailers over their supply chains in terms of product design, costing and production time-scales, is considerable. The UK clothing sector is dependent on large multiple retailers such as M&S.

M&S has maintained an almost dictatorial relationship with its suppliers demanding high quality standards and quick and reliable delivery times. Rannie has described how firms would be squeezed to cut costs at times of economic downturn. The example is given of how in 1979, when M&S decided to shift into a lower price clothing market, suppliers were expected to absorb half of the cost of these changes themselves (Mitter, 1988: 49-50; Rannie, 1984: 148-155). Another downside of linkage with M&S is the way in which firms have become perilously dependent on this single retailer, a problem outlined by Coyle (1984), who has provided an account of the closure of a factory after losing its M&S contract. Indeed, in recent years, M&S suppliers have been hit hard by the declining profitability of the retail chain on top of the virtual abandonment of its "buy British" policy. UK-Apparel and other M&S suppliers have seen their profits fall and share price decline sharply (Barker, 1999), forcing them to shift much of their production overseas through either sub-contracting or FDI. M&S has started to move production away from the traditional suppliers, often using overseas suppliers, themselves operating subcontracted production networks (Whitehead, 1994: 38). This is an issue that has been widely reported in the British press (Denny, 1999: 11; Drapers Record, 1999a: 6; Rushe, 1998: 8) and interviews at both UK-Apparel and M&S headquarters confirmed the extent to which M&S has abandoned the "buy British" policy. The head of womenswear procurement at M&S suggested to me in our interview that the current supply base has been "protected" by its ability to secure M&S contracts, and M&S was in the process of re-shaping and re-organizing its supply base, a process that he described as "letting the market in".[5] The challenges that firms such as UK-Apparel face as the relationship between suppliers and retailers becomes less stable are, therefore, typical of many of the larger firms within the UK garment sector. The ending of supplier contracts with the firm William Baird PLC in 1999 further emphasized the

---

[5] Interview with the head of Womenswear procurement, M&S Baker Street HQ, London (8th June 2000).

continued dependence of large garment firms on production for M&S (Drapers Record, 1999b: 9).

However, this is not to suggest that the UK garment sector is made up solely of large firms producing standardized products. The sector is highly dualistic in structure, with the large scale firms such as UK-Apparel existing alongside very small firms often located in inner-city areas producing short runs of clothing often for the changeable "fashionwear" market (Phizacklea, 1990). In 1986, for example, 99% of all clothing enterprizes employed fewer than 100 people and approximately 74% employed fewer than 9 people (Office for National Statistics, 1986: 12). By 1992, this overall structure had changed very little, with 97% of enterprizes employing less than 100 people and approximately 71% employing less than 9 persons, this is despite of an overall decline in the total number of all clothing enterprizes from 9,284 to 7,173. Although these firms are slightly less important in employment terms (in 1992, enterprizes with less than 100 employees accounted for 41% of all employment) (Office for National Statistics, 1992: 12-13), they have become a permanent feature of UK garment sector. This is an issue that will be returned to later in this chapter where the analysis turns to consider the restructuring of the UK clothing industry that has accompanied the rise of foreign competition in the sector.

UK-Apparel and the emergence of offshore production

Given the ending of the "buy British" policies of M&S, it is not surprising that UK-Apparel operates systems of offshore production. The rise of garment production in low-wage industrialising countries, as well as a greater level of fragmentation within the retail clothing market (especially in the key Womenswear sector) which led to greater competition on price, saw increases in M&S and its suppliers' sourcing from overseas. M&S suppliers sought to maintain their position by moving manufacturing to either wholly owned offshore subsidiary operations or increasing their usage of overseas suppliers. In fact, UK-Apparel's overseas production base was already well established before M&S officially ended its "buy British" policy in the mid 1990s.[6] The company now operates a number of overseas factories; in Morocco and Indonesia as well as Malaysia, in addition to sourcing out production to overseas "partner" factories in a variety of different countries including Portugal, China, the Philippines and Mauritius.[7] By 1997, 36% of the company's entire turnover was made overseas, up from 31% in 1996. The company planned to increase this figure significantly. For example, one company source claims that by the year 2000, 50% of production would be

---

[6] It must be noted however that in my interview with M&S's head of womenswear procurement, I was informed that M&S wanted to remain committed to "buy British", but because the M&S customer wanted the retailer to be more price competitive the company had been forced to increase offshore sourcing. Interview with head of womenswear procurement, M&S Baker Street HQ, London (8th June 2000).

[7] Interview with Quality Director of the Light Sewing Division of UK-Apparel, Cheshire (27th September 1999).

offshore (Moss, 1997: 1), and the industry press has even suggested that the company expects 70% of its production to be overseas by 2003 (Drapers Record, 1998: 2).

A discussion of how the firm went about the process of offshore investment in Malaysia is described in more detail in the second part of this chapter. But first it is necessary to look briefly at the origins of the firm's decision to invest overseas. The offshore investment process for UK-Apparel came about through the purchase of a South Wales based garment firm, SW-Fashions Group.[8] Thus in this chapter, when I am describing the process of FDI into Malaysia, it is significant that this was not something that was undertaken by UK-Apparel, but by SW-Fashions. Interviews with senior company personnel at UK-Apparel indicated that the take-over of SW-Fashions by UK-Apparel, was something more akin to a merger, with senior figures at SW-Fashions taking on some of the most important strategic positions within the structure of the company. The following account of the SW-Fashions take-over is taken from my interview with one such company figure, the Personnel Director, who had originally been part of the SW-Fashions group of companies.[9]

Both UK-Apparel and SW-Fashions were well established M&S suppliers. UK-Apparel were sold the womenswear sections of the SW-Fashions group of companies following a hostile take-over of SW's parent company by one of the UK's largest garment conglomerates. This large conglomerate sold SW-Fashions because it was concerned about the possible implications of over-reliance on M&S contracts. Thus the ladieswear section of SW-Fashions (known as SW-Fashions (Wales) Ltd.) was "parcelled up for sale".[10] At the time, UK-Apparel was only engaged in the production of menswear, and was attracted by the possibilities of diversifying into womenswear that the purchase of SW-Fashions offered. Furthermore, when I asked whether UK-Apparel was attracted by the presence of an offshore factory in the SW-Fashions group, I was informed that this was certainly the case: "It made up the whole business – a nice business in a nice shape, it brought a new dimension".[11] The deal was finalized in October 1991.

Figure 4.1 is a diagrammatic representation of how the Malaysian operations now fit into the overall company structure of UK-Apparel. As can be seen from the area of the diagram identified as "level two", the company is sub-divided into a number of different firms. One of these firms, UK-Apparel (Ladieswear) Ltd, is the old SW-Fashions (Ladieswear) business and is now one of the most important

---

[8] This is a pseudonym for the company.

[9] Interview with UK-Apparel Group Personnel Director, Road Five Cheshire Industrial Estate, Cheshire (19th May 2000).

[10] Interview with UK-Apparel Group PLC Personnel Director, Cheshire (19th May 2000). Although the Personnel Director then qualified this statement – saying that it wasn't officially put on the market, but rather Coats Viyella made it clear that if they got a good offer for it then they would consider it.

[11] Interview with UK-Apparel Group PLC Personnel Director, Cheshire (19th May 2000).

firms within the company, responsible for 48% of company turnover by 1999.[12] UK-Apparel Ladieswear Ltd is itself subdivided into three different divisions (see "level three" on figure 4.1), Light Sewing, Trousers and Skirts and Tailoring. The Malaysian operations (two factories located in the state of Malacca) are part of the light sewing division (LSD), which concentrates mainly on the production of blouses (especially polyester blouses), T-shirts and other casual tops, and summer dresses.

Overall strategic control of the company rests with the firm's senior management at the level of the UK-Apparel Group PLC (level one – "The Group" on 4.1). There are, however, no established headquarters for the Group, and the senior managers that are part of the Group are located across the country at various company locations. It is also worth pointing out in relation to figure 4.1 that these formally separate divisional companies that comprize the overall firm are not functionally quite so distinct. At the Cheshire site (shown at level four on the diagram), for example, there is a blurring of management responsibility between managers of ladieswear and managers of the light sewing division (for example the Group personnel director also takes overall responsibility for personnel issues within the light sewing division).

In terms of the growth of offshore production at UK-Apparel, the years since the SW-Fashions take-over have seen a massive increase in the use of offshore production and sourcing. Indeed, at the time of the take-over, UK-Apparel operated no offshore factories and had very limited offshore experience. Although UK-Apparel had, in the past, operated sourcing offices in Hong Kong, South Korea and Indonesia, these had disappeared by the time of the SW-Fashions take-over.

---

[12] UK-Apparel PLC, *Annual Report 1999*, pp. 5-6. UK-Apparel PLC, *Annual Report 1998*, pp. 5-6.

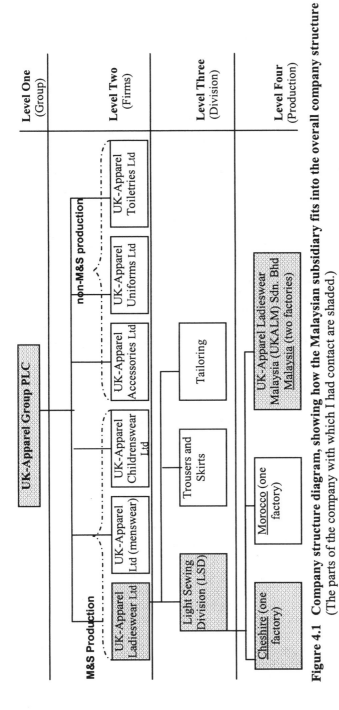

Level One
(Group)

Level Two
(Firms)

Level Three
(Division)

Level Four
(Production)

UK-Apparel Group PLC

non-M&S production

UK-Apparel Toiletries Ltd

UK-Apparel Uniforms Ltd

UK-Apparel Accessories Ltd

UK-Apparel Childrenswear Ltd

UK-Apparel Ltd (menswear)

M&S Production

UK-Apparel Ladieswear Ltd

Light Sewing Division (LSD)

Trousers and Skirts

Tailoring

Cheshire (one factory)

Morocco (one factory)

UK-Apparel Ladieswear Malaysia (UKALM) Sdn. Bhd Malaysia (two factories)

Figure 4.1 Company structure diagram, showing how the Malaysian subsidiary fits into the overall company structure
(The parts of the company with which I had contact are shaded.)

Source: Based on information provided by Personnel Director, UK-Apparel Group PLC, 6th November 1998.

Importantly, the rapid increase in offshore sourcing and use of directly owned production facilities within UK-Apparel has been one of the key impacts of the SW-Fashions take-over. The investment in Malaysia by SW-Fashions in 1991 has become the blueprint for company foreign investment strategies. In fact, I was informed that the take-over made no difference at all to the management of the Malaysian firm, no changes were made and the existing management was retained.

> There has been a total replication of our investment strategies. Malacca is viewed as the blueprint. We now have six Moroccan and three Indonesian Factories, and Malaysia is considered the platform upon which we build our other factories.[13]

The continuity in investment strategies that occurred following the SW-Fashions take-over reflects the fact that SW-Fashions' senior management went on to occupy some of the key positions within UK-Apparel, which had up until then remained largely within family control. These senior management figures included the company's chief executive as well as the personnel director, who now have responsibility across the entire UK-Apparel Group (i.e. they are located at PLC or "level 1" of figure 4.1). The firm has expanded its production rapidly, mainly through offshore investment. In 1991, UK-Apparel employed around 5,000 people (including the ex-SW-Fashions factories in the UK and Malaysia) and by June 2000 this figure stood at 13,000.[14] Furthermore, this increase in employment has largely taken place within the firm's overseas subsidiaries, with UK based employment falling following factory closures in Staffordshire and South Wales.

The changing structure of the UK garment industry

Turning to look in more detail at how the changing structure of the UK garment industry relates to the decision by the company to re-locate production offshore, it is necessary to examine the sorts of challenges that have faced the sector over the past 20 years and how garment firms have responded to these changes. Broadly speaking these changes have been from two different sources. Firstly, as already mentioned there was the threat posed by competition from low-wage newly industrialising countries. Secondly, recent years have also seen real changes in the market for clothing (especially in the key womenswear market) away from the more standardized ("low-fashion") products that change very little each year and towards shorter-run "fashionwear", and the accompanying emergence of niche marketing in clothing products, and some diversification in the retail market.

The result of these changes is seen, on the one hand, in the collapse of the UK model of large-scale garment manufacture based upon the mass production of standard product lines. On the other hand, the secondary, small-firm, sector has not experienced this level of collapse, due to its close proximity to the (UK) retail market enabling it to operate quick response times in the changeable fashionwear

---

[13] Interview with Group Personnel Director, 19th May 2000.
[14] Figures provided by Group Personnel Director, UK-Apparel Cheshire, June 6th 1999.

market and its ability to operate short production runs on these garment lines. Furthermore, the secondary sector's ability to draw upon pockets of low-wage female labour from Britain's ethnic minority communities has further enhanced the competitive advantages of subcontracting production domestically for UK based retailers and the large manufacturers. It is necessary therefore not only to consider how the industry's structure has changed in terms of how and where garments are produced, but also in terms of the impact of economic restructuring on employment, especially in relation to the employment of women and workers from different ethnic groups. This is a very useful discussion to bring in here, because in chapters five and six, it is demonstrated that the case study firm's operations in Malaysia have drawn upon female labour – specifically that of women located within particular ethnic (as well as class) groupings.

The rise of foreign competition

As a labour intensive industry, where labour costs can account for as much as 60% of all production costs (Market Tracking International, 1999: 129; Scheffer, 1994: 10), the UK clothing sector faced considerable difficulties with the emergence of large clothing sectors in low-wage developing countries. As seen in the previous chapter, many states, Malaysia included, came to see export-led growth based on light manufacturing as a way of bringing about development through industrialization. Since the clothing industry generally relied upon high levels of low-cost labour and relatively simple technology, it represented an ideal industry for states seeking to develop their manufacturing base. Table 4.1 gives some indication of the differences in wage costs between Britain, other developed economies, and certain other economies in the developing world that have developed an export sector in garment production as part of the shift toward EOI.

Thus we can see how a country such as Hong Kong which, as one of the first wave NICs, was a major player in the global garment industry now faces competition from a number of countries where labour costs are considerably lower (in fact Hong Kong-based garment companies have themselves exported garment production to these low-wage bases across Asia). The table also provides evidence of wage rates in Malaysia and we can see that these were significantly lower than those found in the UK. In 1990 average hourly labour costs in the UK were US$8.02, and even though these fell slightly to US$7.99 in 1991, in Malaysia comparable figures for the same years were US$0.56 and US$0.62 respectively. Although these figures are based upon guesstimates provided by an industry magazine, and therefore the accuracy of these figures could be queried, they do show us the overall trends, and in this sense are useful indicators of what wages might have been like in Malaysia at the time of SW-Fashions' investment and the expansion of the Malaysian investment that occurred under UK-Apparel.

Table 4.1 Average hourly labour costs in the clothing industry in US\$, 1990, 1991 and 1998

	1990	1991	1998*
Western Europe			
Portugal	2.30	2.15	
UK	8.02	7.99	10.86
Italy	12.58	13.50	13.6
Germany	14.37	14.81	18.0
East and Southeast Asia			
Indonesia	0.16	0.18	
People's Republic of China	0.26	0.24	0.43
Malaysia	0.56	0.62	
Hong Kong	3.05	3.39	5.2
Eastern Europe			
Poland	0.50	0.54	
Hungary	0.92	1.19	
Near East			
Morocco	0.92	0.94	
Turkey	1.35	2.31	1.84

Sources: Winterton and Barlow (1996), 'Economic Restructuring of UK Clothing' in I.M.
Taplin and J. Winterton (eds.), *Restructuring Within a Labour Intensive Industry*,
Aldershot: Avebury, table 3.4, 36.
* Observatoire Europeen du Textile et d'Habillement (OETH) (1999), The EU
Textile and Clothing Sector: A Factual Report, Brussels: OETH, fig. 3.4, 18.

The perceived threat of foreign competition in textiles and clothing from NICs to manufacturing employment in the industrialized world, was reflected in the establishment of the MFA in 1973 (which set up a quota system on clothing imports from East Asia). Since 1973, therefore, trade in clothing was subject to relatively high levels of protection. The protection of textiles and clothing industries by the most industrialized nations reflected a number of factors such as the importance of these sectors to overall employment in the developed world and also the influence that textile and clothing interests – in particular the large textile manufacturing firms – had over governments (Underhill, 1998: 103-109). The MFA ran contrary to the promise of trade liberalization embodied in the GATT, and yet it was justified on the grounds that it provided an opportunity for the developed countries to re-structure their economies away from labour intensive manufacturing.

Yet in spite of the protectionism of the MFA, the low-cost of production in many of the newly industrialising countries meant that from the 1970s onwards, retailers increasingly sourced more of their clothing lines from overseas suppliers (although M&S was initially a notable exception to this trend), thus bringing British clothing manufacturers into competition with low-cost producers in the developing world. The ability, of first the retailers, and later, the manufacturers, to get around the MFA restrictions, eventually led to their demise, as the industry no longer saw the MFA as in its interests such was the extent of transnationalism in the industry (Underhill, 1998: 211).

Throughout the 1980s and 1990s Britain has run a trade deficit in clothing and textiles. In the clothing sector, the ratio of exports to imports fell from 0.50 in 1983 to 0.45 in 1991 (Winterton and Barlow, 1996: 32). Furthermore a breakdown of this data reveals that this worsening balance of trade was especially prevalent in specific segments of the UK garment industry, for example; womens' and girls' tailored outerwear, light outerwear, lingerie and infants' wear. In these segments, an increase in import penetration occurred alongside a sharp decline in the ratio of exports to imports. In other words, UK manufacturers were unable to deal with the problem of rising imports of these products through increases in exports (Winterton and Barlow, 1996: 33). The UK industry remained oriented towards domestic production and faced high levels of import penetration.

But it is important not to overstate the extent to which these imports came from low-wage countries. Countries such as Italy and the US managed to maintain high levels of exports to the UK market. They were aided by the fact that developed states were not subject to MFA quotas, and, therefore, the ongoing trade liberalization between the developed states placed increased competitive pressures upon the UK industry. Although both Italy and the USA have maintained high levels of exports to the UK, this trend is gradually changing and the figures suggest that there has been a continual decline in OECD countries exporting to the UK. The competitive pressure from low-wage countries is therefore on the increase. In 1983, the major low-wage exporter to the UK was Hong Kong, whose exports in clothing to the UK exceeded all those of Africa and Latin America combined. By 1997, however, it was India that was the largest non-OECD country exporting to the UK closely followed by China and then Pakistan (OECD, 1990, 1999). What is more, foreign competition from low-wage countries was often able to get around the MFA quotas by focussing production on different garments which had higher levels of spare quota under the terms of the agreement or even moving production to states which had surplus quotas or preferential treatment under the MFA (Heyzer, 1986: 97) (this factor, for example explains the high level of South Korean direct investment in the Bangladeshi garment sector (Green, 1998a: 11)). Foreign competition was especially intense in the more standardized products such as jeans because retailers could place orders long in advance.

Figure 4.2 Employment in the UK clothing sector, 1971-2001 (projected), by gender and occupational status

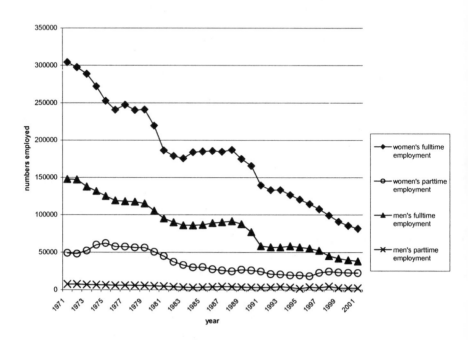

Source: Data provided as excel file, 'Employment in UK Textiles and Clothing Industries', from Institute for Employment Research (1999), *Review of the Economy and Employment*, IER, University of Warwick.

The restructuring of a labour intensive industry?

As has already been mentioned, the larger UK manufacturers had developed their industries on the back of these long standardized garment runs, and it was therefore, the large firms that suffered most from the intensification of foreign competition – a decline intensified by the recession of the early 1980s. Given that most of the UK industry is overwhelmingly domestically oriented, the collapse of consumer demand at a time of increased foreign competition saw a number of bankruptcies in the sector and between 1978 and 1981, the number of firms fell by 16% (Office for National Statistics, 1986: 10). Employment in particular has suffered a massive decrease. This is evident from figure 4.2 (above). What the data presented in this figure reveals is that there was a significant collapse in full-time employment in this sector (in particular women's full time employment which fell from over 300,000 in 1971 to 139,000 by 1991 and was projected to fall to 81,605 by 2001). The decline in part-time employment has been somewhat less sharp, although the numbers employed basically halved between 1971 and 1991. Although it is difficult to speculate why part-time employment has declined less rapidly in this sector, it might be suggested that such patterns are in keeping with general patterns of employment within the UK economy. Furthermore, on a visit to UK-Apparel's Cheshire factory (part of the light sewing division to which the Malaysian factories also belong (see figure 4.1), I was told that the company had real difficulties in filling full time positions in what was regarded as a declining industry and has therefore moved to recruit workers more on a part-time basis.[15]

The job losses charted in figure 4.2 need to be understood not only in terms of the rise of foreign competition in the UK market, but also in terms of the changes that occurred within this sector during the 1980s. For the larger manufacturers, still reliant on mass production of standardized garments, there were very few options available other than moving production offshore.

It has been suggested that British clothing manufacturers were able to stem the extent of the decline in the sector with the application of new technologies such as Computer Aided Design and Computer Aided Manufacture (CAD/CAM) that enabled quick and easy changes in design and production – a shift towards "flexible specialization" and niche marketing (Kilduff, 1997: 1; Zeitlin and Totterdill, 1989). Consequently, the argument has been put forward that the job losses in the garment sector were not only the result of the inability of the UK clothing sector to adapt in the face of low-cost foreign competition, but also the effect of the implementation of labour saving technologies which caused productivity to rise and therefore lessened the need for such labour intensive production processes. However, it is suggested here that it is difficult to really characterize the UK garment industry as moving toward this model of flexible specialization and technological progress. The reorganization of the sector along such lines has been limited by the extent to which large manufacturers have retained a reliance on standardized mass production. In actual fact, the restructuring that was taking place within the UK garment industry during the 1980s effectively amounted to the re-location of the most labour intensive components of the production process offshore. The technological improvements that are available in garment manufacture do not generally alter the fact that the industry remains reliant on sewing machine technology, and has consequently remained highly labour intensive (Bryne, 1998: 3). Technological improvements are concentrated in areas such as product design, cutting technologies and some use of automated handling systems. But it is notable that during the period 1974-1983 (when import penetration was rising and employment in the garment sector fell sharply), investment in the clothing sector actually fell. Hence Winterton and Barlow (1996: 59) comment that "[t]here is little evidence of a high-technology strategy for the clothing industry".

Technological innovations were limited and had very little impact overall on worker productivity. The industry remained largely reliant on low-wage female labour, albeit female labour located in offshore factories or in the secondary small

---

[15] Interview with Personnel Officer, UK-Apparel Ladieswear, Cheshire, 10th June 1999.

firm sector of the UK clothing industry. Furthermore, rather than a shift towards capital-intensive production, Walsh (1991: 283) has charted an "intensification" of the labour process in the industry, highlighting the role of a "fear factor" as employers were able to get employees to work even harder in the face of economic downturn and rising unemployment in the 1980s. With this in mind, one also needs to consider the way in which this intensification of work was reflected in the growth of the secondary small firm and home working segments of the British clothing industry during the 1980s (Mitter, 1988: 50). The restructuring of the industry during the 1980s and 1990s was not the result of new technological inputs and "flexible specialization", but a rationalization based upon subcontracting and the movement of operations overseas. The shift of UK production offshore is discussed in more detail below, but when we look at how the domestic UK industry underwent restructuring during the 1980s, the extent to which the industry increasingly came to rely on more informal working practices and small firm production (often characterized as "sweatshop" production) is significant.

These smaller producers often acted as subcontractors for the larger firms, but they also played a significant role in the production of low-cost fashion garments. Whereas the growth of the large garment firms was on the back of the development of standardized long running production lines for the major retailers, smaller producers often producing for the more flexible "fashionwear" market – women's outerwear - were characterized by short production runs and greater volatility in demand (Phizacklea, 1990). Many small producers during the 1980s actually benefited from a shift away from the retailer's dependence on standardized clothing and towards more fashion oriented consumption. These trends resulted in the growth of the "sweatshop" and homeworking segements of the UK garment sector. For example, the West Midlands Low Pay Unit claims that employment in the West Midlands clothing industry (a centre of inner city sweatshop production) grew by 20% between 1981 and 1987 taking it from 1.5% of West Midland manufacturing employment in 1981 to 2.2% in 1987. Such a rise is especially significant given that it took place during a time when employment in manufacturing as a whole fell by over 17% in the region (Anderson, Bahia, Kaur, and Davies, 1991: 9).

These small firms tended to be run by entrepreneurs from within Britain's ethnic minority communities, were located in the inner cities and generally produced clothing in poor working environments, with longer working hours and lacked the technological advances found in the larger clothing firms. However, both the primary and secondary sectors are characterized by low levels of pay. For example, according to figures from 1992, average annual wages for operative employees in the clothing sector were £6,522 in firms with less than 100 employees and £7,041 in firms with over 1,000 employees (Office for National Statistics, 1992: 12-13). Coyle (1984: 8) therefore has commented that "what unites the industry is the low-wages paid to its predominately female labour force".

Yet, at the same time, the shift towards sweatshop production and the low pay and poor conditions associated with this sector, can be regarded as indicative of the terminal decline in the industry. Rationalization and closure of clothing factories has been concentrated in the large and medium sized manufacturers who despite technological investment, were unable to compete with low-cost overseas suppliers unless they moved their production offshore. The development of this sweatshop sector, reflected the way in which small business sought to meet the competition head on – exploiting cheap female labour in inner-city ethnic communities.

The shift offshore

Given the labour intensive nature of the garment sector, it is notable that large UK manufacturers (in common with other firms across Western Europe) have chosen to relocate production offshore rather than to try and rationalize domestic production. Firms that shift production offshore are generally perceived to experience a rapid growth in profitability on the back of the labour cost savings made (Scheffer, 1994: 10). I would also suggest that the lack of technological innovation in the garment sector is tied in with the way that employers could utilize low paid female labour rather than have to invest in technological research and development. This linkage between cheap female labour and a lack of technological innovation in sewing machine work is highlighted in the way that large manufacturers reliant on the mass production of standardized goods, chose to relocate in offshore locations (where there would be a supply of low-cost female labour) rather than invest in their existing plant and workforce. Thus although the shift to offshore production at first appears to be the result of the declining commitment of the UK clothing retailers to source clothing from UK based producers, such a shift needs to be understood within the context of the ability of the industry to find people (i.e. women) that are willing to work for such low wages (and indeed, the role of garment sector firms in actively constructing women as a low cost source of labour – an argument developed in the final section of this book).

It was the retailers, rather than the manufacturers, who first began sourcing products from overseas (Phizacklea, 1990). Yet at the same time, M&S retained a base of UK suppliers, with these suppliers often subcontracting out production (at home or overseas) or directly establishing wholly owned factories for manufacturing their product in low-wage locations. In theory, the major UK retailers could import all of their goods from overseas suppliers through the establishment of buying offices to source ready made garments and to subcontract out product lines. At M&S, for example, the retailer has cultivated contacts with offshore firms, in particular for the production of some of the most standardized clothing lines. This is a development that has created great concern within UK-Apparel, and other M&S suppliers, and underlined the perceived need within the sector for increased reliance on offshore production. However, such a strategy would require considerable organization as well as involving greater risk and the potential for greater lead times on garment production (Scheffer, 1994: 12). Consequently, many retailers have been willing to accept the higher costs involved in working through UK based manufacturers because the risks are lower. At M&S, for example, the retaining of a relationship with a base of traditional suppliers has meant that the firm is able to work with familiar design teams, and with firms whom it trusts to meet its quality standards, thereby enabling the retailer to have some degree of "exclusivity" or brand image.[16]

Offshore investment options in the garment sector

There are a range of offshore strategies that are available to the UK based manufacturing firms such as UK-Apparel. One such approach has been the development of outward processing trade (OPT), whereby manufacturers would subcontract the most labour intensive sections of the production process to neighbouring low-wage countries. Although OPT has been around since the 1960s (Scheffer, 1994: 9), the OPT process was further aided by the fact that these practices did not count under the MFA regime. For example, US tariffs (where they apply) are only levied on the value added to the garment (Phizacklea, 1990: 40). Within the EU a similar situation exists under EC Regulation 29/1392 which assures that import duties are calculated only on the value added on OPT so long as the materials used were already in free circulation within the EU (Scheffer, 1994: 15). With certain countries, specific quantitative restrictions under EC regulation 638/82 restricts firms engaged in OPT to the use of EC materials. Although even under this regulation the EU allows for a tolerance level of 14% for use on non-EU fabrics (Scheffer, 1994: 15). For an increasing number of countries (especially Mediterranean and Eastern European countries), preferential relations with the EU exist and thus OPT imports are duty free (Scheffer, 1994: 16). Within the European clothing industry it has been German firms in particular who have utilized these OPT practices, exporting ready cut cloth to factories in Eastern Europe for assembly and then importing the made-up garments for the finishing processes (Smith, 2003). In 1998, Germany accounted for 52.2% of OPT imports to EU member states, compared to a 9.9% share for the UK (OETH 1999: 70).

In the UK garment sector, the shift to offshore production by manufacturers has been less oriented towards OPT, with firms preferring to subcontract entire product lines to overseas garment firms, or to directly establish factories in low-wage locations through FDI. The main advantage of FDI over OPT or subcontracting is that, in the long-term, it tends to be much more cost effective for manufacturers and has the added benefit of offering them greater control over offshore production processes (Scheffer, 1994: 56). This control over production is especially useful in terms of maintaining quality standards, a point that will be returned to in the final part of this chapter.

Aside from OPT there are a variety of other subcontracting arrangements available to manufacturers and retailers in the garment industry. The firm might contract out to other firms to produce its garments on a cut make and trim (CMT) basis. In a CMT system the garment is made-up entirely in a low-cost country by a subcontracted firm using materials supplied by the principal firm. These subcontracting arrangements often require working through intermediaries or

---

[16] Interview with Womenswear head of procurement M&S, Baker Street HQ, London, 8th June 2000.

"converters" such as the large Hong Kong and Singapore based garment trading firms, using CMT firms in low-cost locations such as China (Scheffer, 1994: 11). Such a strategy, therefore, involves additional costs in terms of the commissions charged by such intermediaries or agents, but they are often viewed as preferable to FDI, since they involve less risk (in terms of the amount invested). Another option is the granting of manufacturing licences to another firm to produce, as well as, distribute the principle firm's products. Finally, finished garments can be bought-in in accordance with the principle firm's design specifications (Scheffer, 1994: 18-19). In order to control these kinds of sourcing operations, firms will often establish overseas offices in the major source areas, again, these often tend to be in Hong Kong or Singapore (Blyth, 1996: 125).

One of the problems with offshore subcontracting is that it is often very difficult to ensure quality standards and response times (Blyth, 1996: 113-114). Furthermore, concerns have been raised regarding employment standards and practices and the extent to which manufacturers and retailers in the developed world can realistically guarantee that labour standards are being met in their suppliers (especially when we take into account the way in which the garment industry is now organized in terms of vast globalized networks of subcontracted garment production (Green, 1998a)). One of the ways through which UK based firms (and other garment firms based in the developed world) have sought to deal with these problems is via the establishment of more substantive "partnerships" with offshore manufacturers. This is especially the case in the more fast moving fashionwear market where there is need for short runs and quick response times, increasing the opportunity to change a product, or move to another product line. Hence, the popularity of subcontracting to offshore suppliers has increased in recent years, reflecting a declining commitment to domestic suppliers (even in the lower cost small firm sector). Foreign subcontracting accounted for 3% of the turnover of the garment firms sampled by Scheffer in 1983, rising to 15% by 1992, whilst domestic subcontracting fell from 11% of turnover to 9% over the same period (Scheffer, 1994: 136). The shift to offshore production, sourcing and subcontracting has been especially pronounced in the ladieswear sector (Scheffer, 1994: 141), thus suggesting that the original advantage that the UK based small firm clothing sector had in terms of close proximity to the fast changing UK fashionwear market may be becoming eclipsed by the development of faster communications and transportation technologies between UK based large retailers and manufacturers and their suppliers in the developing world (Ram, Gilman, Arrowsmith and Edwards, 2003).

The move offshore by UK-Apparel

This chapter has looked generally at the process whereby UK firms decided to increase their use of FDI and subcontract production rather than utilize a UK production base, here, the focus turns to consider how these overall trends relate to the case study firm. Why did the firm decide to locate production offshore and, more importantly, how did it go about the process of FDI? Having outlined the major options that are available to firms wishing to increase the level of offshore production or sourcing, the discussion now turns to focus on why the case study firm itself decided to invest offshore, and how the process of offshore investment was implemented. Again the issue of labour costs dominates the decision by the firm to establish operations in Malaysia. The significance of labour costs is something that is emphasized in this book and in this chapter attention has been drawn to the way that garment firms have sought to maintain a supply of low-cost labour through offshore investment strategies. However, it is worth bearing in mind that labour cost considerations alone are not the only factor involved in the relocation of production offshore. It is also important to consider why the firm decided to invest in Malaysia specifically, taking into account factors other than merely labour costs, for example, political stability, macro-economic policy, political "appropriateness", incentives to investors and the close proximity to fabric manufacturers within the East and Southeast Asian region.[17]

In terms of company decision-making relating to the move offshore, it is also important to consider the actual management of offshore production in Malaysia looking at how decisions regarding the day to day running of offshore operations are made and implemented. In particular, the focus is on the degree to which there is any kind of convergence between the managerial practices found in the operations of UK-Apparel in Britain and its Malaysian operations.

Company decision-making and the move offshore

Referring back to the company structure diagram provided earlier on in this chapter (see figure 4.1 – page 87) decisions on offshore production are considered to be something decided on by the individual firms (e.g. UK-Apparel Ladieswear) and not by the Group. The Group will, however, have to ratify any decisions that are made concerning off shore investment. It is worth bearing in mind the point raised earlier in this chapter that the decisions concerning Malaysian investment were a slightly different case since this part of the company was not a part of UK-Apparel when the Malaysian operations were first established (the Malaysian factories were established by SW-Fashions). The discussion relating to the decision to move production offshore presented here, therefore, relates to the experience of SW-Fashions, rather than that of UK-Apparel. Although it should be recalled from the earlier discussion, that the process of FDI pioneered by SW-Fashions in Malaysia has come to stand as something of a blueprint for FDI across the UK-Apparel Group. We shall discuss in a moment the reasons for locating investment in Malaysia.

Despite the significance attached earlier in this chapter to the role that M&S played in refocusing the UK clothing industry towards offshore production, senior managers at UK-Apparel were unwilling to view the shift offshore as M&S-led. One senior manager from the UK-Apparel Group claimed that the relationship between the two firms was not at all dictatorial, in fact it was more like a

---

[17] Scheffer (1994: 52) notes, for example, that in the Far East, 90% of the fabrics that are sourced by garment firms are from within the region.

"marriage", a partnership in which they worked together on the various problems that they were facing. Interestingly, Rannie's interviews with M&S suppliers in the 1980s revealed a similar view of the retailer (Rannie, 1984: 148-155). In an interview with M&S's head of womenswear procurement, I was informed that there were considerable benefits to be gained from maintaining a good relationship with their suppliers, commenting that the strong base of suppliers that M&S was able to draw upon gave it a unique strength within the UK garment industry. However, the same interview revealed that M&S wanted these suppliers to engage in an even greater level of offshore production.[18] Of course, SW-Fashions and subsequently UK-Apparel, were not simply dictated to by M&S to establish subsidiary firms offshore. But it is undoubtedly the case that M&S's declining commitment to "buy British" made entirely UK-based production an even less viable option.

As has already been noted in this chapter, labour cost considerations were the primary motivating factor in the decision to shift production offshore. Consequentially, large UK firms have moved some of the most labour intensive sections of their production processes overseas. This trend is evident within the Light Sewing Division of UK-Apparel Ladieswear. Although some production is maintained at the UK factory site in Cheshire, the Malaysian operations generally produce those garments that require more "handling" due to the complexity and number of different operations required for that particular garment (i.e. they are more labour intensive). The Malaysian factories, therefore, tend to produce garments such as blouses, whilst production in Cheshire concentrates on much simpler products such as T-shirts using fabrics manufactured in the EU.[19] In fact, production at the Cheshire plant has been scaled down considerably in recent years. The site has been re-organized to provide mainly warehousing facilities for orders coming in from overseas factories and suppliers. Interviews with a trade union representative at the Cheshire factory revealed very real concerns regarding the future viability of the company's UK operations given the loss of core orders to offshore factories and suppliers.

> When they shut the Welsh factories the MD [managing director] came and assured us that we were not closing. But people were not convinced at all. The branch secretary asked him to address the factory and he stood on a chair and did that. But then we lost the order for jersey shirts, an order that was one of the ones that is made nine months ahead... Now style changes are quicker and we get smaller orders. Managers have left and we have different MDs coming through. The impression is that they are deserting ship. There have been lots of worries, rumours and anticipation about this. Workers really started to worry when the threads ran out. We were convinced that they didn't

---

[18] Interview with head of Womenswear procurement, M&S Baker Street HQ, London, 8th June 2000.
[19] Visit to Cheshire factory (10th June 1999). Factory tour provided by Personnel Officer.

have the orders. So they start to display new orders in the factory. But orders can still be cancelled, so it doesn't amount to much.[20]

If the difference in labour costs between the UK and Malaysia explain the decision to shift production offshore (a position that was emphasized by the Personnel Director in interviews), how do we explain why it was Malaysia in particular that was selected as a site for the firm's overseas factories? After all, table 4.1 revealed that labour costs in Malaysia were higher than those found in other countries in the region (notably China and Indonesia).

Clearly there were factors other than labour-costs that were taken into consideration when the firm made the decision to invest in Malaysia. One such factor that was emphasized in the interviews with Group level management was the issue of "political appropriateness". This is the term that was used by the Personnel Director to refer to the way that company offshore investment strategies need to be perceived as "ethical". The company is keen not to appear ruthless in their decisions, especially given the rising importance of labour standards debates in the garment sector. A range of consumer led campaigns have forced both M&S and UK-Apparel to be very careful about where their products are sourced from and to maintain certain minimum standards for workers (Green, 1998a, 1998b). This commitment to "political appropriateness" should not, however, be confused with the notion that the firm is acting to implement more "progressive" workplace standards in its offshore operations.   These are often very much minimum standards, and furthermore, as will be shown in chapters five and six, they have little to no impact on the way that garment sector employment is based upon the crowding of women workers into low paid menial jobs. The issue of political appropriateness also involves some analysis of the political context that the firm is investing in. It was noted in chapter three, for example, that foreign investors value stable macroeconomic policy-making, lack of political instability a positive attitude towards foreign investment (including incentives to investors) and a stable, pro-business, system of industrial relations.

Secondly, senior managers made the point that there is little advantage to be gained in continually moving production to wherever it is cheapest. I was told that simply by moving out of the UK to a low-wage country, the savings that are made in terms of costs are so significant that there is actually very little difference between where your offshore operations are.[21] Thus despite the fact that labour costs in Malaysia are somewhat higher than those found in neighbouring Indonesia or in China, there are enduring advantages in remaining committed to Malaysia. The firm still makes considerable savings compared to the cost of doing business (and therefore paying workers) in the UK, and Malaysia is considered to be more politically stable and a less controversial site for FDI by the firm. I was told for example by the general manager at UKALM (the Malaysian operations) that UK-Apparel's operations in Indonesia had faced severe problems in terms of getting

---

[20] Interview with GMB Shop Steward, UK-Apparel, Ladieswear Ltd, Cheshire (10th June 1999).

[21] Interview with UK-Apparel Quality Director, LSD (27th September 1999).

products out of the country at a time of increasing political unrest.[22] What is more, since sewing is a relatively skilled production activity, there are advantages to be gained from the maintenance of a skilled workforce at one particular site over a number of years.

Thirdly, labour costs are not the only costs that need to be accounted for when moving production offshore; there are also transportation costs – transporting both fabrics to the factories and clothing from the factories. Hence the re-location of the textiles industry offshore has encouraged the location of factories close to textile producers and at the same time the importance of maintaining a quick response (QR) on certain production lines has also had an impact upon where production is located. Thus on the issue of UK-Apparel's long-term commitment to Malaysia one manager commented to me:

> You can't hop around, you wouldn't get the culture right since it takes a long time to educate a workforce in quality standards and the correct approach to making a garment. If you did hop around, you would get hardly any focus or continuity.[23]

However, perhaps the business could be labelled as more footloose when it comes down to the networks of offshore subcontractors that are part of the clothing commodity chain that UK-Apparel is part of. These are known as "partner" factories (although there is no actual ownership by UK-Apparel of these partner firms) and they perform a variety of roles in the clothing commodity chain for example, producing when there is a shortfall in capacity, or maybe to perform specific tasks (e.g. beading) that UK-Apparel doesn't have the expertise to produce. Sometimes, UK-Apparel will subcontract out entire lines to these partner firms.[24]

Despite the advantages of fully owned offshore operations, UK-Apparel does not have any further plans for new fully owned offshore sites, claiming "we are currently consolidating where we are currently at".[25] In reality, this means expanding existing offshore plants and increasingly depending on subcontracted partner firms. However, fully owned offshore operations such as the Malaysian factories, have a hugely important role in overall company strategy. This is especially the case given the loss of certain core lines to firms that do not have a UK asset base and are sourced directly by M&S. The offshore factories are regarded as a means through which a firm like UK-Apparel can maintain a control over quality standards and speed of response, thus maintaining a high level of service to the retail chain and at the same time benefiting from the lower production costs found offshore. One manager told me, for example, that UK-Apparel's factories were technologically superior, and the company was able to

---

[22] Interview with Factory Manager UKALM (18th August 1999).
[23] Interview with UK-Apparel Quality Director (LSD) (27th September 1999).
[24] Interview with UK-Apparel Quality Director (LSD) (27th September 1999).
[25] Interview with UK-Apparel Group PLC Personnel Director (27th September 1999).

foster a better attitude and culture in its workplaces that aided the overall service that they offered to M&S.[26]

These comments, however, somewhat contradicted those that were made by one of the expatriate managers that I interviewed in Malaysia who argued that UK-Apparel had almost no need whatsoever for UK based operations or even UK based designers and technologists.[27] He was critical of what he saw as UK-Apparel's inability to "think offshore" – that the company still operated as if it were a UK manufacturing company – an attitude impossible to sustain in such a highly globalized industry. These comments reflect, in many ways, those found in a recent trade journal in which it was commented that M&S's "buy British" policies have fostered anachronistic attitudes in the UK industry regarding the extent to which they are prepared to commit to offshore production (Anson, 1999: 14-15). It will be interesting therefore to see how the company continues to respond to the changing demands of M&S in the future and whether further offshore operations will be opened up.

What this discussion has revealed so far are some of the dilemmas that a firm faces in locating production offshore. We will look at the specific issues of how the company manages the communication issues involved in offshore production in a moment, but first it is worth focussing in on the Malaysian factories and discussing why this location was selected as a site for foreign investment.

Malaysia as a site for FDI

The selection of Malaysia as a site for this crucially important first attempt at running an offshore factory came about as the result of a company sponsored project carried out by MBA students at the Manchester Business School to locate a suitable site for investment.[28] The project sought to assess the potential for investment in a variety of different locations that included, as well as Malaysia, Hong Kong, Mauritius, Thailand, Indonesia. The project looked at a number of different factors affecting investment in each of these locations. Firstly, they sought to establish something about the nature of the workforce itself with an emphasis placed upon labour cost and productivity, quality, skill education and labour market flexibility. Secondly, they considered management practices in the location and thirdly, cultural attitudes towards foreign investors in each location. Fourthly, issues pertaining to logistics and shipping were assessed – especially the existence of a "textiles infrastructure", by which they were referring to the availability, quality and ease of transportation and shipping of supplies of fabric and accessories in the region. Fifthly was the nature of the existing industrial structure. Sixthly came quota restrictions under the MFA, and finally the project assessed the suitability of locations as sites for the establishment of manufacturing

---

[26] Interview with UK-Apparel Quality Director (LSD) (27th September 1999).

[27] Interview with Production Manager UK-Apparel Ladieswear Malaysia (UKALM) Sdn. Bhd., Malaysia (18th August 1999).

[28] Interview with UK-Apparel Group PLC Personnel Director, Staffordshire (6th November 1998).

subsidiaries in terms of political factors; government attitudes towards industry and investors, levels of corruption and the political and economic situation more generally in the country.[29]

If these were the criteria that the company used in shaping its decision to invest in Malaysia, what did these criteria actually mean in practice? Why was it that Malaysia was deemed to be an attractive location in terms of these criteria? Labour factors were of particular importance – especially the low-cost of labour relative to the UK – as was the perception that there was a large pool of available labour suited to working in UK-Apparel's factories. The UK-Apparel manager whom I spoke with at length on the investment process in Malaysia was keen to point out that labour costs alone were not the only factor in the decision to invest in Malaysia. He stressed the fact that there were many places in the world where there were much cheaper sources of labour – claiming that the Malaysian labour force was also well educated and English was widely spoken making the task of training, managing and organizing workers much easier. Considerations regarding land costs were also important and the cost of land was a key factor in the decision to locate the factory in the state of Malacca, rather than in the more industrialized states of Selangor and Penang to the north.[30]

In weighing up the risk factors surrounding FDI decision-making, political factors also loomed large. A politically stable environment was perceived as lowering the risks associated with investment. The BN government was also regarded as pro-business and Malaysian government investment incentives also featured as key reasons for why Malaysia was selected. UK-Apparel benefited from a range of investment incentives on arrival in Malaysia. Including the classification of its factory as a Licensed Manufacturing Warehouse (LMW) whereby it was given the same tax relief as firms on FTZs. There was considered to be an openness of culture to foreign investment. When I asked about what this meant in the interviews, the nature of this cultural openness was explained to me both in terms of the government of Malaysia's positive attitude towards foreign investment and a more functional explanation was also offered – that "openness of culture" was in fact to do with the wide use of the English language. This therefore raises issues concerning the extent to which investment by a British firm in Malaysia reflected a form of post-colonial relationship by which the firm felt more comfortable developing its first major offshore venture in a former British colony.

Finally, internationally agreed policies on the trade in garments (the MFA) also featured in the decision-making process. At the time of UK-Apparel's investment, there was no quota imposed on blouse exports to the EU (category 7 of

---

[29] "Why Malaysia?", company document provided by the Personnel Director, UK-Apparel Group PLC (6th November 1998).

[30] Interview with UK-Apparel Group PLC Personnel Director, Staffordshire (6th November 1998).

the EU MFA). This was later imposed, but has not hampered UK-Apparel at all as there remained a large amount of spare quota under this category.[31]

The investment process

Following on from this project, a more in depth feasibility study was done which confirmed the findings of the MBA project – that Malaysia offered considerable advantages as a manufacturing base. A final report was then developed which not only presented the case for locating an offshore subsidiary in Malaysia, it also established the mechanisms through which this process would take place – by formulating an investment strategy.[32] We now turn to the details of this investment strategy. Such examination provides an insight into the way that the company perceives itself in the investment process, and sheds light on how managers at UK-Apparel view the company as engaging with the local social context in Malaysia and expanding upon some of the themes already established in chapter one.

Figure 4.3 is a pictorial representation of how the company formulated its strategy for investment in Malaysia. The diagram is based upon a similar diagram that I was shown during my field research at the firm and also on information gained in the interviews. All of the areas shaded grey in the diagram represent internal company decision-making, and the other areas of the diagram represent those factors external to the investment process. The actual process of investing in Malaysia was very complicated and there was, from the start, a division of responsibility between "UK policy decisions" (strategic decisions that determined the overall direction of the firm's foreign investment strategy) and what they term "tactical decisions" relating to the actual setting up of a factory in Malaysia. This division is represented in the diagram using the two light grey shaded boxes. The UK policy decisions included in the left hand light grey box in the diagram are those decisions made in the UK that related to the investment process in Malaysia. UK policy decisions include levels of transfer pricing (the level at which the firm sets the price of goods transferred within its organizational boundaries, as opposed to through international trade, thereby enabling the firm to overvalue or undervalue profits in order to get around taxation restrictions in host and parent states), the financing of the investment process, numbers of expatriate staff to be sent to Malaysia, levels of technology transfer, decisions concerning the range of products to be produced in the offshore site, and the timing issues (which particular ranges would be sent for production in Malaysia once the factory was up and running relating to time constraints).

The light grey box on the right hand side of the diagram represents the decisions that were delegated to local level during the investment process. These decisions included company location (whether to establish on a greenfield site, and where in Malaysia to locate), the level of equity ownership in the firm, what sort of corporate status it would have under Malaysian law, what levels of investment

---

[31] Interview with Operations Manager, UKALM Sdn. Bhd. (11th March 1999).

[32] Interviews with UK-Apparel Group PLC Personnel Director, Staffordshire (6th November 1998), Cheshire (19th May 2000).

would be necessary prior to the establishment of the factory, the various local negotiations that would be necessary (with state institutions and agencies), and decisions concerning the local labour force.

But figure 4.3 does more than just show how responsibility for the investment process was divided up. It also represents how the company regarded policy decisions as being shaped by a number of "external factors". These external factors are shown in the diagram as "outside" of the company structures and are to do with where the company meets with the "real world" outside of the firm. It is important to note, however, that the use of the word "external" is one that the company itself has used. This is not to imply that I regard the factors shown in the diagram as "externalities". The implications of this conceptualization of the way that the company interacts with the outside world will be returned to shortly.

Looking at the Malaysian tactical decision box in the diagram. We can see that the company views the decisions made at this level as being shaped by external factors such as the cost of local labour, the potential risk of the decision, the nature of investment incentives, and more general logistical problems. The operation of these decision-making procedures on investment resulted in the establishment of a factory on a greenfield site in Malacca, a state in western peninsular Malaysia, conveniently located infrastructurally in terms of transportation to local ports/airports. It had LMW status, the location was deemed suitable in terms of supply of labour since it was a largely rural state and therefore likely to have a large supply of potential workers. The company had minimal levels of expatriate staff (a reflection of the high cost of relocating staff and the concerns of the Malaysian and the state government to keep expatriate posts at a minimum) with, at this stage, even the managing director being recruited locally.[33]

It is important to note that these external factors were not only conceptualized as affecting the day to day running of the investment process in Malaysia, but as affecting certain strategic decisions made by the company in the UK. The company regarded not just the process of investment as shaped by these "externalities" but that investment would have implications for the entire firm because of this interaction between the firm and the local context of investment. Given that this book examines the generalizations found in IPE literature concerning the progressive role of multinational firms in favour of the view that firms actively engage with the socially embedded market, it is significant that the firm itself accepts that the offshore investment process has such a profound impact on the way that the firm is managed.

---

[33] Interview with UK-Apparel Group PLC Personnel Director, Staffordshire (6th November 1998).

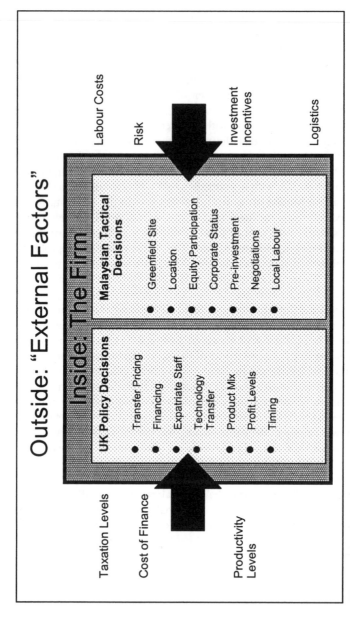

Figure 4.3 How UK-Apparel conceptualizes investment decision-making
Source: Company documents provided by the Group Personnel Director UK-Apparel.

But what is actually meant by external factors and can they really be conceptualized as externalities at all? Is there some boundary between the firm and the social, political and cultural context within which it operates? Of course, the dichotomy between external and internal factors is a far too simplistic conceptualization of investment decisions, but what this discussion has allowed for is an analysis of how the firm itself views the process. The firm places itself in the position of the rational-acting investment decision-maker, responding to external pressures in its decision-making activities. Hence, we do not see two-way arrows in figure 4.3; there is no recognition of how the process of FDI may actually impact upon "external factors" such as labour costs. My argument is that investment decision-making may well have been shaped by the availability of low cost labour, but once the firm invested in Malaysia, it actively sought to construct a low wage labour force through its recruitment and employment practices (see chapters five and six). Furthermore, since the investment in Malaysia represented a "blueprint", it can be said that this was essentially a gendered investment model because of the emphasis given in it to seeking out low cost labour in an industry with long established practices of femininized low paid work.

The management of offshore production at UK-Apparel

The management of an offshore site presents new problems and issues for a firm. The particular focus presented in this book is on those problems and issues associated with the recruitment and employment process in UK-Apparel's Malaysian operations. Such an investigation reveals the extent to which these company practices involve an active engagement with local social structures, norms and values. The discussion here, lays the background for these debates by looking generally at the extent to which managerial decision-making at UK-Apparel Ladieswear Malaysia (UKALM) Sdn. Bhd. (as UK-Apparel's Malaysian operations are known) is UK based or made locally in Malaysia according to the specific problems that managers face in this location. Thus this discussion provides an insight into how company decision-making is made in accordance with the local (socially embedded) labour market. Thus it is necessary to be able to assess the extent to which the firm can really be perceived as an "external", or "westernising" force in the local political economy of Malaysia. The suggestion made here is given the high level of autonomy granted to HR managers in the design and implementation of recruitment and employment practices, these practices overwhelmingly reflect localized conditions, including the specific way in which managers draw upon gender inequalities via their recruitment and employment practices.

Relations between the parent company and the Malaysian subsidiary can be considered on three different levels. Firstly, decisions that are made in the UK and imposed upon the subsidiary – for example minimum requirements concerning quality and labour standards. Secondly, those company policies and practices that are the result of co-ordination and co-operation between departments in the UK and Malaysia. Finally, there are those company policies and practices that are

LIVERPOOL
JOHN MOORES UNIVERSITY
AVRIL ROBARTS LRC
TEL. 0151 231 4022

determined locally – where there is a complete delegation of responsibility down to local level with almost no input from the UK at all.

Of those policies dictated to the Malaysian operations by the UK parent company, the most important are the quality standards that are imposed by the retailer. Within the light sewing division a manager has been appointed to act as a quality control advisor who will visit the offshore sites to ensure that they can meet specific quality requirements. However, these are not the only standards that the UK firm imposes upon Malaysia – perhaps more interesting to this book are those that concern labour standards in offshore locations.

In one of the first interviews that I undertook at UK-Apparel, I was informed of an established set of standards that offshore factories had to comply with. These standards concern a variety of issues including the environment and intellectual property as well as labour (in effect, a code of conduct – although the company did not use this term themselves). These labour standards are basic minimums, but they also cover a number of different issues in employer-employee relations. For example, the company has made it their policy that workers aged under 16 will not be employed in their offshore factories, employees will receive a contract of employment, the company will pursue equal opportunity policies with regard to race, gender, marital status, sexual orientation, age, disability and nationality. In addition to this, the company claims that employees will receive training, will not be required to work overtime, will be paid at least the national minimum wage (or equivalent) in the country that they are employed in, and will not work more than 52 hours per week (exclusive of overtime).[34]

It was suggested to me that the maintaining of these minimum standards in their offshore factories would contribute to UK-Apparel's image as a company producing high quality clothing using a well-trained workforce in a good working environment. What is more, it was felt that such practices would actually enable UK-Apparel to produce clothing more efficiently and effectively.[35] The company operates an employee induction programme across all company factories (whether offshore or in the UK) and it was suggested to me that this programme serves the purpose of monitoring new employee progress and also encouraging employees to regard the workplace as a "happy and harmonious working environment".[36] However, it must be stated that these minimum standards have little to no impact on company employment practices relating to gender divisions in the workplace. Since it is stated in the final chapter of this book that the company actually benefits from drawing upon workplace gender and ethnic inequalities, it is notable that these "equal opportunities" policies exist alongside a grouping of women in low paid work and often with quite overt discriminatory practices in recruitment and

---

[34] Interview with UK-Apparel Group PLC Personnel Director, Staffordshire (6th November 1998). UK-Apparel PLC, *Company Induction Pack*, provided by the Personnel Director, UK-Apparel Group PLC (6th November 1998).

[35] Interview with UK-Apparel Group PLC Personnel Director, Staffordshire (6th November 1998).

[36] Interview with UK-Apparel Group PLC Personnel Director, Staffordshire (6th November 1998).

promotion of workers. Of course, this finding is unsurprising. The rhetoric of equal opportunities is essentially that of a liberal feminism that fails to consider either the structural nature of gender inequality in society or the institutionalized nature of inequality within firms themselves. It can also be said that these minimum standards are so minimal that they have very little impact on the day to day lives of the women working in the Malaysian operations of UK-Apparel.

The second type of relationship between the UK and Malaysia concerns those decisions that are made through a process of engagement between managers in both countries. The interaction between the UK and Malaysia is usually between managers in the ladieswear and light sewing division in the UK with certain managers in Malaysia – especially the expatriate managers. There is daily contact between the managing director of the Malaysian firm and his superiors in ladieswear and the other managing directors in the light sewing division. But the most important department in terms of contact between the UK and Malaysia is the Operations Department. Operations work with the UK parent to determine the overall production targets that the production department will, in turn, strive to meet. Operations, therefore has significant control over the workings of the production department, and operations managers make their decisions based on the requirements of the light sewing division as a whole.

There are however a number of departments with whom the UK has little contact. This includes finance and the technical department. Most significantly, the human resources department (which is responsible for employee recruitment and training) has very little contact with the UK. Even the induction programme that is supposed to be standard in all UK-Apparel factories is less rigorously enforced than in the UK. At the firm's Cheshire site, for example, a personnel officer showed me the detailed files that were kept on new employees monitoring their progress and development,[37] whilst the factories in Malaysia restrict induction to a training school, and employee progress once they are on the production line is solely the responsibility of individual line supervisors.[38]

The responsibility for recruitment (the subject of the next two chapters of this book), lies with the HR department of UKALM. Recruitment practices are, therefore, highly localized. Even managers at the level of the Light Sewing Division of UK-Apparel have little say at all in the nature of recruitment and employment decisions made in Malacca. Another of the more significant factors in the localized nature of the human resources director is the idea that HR managers ought to recruited locally. For example, the HR director at UKALM commented at one point:

> I would say that it would be to the advantage of the company to have a locally recruited HR director who is able to work with the parent company, understands the values of the parent company and how things ought to be brought down to the local level of the

---

[37] Personnel Officer, UK-Apparel factory tour, Cheshire (10th June 1999).
[38] Interview with HR Director, UKALM (10th March 1999).

subsidiary company. You need someone who understands the requirements locally; therefore a local HR director is best.[39]

What the above quotation conveys is that although certain minimum labour standards are conceived within the UK, these are then revised within the Malaysian context in line with localized practices and expectations. The HR director himself, therefore, embodies the fusing together of the global and the local in the subsidiary operations of an MNC. It is also interesting to note that this director is the only senior manager in the firm who is Malay (the other positions are held by Chinese or British managers). It was seen as beneficial to have a Malay HR director given that the overwhelming majority of the workforce is also Malay. The importance of ethnicity in the workplace at UKALM will be explored further in later chapters, but it is worth bringing this issue up at this point because it again demonstrates the way in which the HR director is conceived in terms of translating global management practice down to a local factory level in which structures of ethnicity permeate workplace relations.

The post of HR director is a fairly recent position. The HR director had only been in his job for around six months when we first met in March 1999. Prior to his appointment the company had not given the department a senior manager and the department (then called simply the personnel department) was responsible mainly for the hiring and firing of the non-executive workforce (workers below supervisor level). The decision to improve the status of this department was taken by senior managers in Malaysia in the light of a number of severe personnel problems, in particular the high employee turnover they were faced with. However, it was a decision that was ratified by senior managers in the light sewing division and Ladieswear, and even the UK based Group personnel director had a hand in the appointment.[40] Once appointed, the HR director was sent to the UK for two months for training in order to understand the workings of the business as a whole. Hence, the HR director has a good knowledge of personnel management practices across the whole of UK-Apparel's operations.

Sending Malaysian managers to the UK for training is supported by the Group personnel director since it would allow for some sort of consistency in managerial practice. However, so far the case of the Malaysian HR director is the only example of this. It also seems unlikely that in the future managers will be sent to the UK for training in such a cost conscious industry. Management training therefore is an area in which the company's desire for consistency between the UK and offshore is in fact more a product of *ad-hoc* decision-making, reflecting the local situation. One expatriate manager that I spoke with in Malaysia expressed the view that managerial practices in the Malaysian site were vastly different from those that he had experienced in the UK.[41]

Such issues, therefore, indicate that the level of convergence between the Malaysian and the UK factories is in some ways rather limited. Although the

---

[39] Interview with Personnel Director, UKALM, Malacca (3rd March 1999).

[40] Interview with Group Personnel Director, Cheshire (19th May 2000).

[41] Interview with General Manager, UKALM, Sdn. Bhd. (18th August 1999).

company sets out formal guidelines and basic minimum standards (especially with regard to quality standards), as long as these are met, there is little interference in the day to day running of the plant. Managers from ladieswear and the light sewing division will become more involved in the daily running of the Malaysian site if there is perceived to be a particular problem area that needs work (for example the sending of a quality standards manager to overview the Malaysian firm's whole approach to quality standards, or the involvement of the UK in the appointment of the HR director). However, these examples are generally exceptions and most managers in the Malaysian subsidiary have had very little contact with UK-Apparel's UK based personnel. This general lack of intervention from the UK parent firm into the HR practices found at UKALM is especially significant in terms of an understanding of the impact of FDI on the local Malaysian society, since it demonstrates the way that the firm is operating with and within a local social context, refashioning labour and employment standards to suit local conditions, in Malaysia and *not* performing as a transmitter of Westernising ("progressive") changes. I now turn to expand upon this particular argument, providing the detail of company recruitment and employment practices relating to gender and ethnicity that demonstrate how the firm mobilizes an appropriate workforce. I will demonstrate that the mobilization of women into low-waged sewing machine work is based upon recruitment practices which make use of socially embedded divisions within the local labour market such as gender (as well as age, ethnicity, educational levels, class and rural-urban divisions).

Chapter 5

Recruitment and Employment in the Malaysian Subsidiary: Understanding How the Gender and Ethnic Division of Labour Operates

Introduction

This chapter is based upon primary field research conducted at UKALM. Thus, it is helpful to introduce my research findings with some comments on the chosen methodological approach. Following on from this introductory section, the rest of the chapter provides an analysis of gender and ethnic relations in the workforce at UKALM analysing the significance of recruitment practices. This chapter provides a detailed analysis of a single occupation at UKALM; that of sewing machinist. The reasons for dwelling on this particular job in such detail are twofold. Firstly, in the labour-intensive garment industry these machinists constitute the largest single group of employees. Sewing machinists are therefore essential to UK-Apparel's operations in Malaysia. Secondly, these workers are predominantly Malay and almost entirely female. Thus looking at the job of the sewing machinist provides an example of how recruitment practices act to consolidate the association between a specific occupation and a particular gender and ethnic group. The chapter also considers other groups of workers within the firm, for example workers employed to cut and spread cloth, supervisory and managerial employment. Recruitment practices for all these different types of workers are shown to reflect the many different ways in which the firm draws upon embedded social divisions in its recruitment policies, channelling workers of different genders and ethnic groups into specific occupations.

The argument presented in this chapter is that the recruitment process is a means through which the firm engages with the local socially embedded market. The result of this engagement is the reformulation of entrenched local divisions in the workforce of the firm. In chapters three and four, I looked at the background to UK-Apparel's decision to invest in Malaysia, highlighting how pre-existing social and political arrangements in Malaysia (which included the prevalence of low cost female labour) encouraged the firm to invest there. In this chapter, I carry the discussion forward, looking at what actually happened once UK-Apparel was established in Malaysia in terms of the relationship between the firm and the local political economy that UK-Apparel invested in.

Methodological issues

Before turning to look at the findings from my field research in Malaysia, it is worth considering some of the methodological issues that this fieldwork presents. It is suggested that there is considerable benefit to be gained from undertaking in-depth case-study research of this nature (after all, mainstream IPE writings on the MNC are notable in the extent to which they have not engaged in case study research, preferring to rely on second-hand accounts often from business scholars). This type of in-depth research is necessary in order to evaluate some of the wider claims made in the mainstream IPE literature concerning the supposedly beneficial impact of FDI. The discussion presented here introduces the fieldwork and, considers the difficulties faced in doing case study research on ethnic and gender relations.

Why recruitment?

The focus on recruitment allows for an exploration of the way in which ideas about the gender and ethnic background of workers feed into the gender and ethnic divisions in the workforce as a whole. What this examination of recruitment practices highlights is the role played by management in creating the gender and ethnic divisions found on the factory floor at UKALM. But I want to carry the analysis of recruitment practices further than these assertions about management's role in constructing gender and ethnic divisions in the workplace. It is argued that the role and position held by workers of different gender and ethnic groups in the workforce at UKALM[1] reflects the way in which managers have drawn upon pre-existing gender and ethnic divisions in society. These are therefore not abstract ideas about gender and ethnicity that the firm brought with it from the UK, but rather, the ideas and discourses that managers use in relation to different groups of workers highlights the way in which the firm is viewed in this thesis – as interacting with a labour market deeply embedded in local social practices and institutions. Pearson neatly sums up this perspective with the suggestion that:

> The recruitment of women workers in new industrial situations – either new sectors and processes or parts of the world new to given kinds of industrial processes – does not itself provide capital with suitable labour power. This labour has to be constituted, taking into account the pre-existing sexual division of labour. It is constructed directly by the recruitment, selection, management and personnel policies of individual companies and indirectly by the intervention of the State and negotiation within traditional modes of gender control (Pearson, 1988: 463, cited in Pearson (1998)).

Chapter three has already provided much of the background information regarding gender and ethnic divisions in Malaysian society – showing how these divisions are embedded in local social practices, yet at the same time are constructed

---

[1] This is the full name for the Malaysian subsidiary operations of UK-Apparel Ladieswear. The name is generally shortened to UKALM, and therefore when this abbreviation is used, I am referring to the UK-Apparel factories in Malaysia.

politically by a state actively involved in the development process. The gender and ethnic divisions that the recruiters in this study are perceived to be drawing upon need to be viewed as both socially embedded and politically constructed.

The examination of recruitment presented in this section of the book is to include not just recruitment mechanisms (*how* workers are recruited) but also to look at recruitment within the context of overall employment policies (looking at *why* workers are recruited). Thus I am observing how recruitment practices affect the make-up of the workforce, and also using the concept of recruitment in a broad sense to include things like how internal recruitment/promotion mechanisms operate. The aim is to establish how gender and ethnic divisions of labour operate in the factory and analyse the way in which recruitment practices act to sustain these divisions. Reference will be made to recruitment practices rather than recruitment policies because the aim is to look at what actually happens rather than official statements of company policy. Through examining recruitment practices rather than the formal policies that the company has in place, I was able to appreciate the complex interplay between gender and ethnicity in the process of FDI by a multinational firm. In the following chapters, I reflect in detail on how the firm engages with these local inequalities across all levels of the firm.

This process of engagement is played out in the construction of women as low cost labour – requiring the firm to draw upon embedded social divisions (thus recruitment practices draw upon gendered and racialized assumptions). But at the same time, the construction of gender within the firm also takes place within a global social space as firms across the world replicate these kinds of recruitment practices. It can be suggested, therefore, that recruitment practices reflect the globalized masculinist cultural values that relate to the liberal discourse of the progressive firm introduced in chapter two. We see the articulation of this hegemonic masculinity in the deployment of thoroughly rationalized and regulated recruitment processes that reflect standardized "scientific" western management techniques based upon rigorous measurement and testing methods. In this sense, the focus on recruitment not only tells us something about the way that firms embed themselves within localized systems of gendered social relations, it also tells another story, that of the way in which firms themselves are embedded in a globalized masculinist culture of efficiency.

The fieldwork

The fieldwork presented in this chapter was conducted on two separate visits to Malaysia in March 1999 and August 1999. Most of the data discussed in this chapter, and in chapter six, refers to persons employed in the actual manufacture of garments (production workers) – since these constitute the bulk of the workforce. The chapter will, therefore, focus on the different forms of employment in garment production and the way in which these different jobs are stratified along hierarchical divisions based upon both gender and ethnicity. These workers are found within the production department of the factory. Figure 5.1 (overleaf) shows how the production department fits into the overall organization of the firm. In terms of these departments within the factory, the data presented in this chapter came from interviews and observations in two of the factory departments – human resources and production. I did meet with managers in other departments (operations and finance), although the information gathered in these interviews was less concerned with employment issues, and related more to information presented in earlier chapters of this book such as relations with the UK, fabric sourcing and tax incentives. Figure 5.1 also shows how the production department is further sub-divided into a number of different departments or "floors", typical of most factories in the garment industry. The first is the cutting floor where the production process consists of the inspecting and spreading out of cloth ready for marking out patterns, cutting, and other processes necessary for the pre-assembly stage of garment production (for example, fusing inter lining into collar and cuff pieces or pinning garment pieces together). The second is the sewing floor, where the actual garment assembly takes place on production "lines" (effectively rows of sewing machines). Finally, there is the finishing floor where the garments are pressed, tagged and packed ready for export.

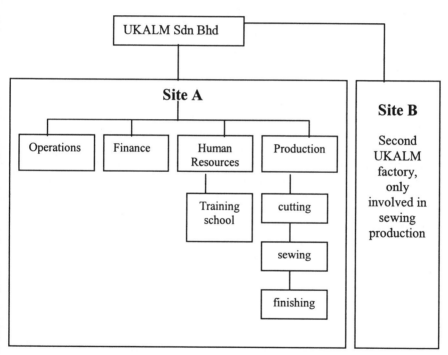

Figure 5.1 The departmental structure of UKALM

Source:　Adapted from Company document, *Departmental Organizational Chart*, provided by Human Resources Director, UKALM (18th August 1999).

As can be seen in figure 5.1, UK-Apparel operates two factories in Malacca. During the first visit I spent three full days at UK-Apparel's Malaysian factories and in August, I spent a day at the main factory. The larger, original factory is located on an industrial estate (although not a free trade zone), which will be referred to as "Site A". As well as being the main production site for UK-Apparel in Malaysia, also located at Site A are all of the non-production departments (e.g. operations, finance, human resources) and the firm's warehousing facilities. Site A is located in a largely rural area about thirteen kilometres north-west from the city of Malacca. The other UKALM factory "Site B" is a much smaller factory located again on an industrial estate, although the area is much more urbanized, being located in a small town some ten kilometres outside of Malacca along the main highway to Kuala Lumpur. The Site B factory basically constitutes an off-site sewing department of the Site A factory. Sewing (garment assembly) is the only production operation done at Site B, and the other aspects of garment production (cutting and finishing) are confined to Site A.

In order to discover the way in which recruitment operated at the firm, I conducted semi-structured interviews with managers who had some responsibility for recruitment to try and establish what their views were regarding workers of different genders/ethnic backgrounds. These interviews were mainly conducted with managers in the human resources (HR) department (figure 5.2 shows how those persons that I interviewed in HR fit into the company hierarchies). Since recruitment cannot be understood without knowing something of the employment requirements of the firm and the nature of work in the firm more generally, I also needed to gain an overview of the work and the workforce at UKALM. Interviews were therefore conducted with managers and supervisors involved in the actual production of garments (figure 5.3 shows those managers and supervisors that I was able to interview in the production department). The research also involved a level of observation since I was taken on tours of the departments involved in the production of clothing and the training of workers. Although the observational data that I recorded did not constitute the major field research technique, it did play an important role in familiarising me with the nature of employment at the firm and allow me to observe the way in which gender and ethnic divisions played out on the factory floor. Another important methodology which falls somewhere between formal interviewing and observation was data that was collected via more informal means, for example, casual comments made by managers when they gave me lifts in their cars, or the lunchtime conversations between managers when I was present.

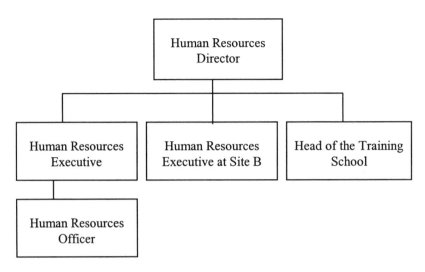

Figure 5.2 Organizational chart of the human resources department

Source: Adapted from company document, *Departmental Organizational Chart*, provided by Human Resources Director, UKALM (18th August 1999).

In nearly all of my visits to UKALM, semi-structured interviewing was selected as the most appropriate research method through which to gain an understanding of the way that managers view the workforce and the way in which the recruitment process operates. Semi-structured interviews enabled me to build a degree of trust between myself and the people I was interviewing and also allowed me to use my judgement as to whether certain questions would be suitable to be asked of certain individuals. Given my lack of background knowledge concerning garment factories, the semi-structured interview was also seen as a way through which I would be able to seek clarification on more technical issues that I was unfamiliar with. Naturally, certain interviews were more structured than others since I was not always sure exactly who I would be able to meet on the different days that I was at the factory. Some interviews were conducted in office space whereby I had a list of pre-prepared questions and was able to record the conversation, whilst other interviews were conducted on a more informal basis. However, I did have a list of themes that I tried to cover with all the different people that I interviewed[2] which included such things as their employment history with UK-Apparel and how they were recruited, their attitudes towards gender and ethnic divisions in the firm

---

[2] The importance of having a number of themes to be covered in the more unstructured interview process is covered by Burgess (1984: 101).

and the problems that they felt UK-Apparel was facing in terms of the recruitment of employees.

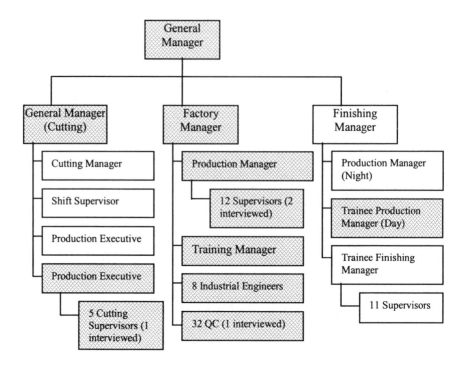

Figure 5.3 Production department organizational chart
(persons interviewed are shaded in grey)

Source: Adapted from company document, *Departmental Organizational Chart*, provided by Human Resources Director, UKALM (18th August 1999).

I interviewed a number of people across the firm. My priority was to discover something about the way in which the firm's recruitment polices were shaped by certain ideas about gender and ethnicity and how this in turn fed into the gender and ethnic divisions in the workforce. Thus the interviews that I decided to conduct were with (a) those managers who had a direct influence over the recruitment process i.e. the human resources department (see figure 5.2) (b) managers, supervisors, trainers and quality control personnel working in the production department who would provide insight into the nature of employment and the sorts of skills and attributes that they looked for in their workers (see figure 5.3) (c) the trade union to give a non-management perspective on the employment and recruitment process and finally (d) with managers, trainers and supervisors to gain an understanding of the recruitment of higher level personnel in the firm (see again figure 5.3).

In terms of the research findings presented in the final section of this chapter concerning managerial and supervisory employment, my research methods were somewhat different since I was able to interview directly a handful of these managers and supervisors concerning their jobs and their experiences in recruitment. However, I did not rely totally on these interviews with managers and supervisors and I found that my interviews with the director of human resources provided very useful information on the nature of managerial/supervisory employment at UKALM and how these positions are recruited. Indeed, I found the task of directly interviewing managers and supervisors about their jobs very difficult, for while these individuals were more than willing to discuss how they viewed the workers that they were responsible for, they were at times very unwilling to disclose rather more personal information. It is to the many difficulties that I experienced in the interviewing process and other problems I faced in undertaking this type of research that the discussion now turns.

Problems and issues faced in the field research

Given the focus of this study on the nature of gender and ethnic divisions in the workforce and how recruitment practices sustain these divisions, I was concerned that my questioning on this subject area would provoke insufficient responses. I was also aware that there is a certain sensitivity about questions, which might be interpreted as an accusation of discrimination and would therefore elicit rather standard rehearsed denials of discriminatory practices. I therefore felt that it was important to describe the nature of my study as broadly as possible – to describe my research as looking at issues relating generally to recruitment and employment, rather than the implications of recruitment and employment on workplace structures of gender and ethnicity. Thus questions regarding the gender and ethnic divisions in the workplace were introduced once the interview was well underway. Hence with human resources managers I would ask them to talk generally about the recruitment process before asking them questions regarding why they felt women were found in certain jobs and not others. Although this approach raises ethical issues, I felt that gaining access as well as being able to get the level of response that I was looking for necessitated these sorts of tactics. Many researchers have adopted these kinds of tactics when undertaking research into potentially sensitive issues. For example, in his research on recruitment and racial discrimination in firms, Jenkins has discussed the way in which he employed "indirect questioning" and a "deceptive candour" in order to gauge the attitudes towards ethnic minorities among employers that he interviewed (Jenkins, 1987: 152).

But there were other methodological dilemmas that I needed to address. Most of these relate to my position as a researcher at the firm. I felt very much the

LIVERPOOL JOHN MOORES UNIVERSITY
LEARNING SERVICES

"outsider" when I was conducting many of my interviews. First of all, I was in an unfamiliar country, secondly I was conducting my interviews in English, a language that was not a first language for nearly all of my respondents (although most of those that I interviewed did have a high level of English fluency), and, finally, I was also unfamiliar with the garment sector having never before visited a garment firm. This posed problems for me as a researcher in the sense that I was worried that people would resent me asking questions that might have revealed rather more confidential company information. In Ram's study of workplace practices in the UK ethnic minority clothing sector, the author writes of the way in which his interviewing of employers in this garment sector was crucially dependent on his position as an "insider" – which he perceives himself as being in terms of his ethnicity as a British Asian, family ties to some of the employers that he interviewed and also practical work experience in the trade. His position as insider not only aided him in gaining access to interviewees, but also, he argues, enabled him to interpret more effectively the nature of workplace practices/shop floor cultures in his case study firms (Ram, 1996: 160-161). In sharp contrast to Ram's work, therefore, in my research in the garment sector, I was overwhelmingly in the position of "outsider". Therefore, how did this position as outsider create problems in the way that I sought to uncover the nature of recruitment at UKALM, how did I cope with these dilemmas, and to what extent was my position as outsider one of advantage?

One of the major difficulties that the perception of myself as an outsider posed in my research concerned the kind of power relationships between me and those that I was interviewing and interacting with at the UK-Apparel factory. Thus it is important to acknowledge the concern in many post-colonial feminist accounts of field research that my own nationality/gender/race/class influenced the way in which interviewees responded to questioning (Scott & Shah, 1993). In this study, one of the ways in which the problem of power relationships in field research methodology presented itself was not so much in terms of my position as "outsider", but in actual fact how my role and position as a researcher in this firm was seen more as that of an outsider who, in someway, had links with senior management and was therefore also something of an "insider". The fact that I was both British and white automatically led to my being associated with the firm's UK operations, or even with Marks and Spencer. I therefore, made sure that it was explained that I was in no way linked to the parent firm, that my interest in the company was purely for the purposes of academic research, and that nothing they said to me would get back to their seniors. However, I was aware of an unwillingness among certain interviewees to discuss certain issues with me – and this problem seemed to be especially the case in those interviews that were conducted in a much more formal setting (for example a company office) with a tape recorder. This role of the researcher as somewhere between insider and outsider is something that has been picked up on in a piece by Lal in which she draws upon her research experience in Indian factories and argues for "the need to constantly negotiate between the positions of insider and outsider, rather than being fixedly assigned one or the other subject position" (Lal, 1996: 193).

Lal's work is very interesting, because she also discusses the way in which people in the factories that she visited generally associated her with management due to her class and educational status and also the way that she had to go through management to gain access to factories. For me, my main contact at UKALM was a senior manager in the position of human resources director. I was therefore, overwhelmingly associated with this particular manager and I was worried that this would cause me problems. One of the worst incidents that I faced followed an interview that I had undertaken with the company's union representative, when the human resources director said that he felt that it would be in the interests of "improving communication" in the firm if I was to "share" with him any information that came out of the interview that might be important for him to know. This put me in a very difficult position ethically because I had given assurances to the Union leader that nothing he told me would be disclosed to the management. Fortunately I was able to successfully evade this request, and still remain on good terms with the HR director.

However, my position as an outsider viewed as having close contacts with management did lead to certain problems in terms of the data that I was able to collect at UKALM. Although the focus of this part of the book is on recruitment, and thereby managerial attitudes to the workforce, it might have been useful to conduct interviews with the women workers at the factory or to conduct some sort of survey of the workforce. I was very much aware of the fact that interviews with the women workers would have been very difficult. This was something that was brought home to me quite clearly when I interviewed a Quality Control (QC) worker, and found that the interview resulted in very little data of relevance to the research.[3] My impression was that this woman was very mistrustful of my intentions and I felt that this was largely because she saw me as an outsider, linked to the HR director and even with UK headquarters. Furthermore, the senior managers at UKALM were not keen for me to conduct what they saw as time consuming surveys or worker interviews and I was aware that if I were to push this issue further it might well jeopardize my access to the firm in Malaysia as well as in the UK. Given that I wanted to conduct research that was qualitatively different from the bulk of research on women and work in Southeast Asia which focuses largely on women's experiences of employment. I felt that having management interviews was, in many ways, far more relevant and useful to the research. Indeed, very few studies have managed to combine interview data from both management and workforce (preferring to focus on interviews with women workers *outside* of the factory environment), with the work of Ong being the most notable exception (Ong, 1987).

There were a number of ways in which I sought to deal with these problems posed by my position as researcher at UK-Apparel's Malaysian factory. First of all, although the issue of access did present certain problems, as I have outlined above, I did however feel that because the main contact through which I was able to arrange access (the director of human resources) was not a British expatriate manager, but a Malaysian, the persons whom I interviewed were aware that I was

---

[3] Interview with a QC, UKALM site A (18th August 1999).

not too closely linked with the UK parent firm.   Secondly, it is important to consider the complexity of the power dynamics that came into play in the interviewing process.   So although I have already noted that I felt that certain interviewees worried that I might be too closely associated with the parent firm (assumptions based mainly upon my nationality and race), my position as a researcher was also affected by my age, my status (as a PhD student), and, of course, my gender.   After all, a large proportion of my interviewees were men at least 10 years older than me and in management positions.   Writers such as Wolf and Scott and Shah have commented that western researchers undertaking fieldwork in post-colonial societies might do well to try and subvert the power dynamics of the interview situation by "interviewing up" – interviewing persons in much higher status positions to the researcher herself (Scott and Shah, 1993: 93-95; Wolf, 1996).   This tactic of interviewing up is something that is evident in my own research, although whether or not it led to more equitable interviewing power dynamics, I am not sure.   One thing that I was acutely aware of was that my position as outsider could be used to my advantage at certain times.   For example, questions could be raised out of curiosity so I could introduce questions regarding female employment at the firm.   Thus I might have asked; "I see that it is mostly women doing the sewing machinist work here – is that usual in the garment sector?" then followed this question with "and why do you think that is?" Therefore benefiting from my position as a young research student operating in an unfamiliar environment.

Women's work as sewers: how recruitment practices sustain gender divisions

This section of the chapter focuses on the occupation of the sewing machinist demonstrating how recruitment practices have sustained a gendered identification of women with this type of work.   The position of sewing machinist is highly feminized, that is to say associated with skills and abilities that are constructed as innately "female".   It is suggested that through the recruitment process, managerial perceptions play a major role in the gendering of sewing work.   The discussion presented below will explore the reasons that managers and recruiters give for the dominance of women in sewing machinist work, thus showing how gendered understandings of skill such as "dexterity, diligence and nimble fingers" are reflected in company recruitment practices.   What is evident from this discussion, is that whilst there are certain qualities that make women preferable employees, there are certain problems associated with the concentration of large numbers of women employees in sewing work.   Yet despite these problems, sewing remains a female dominated occupation, in no large part due to the perceived unsuitability of men to this type of work.

Employment at UKALM is dominated by a single group of employees; the sewing machinists.   Sewing work is the most labour intensive aspect of garment production.   In June 1999 sewing machinists constituted 42.6% of the workforce at

UKALM (or 669 employees out of a total workforce of 1569).[4] But the significance of sewing machinists to this study is not simply in terms of the sheer number of them employed at UKALM, more importantly, this is a job which almost exclusively employs women, and these women workers are overwhelmingly Malay. An examination of the job of the sewing machinist and the means through which machinists are recruited to work at UKALM, therefore, provides an excellent case study of the intersection between gender and ethnicity in the construction of a particular work role. Within the context of the political economy of Malaysian development outlined in chapter two, one can observe how notions of gender and employment are cross-cut with ethnicity. Hence the widespread shift of Malay women out of peasant agriculture and into industrial employment under the NEP is seen in microcosm on UKALM's sewing floor, which is dominated by Malay women workers, therefore underlining how the process of export-led economic development is gendered (Razavi, 1999: 664).

The job of the sewing machinist

In the sewing department the bulk of the employees are machinists. These machinists constitute the largest single concentration of employees in a particular job. At Site A they make up 365 out of a total workforce of 1030.5 and at Site B (where there are no cutting or finishing departments) they constitute 265 out of a total workforce of 392. These machinists are overwhelmingly female and most are Malay. Table 5.1 shows how most sewing machinists are Malay women. But the table also reveals other important trends in relation to the ethnic breakdown of the workforce as a whole. For example, Indian workers constitute 7.8% of the workforce as a whole, but 9.1% of sewing machinists thus having a higher representation in the occupation of machinists in relation to their overall representation in the workforce. Among the Chinese workers, the trend is quite the opposite because whilst 14.2% of the overall workforce is Chinese, Chinese make up 9.4% of sewing machinists. The significance of the way in which the workforce in divided in terms of gender and ethnicity is a theme that will be returned to throughout this chapter.

Production in the sewing department is organized into lines. A line is divided up into a number of different operations each one making up a different stage in the production of the garment. There are usually 32-33 people on a line and there are 17-18 different sewing operations (depending on the garment style) plus a number of non-sewing operations. Sewing operations are graded from A to C with Grade C operations being the most simplistic. There are also about three float machinists per line who are trained in all of the different operations.

A worker will sit at her workstation continually performing the single operation that she has been assigned. Once an operation is completed she will place a sticker on a card above her workstation so that the amount of operations that she completes in a single day can be calculated. Workers are encouraged to

---

[4] Company document, *Distribution of Staff by Race as of June 15, 1999, UKALM Sdn. Bhd.* provided by Human Resources Director, UKALM (18th August 1999).

attain high levels of performance through a bonus payment scheme (see below), an "employee of the month" scheme which gives cash rewards to high performance workers and workers come under pressure from supervisors to attain targets. Supervisors are held responsible for the achievement of production targets on their line – the supervisor that I spoke with complained that these targets were often difficult to meet, especially when style changes are introduced.[5] The company also sets very high quality standards – one quality control officer (QC) will patrol the line and the garment is again checked for flaws before proceeding to the finishing department.

Machinists' pay is daily-rated. Basic rates of pay vary according to the level of skill deemed necessary for performing a particular operation. Those machinists who perform the most difficult A grade operations (for example attaching the collar and cuffs to the garment), and machinists who are multi skilled in a number of operations ("float" machinists) receive the higher basic rates of pay. On top of the basic rate, workers will receive a bonus payment if they achieve their daily target. The performance targets are calculated by the on-site industrial engineers, if a machinist is able to achieve 75% of the target then she is eligible for the bonus payment. In one grade B operation that I was shown, the target was set at 43 operations per hour, it is, acknowledged that such targets result in high-pressure, as well as very repetitive, monotonous work.[6]

How might one explain the dominance of female workers in this sewing machinist work? Part of the explanation lies in the attitudes that managers and recruiters have towards female workers. I raised the issue of why women dominate in sewing with the personnel staff, the head of the training department and also the supervisor who showed me around the sewing department. They all gave the same basic response; that women take greater care, are dextrous, more diligent and more obedient than men. They also commented that there was a certain social stigma attached to men who worked in a job so overwhelmingly associated with "women's work".[7] The human resources executive and officer that I spoke with, for example, called the male sewing workers "the only thorn among the roses" and went on to tell me how male sewers will be given female nicknames by their co-workers.[8] The extent of the social stigmatization of male workers was also revealed in my interviews with the firm's in-house union representative who told me that those men who were working as sewing machinists were "probably not men; something like half man, half girl".[9]

---

[5] Interview with a supervisor in the sewing department (Site A, 10th March 1999).

[6] Interview with a sewing department supervisor (Site A, 10th March 1999).

[7] Examples of interviews where this point came up included those with interviews with the Human Resources Director (Site A, 10th March 1999), head of the training school (Site A, 3rd March 1999) interview with a sewing department supervisor (Site A, 10th March 1999), interview with Financial Director (Site A, 11th March 1999) and interview with the human resources executive at Site B (11th March 1999).

[8] Interviews with HR executive and HR officer (Site A, 3rd March 1999 and 10th March 1999).

[9] Interview with the president of the in-house union (Site A, 19th August 1999).

Table 5.1 Breakdown of sewing machinists at UKALM by gender and race,[10] June 1999

Chinese				Malay				Indian				Other			
Male		Female		Male		Female		Male		Female		Male		Female	
No.	%	No.	%	No.	%	No.	%	No.	%	No.	%	No.	%	No.	%
0	0	63	9.4	12	1.9	531	79.3	0	0	61	9.1	0	0	2	0.3

Source: Company document, *Distribution of Staff by Race as of June 15, 1999.*

---

[10] Although throughout this book I have chosen to refer to ethnicity rather than race, the use of the term "race" in this table is because this is what appears in the company personnel statistics that this table is adapted from.

These kinds of comments are important to consider, because they demonstrate that there is an association between a feminized workforce and certain "feminine" skills and attributes. At UKALM there are clear gendered boundaries in place between certain jobs. Men who move into jobs associated with women's work often find themselves ridiculed – a finding that is consistent with those of other studies of men employed in work constructed as "women's work". Williams, for example, suggests:

> Occupations are structured with the particular gender of the labourer in mind. The positions themselves are not gender-neutral but have built into them assumptions about the kinds of worker likely to be employed in them (Williams, 1993: 2).

Thus it is typical for men employed in "female" positions to face the kind of social stigmatization noted above. But perhaps one of the most interesting examples of how workplace occupations are gendered was seen at the site B factory where a transsexual was employed as a grade A machinist. The company has employed a number of transsexuals over the years, always in sewing operations. The Human resource executive at Site B commented that they tend to be very high performance sewers, very careful about their work and also well disciplined.[11] This example shows, therefore, how skills associated with women's work are regarded as "feminine" skill; that somehow integral to being a woman are these qualities of care, dexterity and diligence.

Recruitment, gender and sewing

I now turn to look at the role that recruitment plays in consolidating the connection between gender and certain skills and characteristics. Furthermore, in investigating this connection, it became obvious that occupations such as that of sewing machinist were not only gendered, they were also associated with a particular ethnic group. The job of a machinist is viewed as requiring a worker with certain "feminine" skills – skills that are regarded as a product of a woman's upbringing in (Malay) society.

The main channel through which workers are recruited is the walk-in interview. One of the first things that I noticed when I arrived at the factory each morning was the long queue of job applicants. The company will sometimes advertize by putting a banner up outside the factory site. It will also make announcements over the tannoy asking whether current staff know of anyone, and there are arrangements with local bus contractors to bring people in for interview. During visits to UKALM undertaken in March 1999, I observed how the company was undertaking a recruitment drive; each morning when I arrived at Site A (at around 7.30 am), there was already a long queue of workers waiting for interview with the human resources officers. All of these workers were young (aged around 16-21) and Malay, and although there were always some men waiting for

---

[11] Interview with HR executive, Site B (11th March 1999).

interview, the vast majority were female and were being interviewed for posts as sewing machinists.

The firm claims that it does not target a particular group of people,[12] but it is clear from observing the job applicants each morning and talking with personnel staff that these applicants tend to be mainly female, young, Malay (and sometimes Indian but rarely Chinese) and from the surrounding rural areas. So how might one explain the fact that applicants for these sewing machinist positions are rarely non-Malays. Of course part of the reason is demographic. It was shown in chapter three, for example, that in 1991, Malacca's population was made up of 176,000 Chinese compared to 301,800 Malays (page 77). Significantly, the Chinese population tended to be located more in urban centres. Thus the fact that the firm is targeting recruitment drives on the surrounding rural areas does suggest that the firm regards Malay females as constituting the natural supply of production workers. Thus it will be shown in this chapter that the job of sewing machinist is not only constructed as feminine employment, but also as Malay employment within the firm.

The recruitment process consists of three stages: an application form, an interview and then a variety of different tests. The sorts of skills and qualities that the firm is looking for in their machinists include neatness and care, patience and an ability to put up with repetitive work, a good eye, dexterity, speed, basic education, an ability to follow simple instructions, sewing skills and previous work experience. These recruitment practices have been thought through in minute detail, and aim to identify potential sewers who will be the most efficient and effective in their work. There is something of a science to the way in which the recruitment process draws upon standardized tests and procedures in order to identify the ideal (most efficient) worker. "Scientific management" is a term that is usually associated with control over the work processes through the rigorous measurement of working practices, but it could equally be applied to aspects of the recruitment process associated with measurement and testing. Such techniques are a normal part of Taylorist western management techniques and foster a culture of control within the firm. I will introduce the nature of the measurement/testing regime for new recruits in a moment, but before doing this, it is useful to think about how these scientific management techniques contribute to the liberal understanding of the rational-acting firm. The firm is merely, to use Dunning's term, an "efficiency seeker"; there is no recognition of the way in which this form of management reflects masculinist biases and assumptions that are implicit to neo-liberal thought. Most notably, there is no recognition of the way in which the recruitment practices themselves that are presented in this chapter reflect gendered assumptions.

Hence, an examination of the recruitment process for machinists also reveals how recruiters seek to identify certain skills and qualities that are overtly gendered. Thus, a great number of these skills and qualities are regarded as either innate to women or skills developed in the household from an early age. The idea that women show greater neatness, care and patience in their work was expressed by

---

[12] Interview with HR executive, Site A (10th March 1999).

various people throughout the factory. It was felt that male workers tended to be less patient with their work and generally took less care. The recruitment process tries to identify workers with these qualities. The interviewer will, for example look at how neatly the application form has been filled in.[13] A careful worker is considered to be one who has a good eye for detail and these skills are tested using a simple test shown in figure 5.4 the first part consists of following the lines across the page using only the eye and the second, again using only the eye, to pick out shapes from the diagram.

In all areas of the factory the view was expressed that women made better machinists because of their dexterity and the care that they take when handling the fabric. Such skills as these are tested using a marble test (the interviewee is asked to put marbles into holes on a grid within a certain time limit)[14] and also a basic sewing machine exercise.[15] It was also felt that women tended to make better sewers because this was a skill they learnt at home. These opinions were clearly articulated by the human resources director when he commented:

> If you look at the history of the industry, women traditionally work in the industry because they have what we call the tender touch. Women have always done the sewing... Who sews in your house for example – your mother or your father? These are skills that women have traditionally monopolized.[16]

At Site B the personnel executive there who undertook the interviewing and selection process suggested that Malay women in particular made good sewers. She felt that Malay households were more traditional than the Indian and (especially) Chinese, and therefore, there was a greater emphasis on women acquiring more traditional skills such as sewing. She told me that in the interview process she will always ask the women whether they like to sew and what sort of experience they have had in sewing.

---

[13] Interview with HR executive, Site B (11th March 1999).

[14] A visit to a Hong Kong owned garment firm in Penang, Penn Apparel, revealed the use of these marble tests in the recruitment process for sewing machinists. Company factory tour with personnel officer, Penang (18th March 1999).

[15] Interview with head of the training school (Site A, 3rd March 1999) and observation of the training school, Site A (3rd March 1999) – these basic tests are conducted in the training school – considered to be part of the HR department, see figure 5.1.

[16] Interview with Human Resources director, Site A (3rd March 1999).

Figure 5.4 Dexterity test

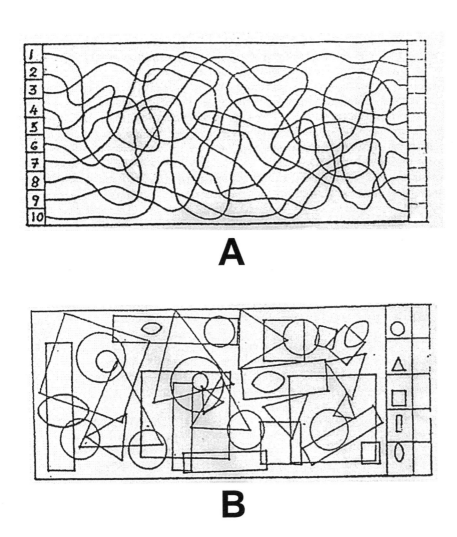

A

B

Source: Provided by the Head of Training School, Site A (3rd March 1999).

Managerial attitudes and problems regarding the recruitment of women

The recruitment process seeks to identify these skills (dexterity, diligence, nimble fingers etc.) in the workers, but it is also a process whereby the firm seeks to employ workers who are likely to stay with the company for the long term. This recruitment target has become very important to the recruitment process because of the severe problem of labour turnover that the company feels it is facing. In particular, it was mentioned that the loss of staff that have been with the company for over six months was especially costly.[17] The garment industry is reliant on the build up of skills in the workforce with good quality machinists taking over six months to reach the performance standards set up by the company (both in terms of quality and quantity). Linked to the problem of high labour turnover is the problem of employee absenteeism – which is viewed as related to women's family responsibilities. A supervisor from the sewing department commented that this was one of the major problems that he faced on a daily basis, requiring him to constantly re-organize the production lines that he has responsibility for to ensure that targets are met.[18]

The problem of high labour turnover amongst experienced machinists is viewed by the recruiters as stemming from women's position in society. This was shown by the type of questions that the recruiters will ask in the interview. For example, the interviewee will be asked whether she is married or has any plans to be married and whether she has children. The Human Resources director expressed, a clear preference for women without family responsibilities:

> I *am* looking for unmarried ladies to take on the job of sewers, but in actual fact what I am looking for are people who aren't going to give me a problem, so I also consider women who are past the childbearing age. What I don't want is somebody with a young family – problems will arise there.[19]

However, the company has experienced considerable problems in attracting young unmarried women. Younger women are seen to prefer the better paid jobs found in the electronics sector. These jobs are not only better paid, but are regarded as easier, less intensive work and the jobs carry more employee benefits. This line of discussion is developed further in chapter six where it is suggested that married women constitute a relatively new source of low cost labour for the firm. In some ways the difficulty in attracting young unmarried women was side-stepped by the human resources director who suggested that very young school leavers (under the age of 18), generally did not make very suitable employees anyway since he considered them to be lacking in maturity.[20] Furthermore, despite the desire of the human resources director to attract women without big family responsibilities, his

---

[17] This point was raised by both the Human Resources Director (various interviews) and the Finance Director, Site A (11th March 1999).

[18] Interview with a sewing department supervisor, Site A (18th August 1999).

[19] Interview with HR Director, Site A (3rd March 1999).

[20] Interview with HR Director, Site A (3rd March 1999).

executive level staff (the ones that do the actual recruitment and interviewing of machinists) are more practically minded. For example, they will not rule out employing a woman who has young children so long as she can make suitable arrangements for childcare. Women will also be asked questions about what her husband does (will his work involve moving around the country?) and whether her husband is aware of or approves of her seeking work. Thus the married female worker is viewed in relation to her husband; her career is seen as secondary to his. The Site B factory, for example, is located near to a military establishment and the HR executives have come to realise that this creates potential problems in trying to hold on to a stable workforce since the wives of military personnel are likely to regularly move with their husbands.

Though employment of married women may have risen at the firm, what has not altered in company recruitment practices is the explicit preference for women workers in sewing machinist work. The human resources director was of the opinion that women are more likely to see sewing as a long term career than men. So although married women may have attendance problems due to their family responsibilities "the problem with the guys is that they don't see sewing as a long term profession".[21] What came across from the interviews, therefore, was that the recruiters see the (female) worker as a person living in a social context. Thus this same social context that makes women preferable employees to men also acts to prevent certain types of women from working at the factory. However the restrictions that the recruiters place on employment of certain types of women are themselves limited by the availability of workers. The company has been constantly expanding its labour force since it opened (see figure 5.5) and was, at the time of the visits in March 1999, seeking to recruit an extra 655 machinists by the end of the year. Much of this expansion was taking place during a time of severe labour shortage in the Malaysian economy. Despite the fact that the Malaysian economy has now gone into recession, there are still considerable difficulties in trying to find people to work in the lower paying end of the manufacturing sector. The HR Director commented on the labour shortage:

> The day will come maybe in ten years time when Malaysians don't want to work as operators on the shop floor because this is too low a job, just like today where nobody wants to be a petrol pump attendant.[22]

---

[21] Interview with HR Director, Site A (3rd March 1999).
[22] Interview with HR Director, Site A (3rd March 1999).

Figure 5.5 Numbers employed at UKALM as sewing machinists and non-sewing machinists, 1989-1997

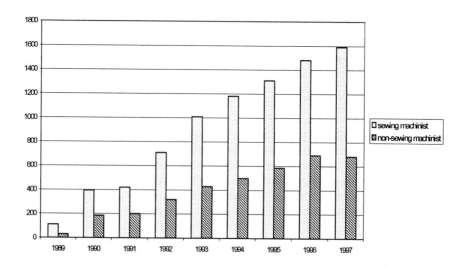

Source: "UKALM – Employee Build-up", document provided by HR Director (3rd March 1999).

But despite the difficulties in recruiting sewing machinists, the firm displays an unwillingness to employ just anyone in these positions. We have already seen, for example, the view put forward that men are not best suited for sewing machine work. In fact, during the three-month period of September to November 1998, company records show that 768 people walked in for interviews, yet only 125 were offered jobs at the firm. The HR director claimed that there was only a 16% success rate from interviews, a fact that he attributed largely to the walk-in interview system; "we can't control who walks in here".[23] But the low success rate from interviews also reveals the way in which the firm has very clear ideas concerning the type of worker (her skills, family situation, age, ethnicity, attitudes and behavioural characteristics) that they wish to employ.

Another significant characteristic of the worker who tends to stay with the firm is that she is from the rural areas and not the urban area. This, therefore, goes part of the way in explaining the predominance of Malays in sewing machine work (as seen in table 5.1, page 125). As has already been described in the previous chapter, rural Malaysia has remained demographically Malay because NEP policies aimed at adjusting the ethnic imbalances in the economy were centred more on the development of modern, urban, industrial areas. The villages, or *kampungs,* remain Malay dominated. What this preference for rural women

---

[23] Interview with HR Director, Site A (3rd March 1999).

implies is a preference for Malay women. These preferences, therefore, tie in with the earlier discussion of the way in which Malay women were viewed as coming from more "traditional" household backgrounds. In chapter four, it was shown that the expansion of employment opportunities for Malay rural women in manufacturing industry reflected the demand for low cost labour in an expanding labour intensive manufacturing sector. These claims that rural Malay women are more suited to sewing machinist work need to be evaluated in terms of the need for employers to seek out low wage, relatively skilled and also reliable sources of labour – a claim that will be evaluated in more detail in chapter six.

Gendered jobs: The production department

Recruitment practices have sustained a gendered association between women and sewing work. But are these trends mirrored in the recruitment and employment of workers across the production department (i.e. in non-sewing production work)? The discussion here will look at the non-sewing production workers – those categories of employees who are classified as skilled, semi-skilled and un-skilled production workers and who are involved directly in the production of garments. The aim is, to look at how different jobs within the production department become defined in terms of masculine or feminine characteristics. In order to illustrate how this process takes place, a comparison of different jobs in production is presented. Looking, firstly, at gender divisions in the cutting department and secondly, at the finishing department where there has been a general loosening of the association between gender and occupation.

The focus of this comparison is much more on questions of gender rather than ethnicity. This is due to a number of factors. Firstly, the greater willingness among managers to discuss gender compared to the more politicized issue of ethnicity. Secondly, in production work, the gender divisions were much starker than those based upon ethnicity. Finally, the fact was that the really significant ethnic divisions were not found among production workers, but between production workers and supervisors/management, thus a more indepth commentary on the nature of ethnic divisions in the workforce is provided in the final section of this chapter.

Gender divisions and hierarchies on the cutting room floor

I was shown around the cutting department by Rosnah, a young Malay woman who had worked her way up in this department to the role of production executive (a lower managerial position). In this department there was a higher level of male employment although women still constitute a large proportion of the workforce usually in the lower paying lower skilled jobs. My purpose here, therefore, is to try and unpack the way in which "women's" and "men's" jobs in this department have developed and how these have become associated with different levels of pay and occupational status. In cutting there are a variety of different jobs. These include the cutters (who cut the pattern pieces), spreaders (who spread out material and patterns ready for cutting), those employed in the inspection of cut panels, operators of the fusing machine (which fuses the interlining between cut collar and cuff pieces), and finally, employment in pinning. These jobs have, as a whole, become rigidly associated with either male or female employment.

Men dominate the cutting jobs. There was only one woman out of seventeen currently employed as a cutter (and she was still a trainee). Like cutting, spreading of the fabric is also mainly done by men. Women workers are found in the fusing section, pinning, and panel inspection. Rosnah explained to me that in the garment sector, spreading and cutting were traditionally seen as male jobs. They were viewed as more manual and physically demanding. She claimed that the firm now saw no problem with employing women in these positions since the work was not especially heavy and argued that the firm had been influenced in its decision to start employing women as spreaders and cutters by the UK parent company that had been employing women in these positions in its UK plants.[24] Thus we can see here some limited evidence of the firm's commitment to equal opportunities (as laid out in its code of conduct) having an impact on working practices within the firm.

Rosnah's views did, however, conflict somewhat with those expressed by others at the factory. The union president, for example, told me how cutting was "rough work", and that women would experience difficulties in operating certain pieces of machinery such as the band knife (there is, of course an issue here concerning the way that male dominated trade unions have sought to preserve the superior status of masculinized "craft" industries within factory environments). The job of a cutter is seen by many as one of the more dangerous jobs with cutters often wearing chain mail gloves, masks and goggles. It is also regarded as one of the most highly skilled jobs in the factory and consequently these are among the highest salaries for non-executive staff at UKALM (cutters work within a salary band of RM 850 to RM 1,100 per month). Training for cutting takes about three months, they are usually recruited from spreading.[25] They are a stable workforce with an average length of employment of around five to six years.

The low labour turnover among cutters is a real contrast with other sections of the cutting department such as panel inspection and fusing where the high labour turnover was explained in terms of low pay and the monotonous nature of the work. Fusing is seen as one of the most simplistic jobs in the factory. It requires no training at all, workers simply have to lay out the pieces of collars and cuffs that are to be bonded with the lining in the fusing machine. Although most of the employees in this section were young women, there were also some deaf people in this section many of whom were male. Women and deaf employees are regarded as more likely to stay than (hearing) male workers. Indeed it was felt that most male workers are not suited to fusing because they are easily bored and prone to discipline problems. Thus managers will try and ensure that the men are transferred into spreading as soon as a vacancy arises.[26]

---

[24] Interview with production executive, cutting, Site A (10th March 1999).

[25] These figures are compared with the earnings of sewers in chapter six.

[26] Interview with production executive, cutting, Site A (10th March 1999).

Interestingly, labour turnover in spreading is not a problem despite relatively low wages of RM625-810 per month.[27] This low turnover reflects the possibility that these workers have of progressing into a cutting position. Thus it can be seen that in the traditionally male occupations within this department (i.e. cutting and spreading) there is a possibility of career advancement into a high status, relatively high wage skilled position. The example of the fusing department also shows how perceptions about female docility disadvantages them in gaining promotion into the higher skilled/paid jobs in the department as the less well disciplined men are actually transferred out of the fusing section into higher status jobs.

Changing gender roles? The case of finishing work

The discussion of gender work roles in cutting provides quite a contrast to the finishing floor where the association between gender and certain jobs has become less clear-cut. The entry of a significant number of male employees into the traditionally female occupation of pressing has led to a redefining of the skills needed to do this job along more "masculine" lines. The finishing floor is where garments are brought to be pressed, tagged and packed ready for export. One of the main jobs in this department is that of presser. Pressers work standing at ironing boards ironing garments, or they work as operators of the "big jim" machine (a machine that removes creases from garments by blowing hot steam through them). Other jobs on this floor include hanging and tagging clothes, the final inspection of garments, or working as packers in the "vac pac" machine which vacuum seals garments in plastic packaging.

Like the sewing department, the finishing department is organized into lines with workers employed on a piece rate bonus system of payment. Basic salaries for the pressers were RM 22.88 per day, and spreaders meeting the performance targets got paid RM33.16 per day. The rates of pay for pressers therefore, were the same as those received by grade B machinists on the sewing floor. However, whereas the sewing work is dominated by Malay women workers, this is not the case in pressing work. In finishing, the manager who showed me around the floor estimated that half of the pressers were male.

The finishing manager told me that, in the past, it had been almost entirely women employed as pressers but this had changed over the last five years. He suggested that the main reason for the shift towards employing higher levels of men in the finishing department came down to a realisation among managers and supervisors that men were just as capable as women at meeting company standards in finishing work. This is an important point, because it demonstrates the extent to which socially constructed ideas about what constitutes "women's work" actually influences company recruitment practices. Although ironing might have been perceived to be "women's work" in the past (mainly because women are regarded as being more careful than men in the "handling" of garments), this was not the case any more. Indeed, I noted that the job of presser was being redefined along more masculine lines as the finishing manager began to speak of the quite

---

[27] n.b. at the time of my visit to Malaysia, £1 sterling = RM6.

physically demanding nature of finishing work with workers being required to stand and work in hot temperatures. The manager went as far as to claim that he thought that women were not physically suited to this kind of work.[28]

But another issue that this manager raised was that women had been recruited in the past to work in finishing because they were deemed easier to control. When I asked him whether the male workers were more likely to be ill-disciplined, the manager answered that this was the case. He commented that many of the female supervisors in finishing had found some of the male employees difficult to control, and told me that he would often have to step in to sort out discipline issues between male workers and their female supervisors. But despite these problems, the manager was still of the opinion that men made good pressers firstly, because of their physical suitability to the job and secondly, that women workers faced attendance problems due to their family responsibilities commenting "the men, they have less family problems because in our Malay culture when a woman has family problems she will go home".[29] These views, therefore, provide a very interesting contrast with those views expressed by managers concerning the sewing machinists. The job of presser has, to a certain extent, been reconstructed as a job where "masculine" skills and attributes are built into the nature of the job. What can be observed in this situation is that when men are willing to do certain jobs within the factory, the skills that women are supposed to possess (i.e. "nimble fingered" manual dexterity or "handling" skills) start to be perceived by the employer as less valuable in comparison to other more "masculine" skills. Women are viewed as more likely to take time off work, as the family member most likely to have responsibility for children, and this influences the preference for male employees in a previously feminized occupation. There has been a shift towards greater male employment in pressing work, and yet this type of work is relatively low paid work compared to other jobs in the factory that are considered to be "male" work and generally pay higher wages and have better promotion prospects. The significance of the trend towards higher male employment in a traditionally female job is that it shows how the association of a particular job with a particular gender is related to a process of sex-typing of certain jobs as "male" or "female".

Given the relatively small number of persons employed in the finishing department, it is difficult to draw any firm conclusions regarding the significance of these changes in terms of recompositions of gender relations within the workplace. What needs to be borne in mind is that, despite these changes within the finishing department, sewing machinists remain the largest single group of employees at UKALM, and are considered by the HR managers to be the group of workers that the firm is most reliant upon. In the sewing department, little has altered in terms of the gender or even the ethnic divisions within the workforce. At UKALM sewing has always remained a job performed by Malay females and thus the loosening of gender roles that is occurring in finishing must be offset against the overall situation in the production department whereby the bulk of women are

---

[28] Interview with acting finishing manager, Site A (10th March 1999).
[29] Interview with acting finishing manager, Site A (10th March 1999).

found in sewing machine positions, whilst men are generally employed as spreaders, cutters, and industrial engineers.

Managerial and supervisory employment and recruitment practices

The preceding sections of this chapter have shown how recruitment practices act to sustain gender and also ethnic divisions within the workforce working in skilled and semi-skilled production jobs. I now turn to look at the issue of recruitment from another perspective – that of the managerial and supervisory staff. There are a number of reasons why recruitment and employment practices for these occupational categories is being treated separately from those production workers already discussed in this chapter. Firstly, the methods of recruitment are quite different for these more senior positions. Secondly, the nature of the work is very different. Thirdly, in light of these differences in the recruitment and employment of managers and supervisors the findings presented in this section will demonstrate how the interplay between the firm and local structures of gender and ethnicity have led to quite different patterns of employment. And finally, from the point of view of my field research, unlike the production workers, I was able to directly interview a number of managers and supervisors about the nature of their work and how they were recruited, thus providing a somewhat different perspective on the way in which recruitment practices interact with local socially embedded structures.

Again it is shown that the firm draws upon local social divisions (based upon both ethnicity and gender) in its recruitment strategies. Although at first glance the managerial recruitment practices in place at UKALM do not seem to favour either women or men (numbers of men and women employed as managers are roughly equal – see table 5.2, page 140), it gradually became clear through my interviewing that the recruitment process did, in fact, act to build up barriers that prevent certain groups from entering into managerial employment. It was shown earlier in this chapter, for example, that internal recruitment practices act to confine women to low paid work where there is little opportunity for training. But what is also clear is that whereas the firm targets relatively uneducated Malay females for sewing machinist work, the recruitment for higher-ranking positions within the factory has tended to favour Chinese employment. A variety of reasons could be presented for explanations of the relatively high levels of Chinese employment at supervisory and managerial level. On the one hand, these practices reflect the way that employment opportunities for the educated urban Chinese have been largely confined to the private sector (with increased numbers of educated Malays finding employment in the public sector). Yet on the other hand, the recruitment practices themselves have acted to consolidate connections between managerial employment and the Chinese. Informal *ad hoc* recruitment practices for managerial staff have meant that the Chinese have benefited disproportionately because of their access to ethnic recruitment networks. There may well, therefore, be high levels of female employment at managerial and supervisory level, but this employment is largely confined to Chinese women. In this sense, what the case study evidence suggests is that certain (privileged) groups of women do, in fact, benefit from the opportunities available within this MNC. However, for the bulk of the firm's (largely Malay) female workforce, these opportunities do not exist, thus highlighting how different types of women experience global restructuring in different ways.

Another issue that comes out from the analysis of managerial/supervisory recruitment, is that the *ad hoc* approach to recruitment of this group is a real contrast to the highly regulated recruitment process for sewers. The recruitment practices at UKALM that have been overviewed thus far, aimed at securing the most efficient work force possible in sewing. These practices are infused with notions of gender and ethnicity, yet it is in the managerial and supervisory jobs that recruitment practices come to reflect much more strongly a localized culture of ethnicity. Recruitment for sewing machinists was tied in with established global practice across the labour intensive ("efficiency-seeking") garment sector in which firms aim to keep labour costs at the minimum whilst ensuring an efficient productive workforce. These concerns (and the standardized recruitment practices that accompanied them) have been markedly absent from recruitment practices for the more senior level staff at UKALM. The discussion below will demonstrate the clear differences between the recruitment of production workers and the recruitment of managerial and supervisory level staff.

Non-managerial supervisory employment

Two jobs found within the production department that fall someway between that of the actual production workers and the managers are those of the supervisors and the trainers. Although supervisors are considered to have a somewhat higher status to trainers in terms of company hierarchies, they both take a similar role – patrolling the production lines, ensuring that workers meet the production targets. Yet in terms of both gender and ethnicity, there are quite distinct patterns of employment in these two jobs. Compared to the workforce as a whole (which was described in the previous two sections as overwhelmingly female and Malay), there is a much greater level of Chinese employment in these higher occupational categories. For example, Chinese make up 14.2% of the firm's overall workforce, yet occupy 51.4% of the supervisory posts. By contrast Malays make up 76.6% of the workforce but 43.2% of the supervisors and Indians, who make up 7.8% of the workforce are equally underrepresented accounting for 5.4% of supervisory employment.[30] With the supervisors, one can also observe a much higher level of male employment.

The job of the supervisor is to take responsibility for the overseeing of a single production line. They have a number of responsibilities which include; ensuring that workers on his or her line are punctual and meeting targets, organising the workers and the machinery on a line to ensure that production targets are met and dealing with day-to-day problems. The job of supervisor is a

---

[30] Based on calculations from company document, *Distribution of Staff by Race as of June 15, 1999 UKALM Sdn. Bhd.*, provided by Human Resources Director (18th August 1999).

highly stressful one since the supervisor comes under intense pressure from management to meet high targets in terms of both quantity and quality and also has to deal with worker problems such as absenteeism (a major problems that came across in all my interviews with supervisors) and any difficulties that workers may have with particular procedures or targets. On the sewing lines in particular, given the labour intensity of these operations, the supervisor faces the pressure of taking responsibility for a large number of employees. Although the supervisor has sole responsibility for the line (or "ownership" as the British factory manager referred to it as)[31] they are often aided in the tasks assigned to them by a trainer and a quality controller (QC). This set-up with the QC and trainer on the line relates specifically to the sewing floor. Trainers are former highly skilled sewing machinists who have moved into a training role and are assigned to work with the sewers on a particular line. Additionally, in cutting and finishing work where the work is less labour intensive there is often not the need to have a QC on each production line.

Even between these jobs (supervisor, trainer and QC) there are social divisions and hierarchies that run along the lines of race and gender. For example, trainers are overwhelmingly female whilst among QCs and supervisors there is more of a mix of both sexes. The reason why trainers tend to be female is largely due to the fact that they are training the workers in sewing skills and are therefore must have a background in sewing production. The trainers are recruited from both inside and outside the factory, although the trainer that I was able to interview had been recruited externally.[32] Interestingly, there is a much higher proportion of Chinese women employed as trainers compared to the proportion of Chinese workers employed as sewing machinists in the factory as a whole. This is a general trend across the factory; Chinese predominate across the higher paying occupations in the factory. For example, outside of the production department, the training school is headed by a Chinese woman and staffed by two trainers who both are Chinese.

Returning to the job of the supervisor, how is this type of work subject to divisions of gender and ethnicity? The ethnic and gender divisions among the supervisory staff appear at first to be rather equitable. For example, in table 5.2, we can observe how Chinese account for 19 of the supervisory positions, whilst Malays account for 16 and one supervisory post is held by an Indian. In terms of gender there is again no significant pattern; 5 out of the 19 Chinese supervisory posts are held by men, whilst 10 of the 16 Malay supervisors are male (the one Indian supervisor is also male). But what is really significant from the point of view of these figures is that most supervisors are concentrated in sewing, an area of the factory which is overwhelmingly staffed by Malay women sewing machinists and yet there are relatively high levels of male and Chinese employed as supervisors.

---

[31] Interview with General Manager, Site A (18th August 1999).
[32] Interview with a trainer, Site A (18th August 1999).

Table 5.2 Distribution of managerial and supervisory staff at UKALM by race and gender, June 1999

Level	Chinese		Malay		Indian		Others	
	Male	Female	Male	Female	Male	Female	Male	Female
Senior Management	0	3	1	0	0	0	0	0
Management	14	17	7	6	1	0	0	1
Supervisory	5	14	10	6	1	1	0	0

Source: Company document, *Distribution of Staff by Race as of June 15, 1999 UKALM Sdn. Bhd.,* provided by Human Resources Director, UKALM (18.08.99).

When managers were asked in interview about the role of the supervisor in the factory, some very interesting, gendered, assumptions were unveiled. I asked managers what skills were needed for the job of supervisor and they all mentioned things like an intrinsic ability to get on with the workers. Some managers even went as far as to suggest that women supervisors find it easier to relate to the (female) workers that they have responsibility for; that they have some kind of natural empathy with other women.[33] A male supervisor expanded upon this point of view, suggesting that the female supervisors tended to have more in common with the women workers, not least because "women already know how to sew".[34] However, these gendered discourses relating to feminized supervisory skills do not translate into an advantage within the workforce. Thus when I asked whether women might be preferred as supervisors I was told that this was not the case at all.[35] Women are recognized as bringing certain skills and attributes to the job of supervisor, but the job is not constructed as one that fundamentally requires these qualities.

Recruitment practices operate differently for supervisory level staff compared to that of skilled and semi-skilled production workers. Conversations with the director of human resources highlighted how the loss of supervisory staff creates major problems for the firm and consequentially, they will cast their recruitment "net" as widely as possible in seeking new supervisors. The director of human resources had, for example, been in Penang (a major location for manufacturing in Malaysia) to seek out potential new supervisors. The HR director felt that a good potential supervisor would be someone with good quality supervisory experience in industry (preferably the garment industry), decent educational qualifications and some training in how to manage a workforce. Recruitment will therefore often take a much more formal route – for example placing adverts or employing the services of "head hunters".[36] However, this style of recruitment is relatively new and even with these techniques in place, the HR director told me that he had experienced problems; providing the example of his attempt to recruit a woman into a supervisory position which fell through when her husband expressed his unwillingness to her taking a job that would take her away from the home.[37] Such an example confirms the idea put forward earlier, that the perceptions that managers and recruiters have regarding women and employment in the factory, are themselves a broader reflection of the role and position of women in Malaysian society more generally.

Returning, to the issue of the recruitment of supervisors, it became apparent in my interviews that recruitment practices had created something like a "core" group of male Chinese supervisors, who were, until the recent arrival of the

---

[33] Interview with acting finishing manager, Site A (10th March 1999).

[34] Interview with a supervisor from the sewing department, Site A (18th August 1999).

[35] Interview with acting finishing manager, Site A (10th March 1999), training manager, Site A (18th August 1999) and informal conversation with the supervisor in the fusing section, translated by the production executive, cutting, Site A (10th March 1999).

[36] Interview with HR Director, Site A (18th August 1999).

[37] Interview with HR Director, Site A (18th August 1999).

(Malay) HR Director, viewed as the most likely candidates for promotion into managerial positions. Thus despite the human resource director's recent changes in the way that supervisors are recruited, prior to his arrival at the firm (only one year previously) recruitment of supervisors had been done on a much more informal and *ad hoc* basis. Whereas some supervisors were recruited internally, it does appear to be the case that a large proportion of the Chinese supervisors were recruited externally via networks of family friends. I was able to interview two Chinese male supervisors who openly told me that they had got their jobs because they knew the old MD and/or a certain production manager (both Chinese males). For these supervisors, their networks of friends were much more important in getting their jobs than any formal recruitment process. Both supervisors only had a single interview and there were no tests at the interview. Both of these supervisors saw their job as a route into managerial employment, indeed one of them had been covering the job of a finishing manager for several months.[38]

Managerial employment

At the level of managerial employment, my interviews revealed that very similar processes of utilising personal contacts to get jobs had taken place amongst the Chinese managers whom I interviewed. This is not surprising because supervisory employment is viewed as a route into management, with many managers having worked previously as supervisors. Although it ought to be emphasized that this was not the only way through which managerial staff were recruited, the use of these networks of personal contacts as a means of recruiting management staff does go some way in explaining the relatively high prevalence of Chinese and/or men in management positions. Both management and supervisory jobs are, on the whole, recruited via very informal means. Despite the HR director's determination to implement more formalized recruitment and promotion arrangements at the firm, as yet no formal recruitment mechanisms have been put in place for the recruitment of managerial staff. I argue that it is these *ad hoc* recruitment mechanisms which have helped to sustain patterns of ethnic inequality in supervisory and managerial work.

Table 5.2 (page 140) shows the breakdown of management by race and ethnicity. We can see that three of the four senior managerial positions in the factory (operations manager, finance manager and finance director) are held by Chinese women, whilst one post (that of Human Resources director) is held by a Malay male.[39] The predominance of Chinese in managerial employment is shown further in the figures on lower level management, which show that 31 out of the 46 managers are Chinese compared to just 13 Malay managers, one Indian and one

---

[38] Interviews with two of the sewing department supervisors, Site A (18th August 1999).

[39] These statistics do not include expatriate staff. Senior managerial positions held by British staff are those of managing director (MD), general manager (GM) and the factory manager at Site B. There are also expatriate staff employed as the production manager at Site Two and in two technical managerial positions.

mixed race. Interestingly, women make up over half of these managers and we can see that 17 of these managers are Chinese women.

Considering the high level of Chinese managerial employment, this is something that has been noted in a number of studies of the Malaysian manufacturing industries (Ackerman, 1980; Ong, 1987; Rasiah, 1993). It is thus impossible to explain the prevalence of Chinese in management positions at UKALM without reference to the broader political economy of ethnic relations in Malaysia that was outlined in chapter three. The NEP has operated to draw educated Malays into the public sector, whilst at the same time witnessing the expansion of a Malay proletariat as the rural Malay peasantry came to work in the newly expanding manufacturing sector. In this sense there has been a lack of educated Malays to take on managerial positions in industry. At the same time, the traditional dominance of Chinese in the private sector and the lack of employment opportunities in the public sector for educated Chinese also helps to explain the prevalence of Chinese in Managerial positions. It is again worth referring back to Rasiah's study of the garment sector mentioned in chapter three (page 77) because he notes that there is a level of intra-ethnic networking that goes on in the recruitment of managerial employees. The prevalence of Chinese in managerial positions in his case study factories reflected a sense of solidarity among Chinese business-men who saw recruitment of other Chinese into their firms as some form of counter measure towards what they perceived to be the discriminatory practices of the NEP (Rasiah, 1993: 10-11).

In an interview with the firm's training manager (a Chinese man), I was told that he had got his job through personal connections with the previous MD. Although this manager did have previous managerial experience, this had been in a bar rather than in a factory and the manager's educational qualifications were limited to SPM (the Malaysian equivalent of the British GCSE, taken at around age 17). When I asked this manager about the interviews that he had for the position he responded that he only had one interview; "I was asked a few simple questions like can I work alongside a lot of girls, about my past experience and that's all".[40] This manager's gender was not deemed to be especially significant when he was recruited for the job. He was asked a few, rather jokey questions about whether he could work alongside a lot of "girls", but this was not deemed to be a significant barrier to entry into the job. So it is again an interesting contrast with the recruitment process outlined in 5.2 for sewing machinists, where gender is regarded as an essential aspect of what constitutes a good worker. Although my interviews with managers were not comprehensive, I did find the interview with the (male Chinese) training manager outlined above in total contrast to interviews that I undertook with Malay female managers. For example, Rosnah, the cutting floor manager who had been recruited internally, had higher levels of educational attainment than the training manager. Or, Saadiah the HR executive who was a graduate from a New Zealand university and was recruited to work in personnel having had considerable work experience within the garment sector.

---

[40] Interview with training manager, Site A (18th August 1999).

My interview with the company union president also gave me an insight into the extent to which these networks had been in operation as a recruitment mechanism. The union president, a Malay man employed as an industrial engineer, complained that many of the managers at the firm had got their jobs because they had contacts in the firm and not on the basis that they were the best person for the job. The union president felt that this was the major reason for the predominance of Chinese in management and supervisory positions. He commented that:

> When I first came here the general manager was a China-man. I see that a Chinese comes in as a supervisor, and then another Chinese comes in as a supervisor. Why are there no Malay I ask – because Malays also have certificate and experience in these sorts of things. I know why, it is because of race.[41]

The union president felt that over the past year things had been improving at UKALM, especially with the establishment of the position of Human Resources director – a post now filled by a Malay man. So when I asked him whether he felt that Chinese supervisors and managers had used personal contacts to get their jobs he responded:

> Yes exactly! Before Syed [the HR Director] came here, only Saadiah was there as the executive personnel officer. So they bypass Saadiah and go direct to the general manager and then start work. If they had followed procedure, personnel should have interviewed first. Several people, still working here, went directly to the general manager and had no interview with personnel. Now it's very different; Syed is very good.[42]

I had a clear sense that the union president's respect for Syed not only stemmed from the way in which the Human Resource director had instigated a shift away from these recruitment practices based upon ethnic cronyism, but also because Syed was Malay. The union president therefore seemed to regard Syed as more likely to look out for the interests of Malay workers on the basis of his own ethnicity. In this respect, the political economy of ethnicity in Malaysia, and the overlapping tensions and hierarchies that are part of this economy, can be seen to be operating in microcosm at UKALM. The Trade Union at UKALM itself reflects ethnic divisions, with almost no Chinese members. Although almost all of the firm's Indian employees have joined the union, the union is dominated by Malays who have also taken all of the executive positions within the union. Syed is therefore able to develop a close relationship with the trade union on the basis of ethnic identity,[43] whilst Chinese workers are likely to see Chinese managers as the ones most likely to look after their interests (and evidence suggests that Chinese managers have done just this). When I asked the union president what steps the

---

[41] Interview with the in-house trade union president, Site A (18th August 1999).

[42] Interview with the in-house trade union president, Site A (18th August 1999).

[43] Similar practices are observed by Wendy Smith in her study of a Japanese multinational operating in Malaysia. Smith suggests that the Malay HR Director has developed close linkages with the majority Malay workforce (Smith, 1994: 179).

union had tried to take in the past against these discriminatory recruitment practices, he told me that although they had raised the issue with management, "because the GM was still a Chinese, we couldn't do anything, we just strive in our hearts and wait and see".[44]

Indeed, the HR Director was keen to see these sorts of practices stamped out. For example, he was trying to introduce policies that would lay down minimum standards for applicants for managerial and also supervisory employment. The HR Director was critical of the standard of managerial and supervisory employees that he saw at the firm, claiming that "it isn't enough to make someone a manager just because he has been a bar manager or whatever"[45] (this was a clear reference to the training manager). What this will mean therefore is less of a reliance on personal contacts as a recruitment mechanism, but as to whether this will seriously change the ethnic balance of the management staff is difficult to say. After all, the recruitment of managerial staff will go on within the context of a Malaysian political economy that is deeply segmented along the lines of ethnicity.

What one can observe from this discussion of managerial and supervisory employment is that there is a local culture of ethnic recruitment networks that has been in operation at the factory. These are locally constructed ideas about who and how to recruit and not a reflection of management recruitment strategies that had been brought with the firm from the UK.

Conclusion

This chapter has shown how the need to secure a low wage supply of sewing machinists manifests itself in recruitment practices that reflect gendered assumptions relating to the skills and aptitudes of female workers. This is a highly regulated process and has led to the appointment of a new HR director in order to try and understand the problem of labour turnover in the firm. The gendered nature of the recruitment process for sewing machinists reflects the needs of the firm to seek out the most efficient (i.e. low wage and hard-working) workforce possible. Such ideas of efficiency are part of the global liberal culture within which the discourse of the progressive firm is framed, and they reflect deep-seated gendered assumptions, which statements concerning equal opportunity (in effect a strategy that reflects the way in which firms regard themselves as gender neutral agents of change) do little to change.

The global culture of efficiency and equal opportunity that shapes the gendered nature of employment in sewing is, of course, cross-cut with localized divisions and hierarchies – not least in terms of the assumptions relating to ethnicity and employment that characterise workplace relations across the whole of the Malaysian economy. But it is in the recruitment of managerial and supervisory level staff that these communal tensions emerge most clearly. Such a finding is very relevant to this study because it indicates the extent to which globalized

---

[44] Interview with the in-house trade union president, Site A (18th August 1999).
[45] Interview with HR Director, Site A (10th March 1999).

liberal notions such as efficiency and equal opportunity have not impacted upon employment practices in masculinized occupations. The interests of a localized masculinist elite are, therefore, protected by the operation of recruitment practices that reflect masculinist managerialist assumptions concerning the need to control feminized occupations.

In the next chapter, the various arguments brought up in this chapter will be subjected to greater analysis as I turn to look at how these divisions within the workforce are related to the construction of women (especially Malay women) as a low paid source of labour for the firm.

Chapter 6

Company Recruitment Practices and the Impact of FDI

Introduction

A garment sector firm such as UK-Apparel presents a good example of a firm that has sought to maintain its competitive position through expanding production offshore, enabling it to benefit from low-cost labour – a process that has been enhanced by developments in communication technologies and transportation. Operating a number of overseas factories and engaging in subcontracted production networks, it is just the sort of firm that economic liberals might view in terms of it being an agent of globalization (along the lines of Dunning's model of the "efficiency seeking firm" (Dunning, 2000: 29) drawing previously marginalized areas of the world into the global market economy. However, as I suggested in chapter one, the liberal perspective on the firm tends to overstate the beneficial impact of FDI on host countries, and fails to analyse the differential impacts of FDI on groups within the population. As a result, when the liberal mainstream actually deals with issues of women's employment in MNCs, the general assumption is made that FDI benefits women, with no analysis of the gendered hierarchies and inequalities that characterize global transformations such as the spread of multinationally organized firms. The liberal perspective (a) assumes that FDI is a gender neutral process and therefore, women's participation in multinational employment has the potential to undermine gender inequality and (b) is a model that fails to recognize the gender inequalities that are integral to its functioning.

In the previous chapter, the suggestion was put forward that the notion of the efficiency seeking firm needs to be replaced with a gendered understanding of FDI, in which the firm plays an active role in gender construction. It was shown, for example, that the notion of gender neutrality of modern (Western) management practice, articulated through the language of equal opportunity, cannot be substantiated – recruitment practices reflect both globalized and localized notions of women's natural skills and women's place within society. As suggested in chapter two, the firm can be recognised in this sense as operating at the intersection between a globalizing hegemonic masculinity and localized gendered social practice shaped by the experience of state-led economic development. In this chapter, I turn to look more specifically at the way in which the firm has been understood within mainstream IPE thinking in terms of the transmission of progressive modernizing values into "backward" host states. The aim of this chapter, then, is to provide the empirical support to the claim made at the start of this book that FDI does not have a progressive impact upon host states, rather, it benefits from embedded gendered and racialized divisions and inequalities that it has played a role in constructing.

An overview of the claims that are being assessed

In chapter one it was shown that the attraction of FDI into export industries is often encouraged on the grounds that it creates employment opportunities in labour intensive sectors (World Bank, 1990; 1995: 42-43). The creation of new jobs is obvious in a firm such as UKALM where production is based upon labour-intensive manufacturing techniques. The employee build-up charts shown in chapter five (page 132) indicate that the firm has created large-scale employment opportunities. The opening up of a secondary factory (Site B), which is only involved in sewing production, has extended these employment opportunities into a further area of the Malacca region. Furthermore, one could identify that there are possible knock-on effects in terms of employment for those firms that act as suppliers and sub-contractors to UKALM. For example, the firm subcontracts out any embroidery work to a couple of local firms. More importantly, claims have been made regarding the positive impact of FDI on female workers emphasising the creation of jobs, outside of the home, for women in MNCs. Again it has been shown that this is the case at UKALM, with over 98% of the sewing machinists (who make up around 43% of the entire workforce) being women, (79.3 % of these women being Malay).[1] Thus the suggestion is made that women are drawn out of the household sphere and into the "formal" market-based economy and this has the potential to undermine traditional gender relations.

The more significant claim made regarding the impact of FDI on employment is that the MNC not only creates job opportunities, but jobs that are better paid, have better working conditions and better training programmes than local firms based in the same sector. This forces local firms to adapt to these standards and, consequently the firm is viewed as acting as something of a "role model". It was shown in part two of this book that the firm is concerned with its operations offshore being deemed to be "politically appropriate" and, like many garment sector firms, has adopted a set of core minimum standards that must be applied to all offshore factories and sourcing partners. At UK-Apparel, these minimum standards were put together in a document in July 1998 in which the claim was made:

> The only criteria for the selection for employment will be the candidates ability to do the job required. As far as is reasonably practicable (having regard for local cultures, religious beliefs practices etc.) We will pursue a policy of equal opportunities for all

---

[1] UKALM, *Distribution of Staff by Race as of June 15, 1999 UKALM Sdn. Bhd.*, company document provided by Human Resources Director, UKALM, 18th August 1999.

regardless of sex, sexual orientation, marital status, creed, colour, race, religion, age, disability, nationality, ethnic or national origin.[2]

What is made apparent in this chapter is that such strategies do not deal with the established patterns of gender segmentation within the garment industry whereby women are grouped in the lowest paying occupations (e.g. as sewers or fusers rather than as cutters or technicians) which lack any real opportunity for career progression (unlike, for example, the job of spreader). The question therefore is not whether MNCs are any worse employers than local firms but, as Elson and Pearson have suggested, it is worth singling out the MNC in debates regarding women's employment because MNCs are regarded as possessing a "transformative capacity" above and beyond that of local employers (Elson and Pearson, 1989).

Rather than acting as a "role model" or demonstrating a "transformatory potential", the case study firm acts to shore-up and thereby, benefit from gender divisions and inequalities. The gendered nature of employment within UKALM is not simply a reflection of the embedded nature of gender (and ethnic) inequality within the political economy of Malaysia. They are also an indication of the active role of the firm in the (re)construction of these gendered inequalities with the firm targeting specific groups of women workers (in this case married Malay rural women) in order to ensure a supply of low-cost labour.

The trends noted in this chapter fit largely with the findings of authors such as Fussell and Pearson noted in chapter two, who claim that more economically mobile women will seek employment in other sectors (for example in electronics or the service sector) leaving the lower wage more labour intensive industries such as the garment industries to search for new sources of low-cost labour (Fussell, 2000 63, 69-72; Pearson, 1995: 161).

As a subsidiary of a UK garment firm concentrated in labour intensive production, UKALM needs a source of workers that are cheap yet also productive and easy to control. The firm mobilizes this kind of workforce through its recruitment system. An analysis of how rates of pay vary across the firm by gender and ethnicity is, therefore, linked to a discussion of the process whereby jobs become defined as exclusively "male" or "female". Thus revealing the systematic devaluation of the sorts of skills and attributes that female workers bring to the jobs that they do, a process that enables the firm to construct the job of sewing machinist as low paid. In the final part of this chapter, ideas regarding how the firm constructs gendered identities within the firm based around regimes for the control of workers are introduced. We can see that this process also serves to disadvantage women workers, with managers viewing women as best suited to monotonous work because of their perceived "docility", effectively locking them into the lower paying echelons of the occupational hierarchy. Consequentially, the "transformatory potential" of the MNC is witnessed not in the destruction of gendered workplace relations and divisions in the local society, but in the active (re)constitution of these practices within the workplace.

---

[2] UK-Apparel Group PLC, *World Class Operations: Protecting People, Property, Product and Environment*, document supplied by Personnel Director, 6th November 1998.

LIVERPOOL
JOHN MOORES UNIVERSITY
AVRIL ROBARTS LRC
TEL. 0151 231 4022

Pay and gender inequalities in the workforce at UKALM: an overview

Tables 6.1 and 6.2 show figures for the rates of pay available to workers at UKALM (excluding "executive", i.e. managerial employment). Table 6.1 shows the rates for workers who are paid monthly and 6.2 shows the figures for those paid on a daily rated basis. The most highly paid non-executive job is that of supervisor with a maximum monthly earnings potential of 2,200 RM followed by the job of trainer (maximum monthly income 1,380 RM) and cutter (maximum monthly income 1,100 RM). On the basis of the rates of pay shown in 6.2, it is difficult to suggest that the workplace at UKALM is characterized by gender inequalities in terms of pay given that 21 out of 37 supervisors were female and all of the trainers were female whilst all of the 17 cutters employed at the firm were male (although there was one female trainee). But, as was shown in the previous chapter, the divisions that exist within the workforce at UKALM are based largely on the crowding of Malay women into sewing machinist work. Importantly then, when we break down the figures on supervisory employment in terms of ethnicity, we find that of the 21 female supervisors, 14 were Chinese.[3] The job of trainer is also dominated by Chinese women. Whilst the cutting jobs employ mainly Malays, these are very much male dominated jobs. There are therefore, some very interesting intersections between gender and ethnicity taking place on the factory floor, but at the same time, there is very little evidence that Malay females are making inroads into the occupational hierarchy at UKALM.

Considering tables 6.1 and 6.2 from the point of view of the evidence provided in the previous chapter, what is notable is that when a comparison is made between those jobs that are daily and monthly rated, almost all daily rated jobs are female dominated and also dominated by Malay employment (although Indian women are also disproportionately represented within these groups of workers – especially in non-sewing positions). Jobs that require very little skill overall, such as the jobs of spreader or the operatives of the "vac-pac" machine (which vacuum packs clothing ready for shipping) yet are dominated by male employment are monthly rated. The significance of earning a monthly wage is not simply a matter of status or stability in earnings (given that there is no piece rated bonus system in place for these workers), but also, in the main translates into higher rates of pay.

---

[3] UKALM, *Distribution of Staff by Race.*

All of the jobs listed in figure 6.2 are dominated by female employment with the notable exception of finishing work where male employment has come to play a more significant role. The employment of men in the finishing department in jobs previously viewed as exclusively female suggests that there is some merit in the suggestions that in a globalizing world economy, men's employment conditions are becoming more "like women's"; that the downward pressure on wages and working conditions in industries such as garment manufacture is leading to an equalization in the wage inequality between men and women, mainly because men are now being forced to accept lower wages[4]. However, on the limited evidence of this trend available from the case study firm, it is difficult to substantiate these kinds of claims. In fact, the overwhelming trend at UKALM is that it is mainly women workers who are found in the lowest paying segments of the workforce and also the sections of the production process that are the most heavily supervised (especially in sewing), receiving payment on a daily basis and facing penalties if production targets are not met.

Figures relating to rates of pay at UKALM do however raise certain issues relevant to recent feminist economics debates regarding the way that industries based in highly labour intensive sectors have sought to keep wages as low as possible. Such a strategy is often characteristic of countries that have pursued a "low road" economic development strategy based upon the expansion of labour intensive industries in low technology, low skill, sectors such as garment manufacture (Sen, 2001). The suggestion is that these industries will seek out new sources of low-cost, generally female, labour rather than look to upgrade employee skills and workplace technologies. This is not to suggest that wages have not risen considerably in the Malaysian garment sector; it was shown in chapter three, for example, that there has been a narrowing in the wage inequality in this sector. However, wage increases in the garment sector have not kept pace with the rates of increase in other manufacturing industries, a trend that is revealed in table 6.3.

---

[4] Pearson (1995: 156-157) raises this suggestion as one possible explanation for declining wage inequality in Mexican export industries.

Table 6.1 UKALM salary band for monthly rated, non-executive staff, March 1999

Position	Starting salary	Mid-Point salary	Maximum salary
Supervisor	RM 1,200.00	RM 1,700.00	RM 2,200.00
Trainer	RM 600.00	RM 850.00	RM 1, 380.00
Cutter	RM 600. 00	RM 850.00	RM 1,100.00
Fabric Inspector	RM 550.00	RM 780.00	RM 1,010.00
Vac Pac	RM 480.00	RM 680.00	RM830.00
QC	RM 450.00	RM 640.00	RM 830.00
Spreader	RM 450.00	RM 640.00	RM 830.00

Source: UKALM, *Pay Policy for Non-Executive Staff*, Company document provided by HR Director, UKALM, March 1999.

n.b. at the time of this study there were approximately 6 RM to £1 Sterling.

Table 6.2 UKALM salary structure/band for daily rated staff, March 1999

Position	Starting	Confirmed	Bonus rate
Sewing floor			
Grade A Machinist	RM 23.71	RM 26.00	RM 37.68
Grade B Machinist	RM 21.03	RM 22.88	RM 33.16
Grade C Machinist	RM 19.00	RM 20.80	RM 30.14
Float Machinist	RM 24.31	RM 28.65	RM 30.14
Pre-Sewing Operator (PSO)	RM 24.31	RM 28.65	RM 30.62
Float PSO	nil	RM 24.28	RM 26.08
Finishing Floor			
Pressers	RM 21.03	RM 22.88	RM 33.16
Float Pressers	nil	RM 24.28	RM 26.08
Big Jim*	RM 19.00	RM 20.80	RM 30.14
Stain Remover, Laundry	RM 18.42	RM 20.80	Nil
Bagging, Kimball Tag, Insert Hanger, Button-Up, Bag Label **	RM 17.17	RM 18.72	RM 27.12
Presser, Bagging, Kimball Tag, Insert Hanger, Button-Up, Bag Label, Service Girl (evening)**	RM 10.66	RM 11.09	n.a.
Shift allowance	RM 1.63	RM 1.70	n.a.

Source: UKALM, *Pay Policy for Non-Executive Staff*, Company document provided by HR Director, UKALM, March 1999.
*This relates to the operators of the machine that is designed to remove creases from garments by blowing hot air through them.
**These jobs relate to all the various different processes involved in the finishing of garments.

Table 6.3 Wage increases in selected Malaysian manufacturing industries, 1990-1997

Industry/earnings	Average earnings per month (RM)		Percentage increase in wages 1990-1997
	1990	1997	
Manufacture of wearing apparel except footwear			
Male earnings	714	969	35.71
Female earnings	463	780	68.47
Manufacture of electrical machinery, apparatus and supplies			
Male earnings	1138	1820	59.92
Female earnings	445	966	117.07
Manufacturing Industry average			
Male earnings	885	1449	63.72
Female earnings	443	912	105.86

Source: ILO (2000), *Yearbook of labour statistics*, table 5A and table 5B, 937.

What the data in table 6.3 shows is that female wages in other sectors of manufacturing industry have risen much faster than the garment sector. Between 1990 and 1997, average female wages in Malaysian manufacturing rose by over 105%, compared to just 68.47% in the garment sector. It is relevant also to compare these rates of increase in wages with the electronics sector, because UKALM competes with local electronics employers for female employees to work in assembly line positions. In electronic and electrical industries, female wages between 1990 and 1997 rose from 445 RM per month (a figure lower than the average monthly wages paid in the garment industry in that year) to 966 RM per month, well above the figure of 780 RM per month, the average wage in the garment sector.

Part of the reason for the low wages in the garment sector compared to electronics is the limited technological upgrading that has occurred in the garment sector. Ishak Shari has argued that the higher wages and levels of training associated with more capital intensive, high technology industries are only really found in electronics industries (especially the semi-conductor industry) with most other manufacturing industries remaining largely reliant on labour intensive production processes (Shari, 2000: 121). Wage differentials between the electronics sector and the garment sector have therefore been exacerbated by the formers' shift into capital intensive production. The benefits of these changes within the electronics sector for women workers are seen not only in improvements in wages, but also in conditions of work as less labour intensive production processes have meant that there is a much lower likelihood that women workers would be exposed to the more dangerous work processes in the electronics industry. Interviews at UKALM revealed that the major competitor for female employees, especially young female employees, were the large multinational electronics firms that have located in Malacca. Such is the extent to which these firms have been successful in attracting young female workers, that the HR executives at UKALM tended to regard young workers as unlikely to stay with the firm; they would leave UKALM when an opening in an electronics firm arose.[5]

Since the 1970s, electronics firms have also been able to attract workers from much further afield. Electronics firms have established practices of sending agents into the rural states of Malaysia to recruit young single women. The agents will promote to potential women workers the many benefits of factory employment and certain electronics firms have established housing accommodation or hostels for these women workers (Ariffin, 1994b: 53). There is little evidence of these practices occurring in the garment sector with women workers usually recruited locally (Beaudat, 1993: 146). Furthermore, despite evidence suggesting that garment sector employers would like to employ women who have completed their secondary education, in reality well-educated young women are more likely to seek better paid employment (for example in the electronics sector, but also in the public sector). Thus the average female garment worker has completed just six years schooling (Beaudat, 1993: 53).

---

[5] Interview with HR Executives at Site A and Site B (March 1999).

How then did the garment sector manage to keep wage costs down despite the competition for female workers from other manufacturing sectors, such as electronics (and also from the service sector)? Specifically, how might the study of employment and recruitment practices at UKALM lead to a greater understanding of these trends? Part of the answer to this question lies in the ability of the firm to construct female employment in such a way that it is associated with low paid work. Low wages are associated with systems of payment that act to devalue the skills that women workers bring to the workplace. At the same time, garment firms have sought to secure new supplies of low wage labour through the employment of rural Malay married women with children. In this sense, the firm has identified a group within the local population and recruitment strategies have targeted this group of workers because the company has been able to employ them in sewing machinist work and at the same time keep these workers wages as low as possible. Thus whilst younger workers have sought to find employment in the better paying electronics sector, given the labour intensity of the technologically unsophisticated garment sector, the firm has been forced to look for new sources of low-cost labour. In this sense it is very difficult to view the MNC as acting to raise employment standards and increase wages for women workers in the way that is assumed in the liberal literature on the firm.

Pay, skill and gender: comparing sewers and cutters

It is suggested here that the low wages associated with women's work are a reflection of the way that skills associated with women's work are generally undervalued. In order to do this, a comparison of the income of Grade A and float machinists with that of the cutters is presented. This analysis of pay is then linked to a discussion concerning how the gendered workplace discourses articulated by managers at UKALM contribute to the process whereby women's work is undervalued within the factory.

Figure 6.1 Calculations of the minimum and maximum potential earnings of confirmed* grade A machinists in various months (1999)

			Monthly Wage (RM)	
Month	Number of working days	Number of days holiday	Minimum (does not get any bonus payment)	Maximum (gets all the bonus payments)
January	21	6	546	721.2
February	20	5	520	650
March	22	1	572	817.28

Source: Adapted from information provided by the HR department on company pay policies for non-executive staff.
*Only after a 3-month period if speed and quality of work meets company standards are the machinists confirmed.

Figure 6.2 Calculations of the minimum and maximum potential earnings of confirmed* float machinists in various months (1999)

			Monthly Wage (RM)	
Month	Number of working days	Number of days holiday	Minimum (does not get any bonus payment)	Maximum (gets all the bonus payments)
January	21	6	601	631.2
February	20	5	573	602.55
March	22	1	630.3	671.67

Source: Adapted from information provided by the HR department on company pay policies for non-executive staff.

There is a huge disparity in the wages earned by cutters compared to those of sewing machinists. This is significant because grade A and float machinists and cutters are all regarded as skilled jobs.[6] Despite the assertion by one of the personnel executives that the sewers "can really earn" because of the piece rate-bonus system,[7] the wages are significantly lower than cutters' and actually even lower than those received by the spreaders. Tables 6.1 and 6.2 present data on employee earnings from grade A machinists and "float" machinists (a sewing machinist who is multiskilled in all of the various operations). Looking at this data, one can observe how the system of payment leads to vast fluctuations in a worker's levels of pay. As outlined in chapter five, these workers are paid on a daily rated basis with bonus payments if they meet a specified daily target. Workers will continue to receive the basic rate of pay during holidays (of which there are many in multi-ethnic Malaysia), but will not receive any bonus payments for those working days lost. In the month of January 1999, for example, there were 21 working days of which 6 were public holiday (due to the *Hari Raya* or Eid Islamic festival), thus there were only 15 days during which workers could earn the bonus rate of pay. This means that if a grade A machinist failed to achieve the bonus rate for the entire month of January, she would earn 546 RM and if she achieved the bonus on all of the 15 days she would earn 721.2 RM per day. In February 1999, the Chinese New Year holiday also meant that workers could only hope to achieve bonus payments on 15 days out of 20, making the maximum payment that a grade A machinist could earn for that month just 650 RM.

Compared to the sewers, cutters are on significantly higher wages. The starting monthly salary for a cutter is RM600 rising to a midpoint of RM850 and a maximum of RM 1,100. Even the relatively low skilled spreaders can potentially earn more than the sewers. The spreaders starting salary is RM450 rising to a mid point of RM640 and a maximum of RM830. Importantly these salaries are much more reliable sources of income. A sewer's pay can suffer immensely if she regularly fails to meet the bonus rate.

So how do we explain this disparity in wages? It is certainly not the case that low wages can be explained simply by looking at the supply and demand for workers. There is very high demand for workers in sewing but the firm is very reluctant to raise wages. After all, sewing machinists make up 44.3% of the total workforce at UKALM, by far the largest single category of employees,[8] making it in the interests of the company to structure their salaries in such a way that wage costs are kept to a minimum.

Another way of explaining this disparity in wages is to consider the view that wage rates are linked to the level of skill needed to do the job. It could be argued that the job of cutter requires greater skill and training takes longer. This is true to a certain extent, training to be a cutter takes around three months whereas the most difficult sewing operations will take a maximum of two months to learn. However,

---

[6] Interview with HR Director, Site A (3rd March 1999).
[7] Interview with HR Executive, Site B (11th March 1999).
[8] UKALM, *Personnel Statistics Consolidated as at Period 1,* 12.2.99, provided by Human Resources Director, UKALM (10th March 1999).

in my conversations with the head of the training school, she mentioned that they will only train experienced machinists in the Grade A operations.[9] In other words, these machinists would have already spent a significant amount of time training in other operations and basic sewing machine techniques. Indeed, the financial director claimed that it takes at least six months for a machinist to be fully competent.[10] There is the possibility that sewers could progress to the position of trainer on the lines. Trainers are usually all women and some have been recruited internally (although the fact that many trainers were Chinese made it unlikely that they had worked their way up through the (Malay and Indian dominated) factory floor). Indeed, most of the trainers currently employed at UKALM were recruited from outside the firm.[11]

The discussion of gendered wage inequalities touched upon in this comparison of sewers and cutters raises broader questions relating to how the skills that women bring to the workplace are valued. Thus in order to understand the disparity in wages, it is necessary to look at how skills are defined (Elson and Pearson, 1981: 23-24). The discussion here suggests that the association between women's work and low pay is linked to perceptions concerning the way in which many of the skills that women bring to the job are developed in the household rather than on-the-job. This is evidenced, for example, in the way that the company seems to regard women as natural sewers and will ask women at interview whether they like to sew. It can also be argued that women bring to the job other skills such as diligence and dexterity which are seen as natural attributes rather than actual skills necessary for doing the job. Women's skills are naturalized, viewed as innate rather than a product of training, and therefore not something that can command higher levels of wages. Diane Elson suggests that the devaluation of these feminine skills compared to the "technical" skills associated with male labour is what is at the heart of the "fable" of nimble fingered female worker.

> ...nimble fingers are not just a physical attribute. The nimbleness comes from the mind as much as the muscles. It requires concentration, patience and meticulousness. Again, these are all attributes that girls are typically encouraged to develop, much more so than boys. Employers find girls quick to achieve proficiency because they are already trained in the art of manual dexterity. But because the training hasn't cost the employers anything, it tends to go unrecognized. It is attributed to nature – and it's not reflected in higher pay (Elson, 1983).

Such is the salience of the view that women are somehow naturally suited to sewing machinist work, it remains the case that training in a "craft" skill such as cutting is somehow much more valuable than that received by the sewers. This is a point that has been made by a number of feminist writers. In particular by Phillips and Taylor who have put forward the argument that:

---

[9] Interview with head of the training school, Site A (3rd March 1999).

[10] Interview with Financial Director, Site A (11th March 1999).

[11] Interview with Training Manager, Site A (18th August 1999); interview with a trainer from the sewing department, Site A (18th August 1999).

> Far from being an objective economic fact, skill is often an ideological category,
> imposed on certain types of work by virtue of the sex and power of the workers who
> perform it (Phillips and Taylor, 1980: 80).

The gendered discourses surrounding notions and definitions of skill are
fundamental to discussions of workplace inequalities and gender relations. The
ubiquity of these gendered discourses was evident in nearly all of my interviews –
managers and supervisors all held the view that women workers possess these
innate skills[12] and when combined with discourses relating to the traditional nature
of rural Malay society, workplace gender inequalities are presented as reflecting
some sort of natural social order. This is, then, a real contrast to the image
presented in mainstream approaches to gender and FDI of the modernising MNC
that acts to breakdown gender inequalities both outside and inside the factory as
women become more and more incorporated into the global capitalist system.

*Shifts in workplace gender relations: control, resistance and the employment of
married women*

Having already considered how understandings of skill contribute to the
devaluation of women's work, it is important to consider some of the other
managerial perceptions concerning female workers that act to confine women to
sewing machine work. Interviews at the firm revealed that women are viewed as
more submissive and docile, that is, less likely to act in an insubordinate manner
or, to become involved in trade union activities. But the fact that the firm finds it
easy to control women workers is a reflection not only of gendered behavioural
norms in Malaysian (especially Malay) society, but also a reflection of the way that
for many women at UKALM, better alternative forms of employment are not
available. Thus we see that although young, economically mobile and relatively
well educated women seek out employment in the more highly paying electronics
sector where employment standards also tend to be better, for the women employed
at UKALM who are often married with children and lack a considerable amount of
formal education, this is often not a viable alternative. The theme of tight control
over the labour process in order to secure efficiency has already been introduced in
the previous chapter. What can be seen, is that the firm is, again, targeting groups
of women who can be easily controlled. Thus, again, we can see the gendered
assumptions (women are docile and therefore easy to control) and opportunist
behaviours (the need to target particular groups of women who will be especially
easy to control because of their economic circumstances) that lie within globalised
management techniques.

---

[12] This view wasn't only evident at the UKALM factories, but also came across in
interviews with management staff that I met with on visits to other manufacturing firms
such the Hong Kong owned Penn Apparel Sdn. Bhd. Interviews with personnel manager
of Penn Apparel Sdn. Bhd., and factory tour with company personnel officer, Penang
(18th March 1999).

Issues concerning how the firm benefits from the recruitment of these rural Malay women, however, must be offset against the possible gains that this experience of employment in the formal sector brings to women themselves. A group of women are being targeted that prior to the 1980s would not have had access to formal waged employment. Furthermore, in terms of issues of control within the factory, it is not entirely fair to characterize all the female sewing machinists and other women employed in operative work as submissive since there are examples of women workers at UKALM exerting a certain level of resistance to factory control. There are, therefore, contradictory processes at work as women enter employment in the export sector that impact upon gender relations both inside and outside the firm. Thus the discussion of the control of women as secondary workers that is developed below needs to take into account the way that the shift of women workers into factory employment is accompanied by a "decomposition", "recomposition" and "intensification" of gender relations.

These ideas of "decomposition", "recomposition" and "intensification" are found in the work of Elson and Pearson which draws out the interconnections between locally established gender relations and the production of gender relations in the workplace (Elson and Pearson, 1981: 31). A process of decomposition could be seen in the way that waged employment increases the status and power that (usually) young women had within the household (Elson and Pearson, 1981: 31), whilst the processes of recomposition and intensification refer to things such as the new and existing forms of gender subordination that the female workers confronted in the factory setting (Elson and Pearson, 1981: 32). These ideas have been highly influential within studies of women and work in developing countries, especially in those studies that are concerned with women's experiences of factory employment (Wolf, 1992).[13] Elson and Pearson's work remains useful to this book because their concepts of decomposition, recomposition and intensification are not a deterministic frameworks but heuristic devices that pick up on the contradictory processes at work as women enter paid employment. Although this book is concerned with how the firm itself has drawn upon gender divisions in society rather than a study of women's experiences within that firm, these concepts remain relevant to an assessment of the extent to which the firm benefits from the inequalities that its recruitment practices perpetuate.

Control of workers and workplace resistance

In a labour intensive sector, the ability to control labour is important because it enables the firm to raise productivity and quality standards. The way that the firm draws upon gender divisions in society concerns not only a desire to keep wage costs down but also to maintain control over the workforce (Ecevit, 1991: 68). The preceding discussion regarding the differences in systems of payment between daily and monthly rated staff at UKALM also needs to be understood in terms of the way that these systems of payment contribute to greater levels of control over

---

[13] The use of these concepts has also been widespread in studies of women and development in Malaysia e.g. (Buang, 1993; Maznah Mohammad, 1996; Ong, 1987; Stivens, 1996).

workers. By structuring the salaries of machinists along the lines of a piece-rated
bonus system and subjecting them to constant supervision on the line by the
supervisor, trainer and QC, the company places huge pressure on the women to
achieve targets.[14] The sewing machinist is assigned to a particular station in the
assembly line where she repeatedly performs a single sewing operation over and
over again. By contrast in the more male dominated occupations workers have
more freedom to move around the factory. For example, I observed the spreaders
and cutters engaging in conversations on the factory floor and taking the occasional
break; something that would be near impossible to do on the sewing assembly line
or in the finishing department.

     These observations relating to the dominance of female employment in the
areas of production where control over the labour process is most intense are again
linked in with ideas that women are more suited to repetitive and fiddly operations
than men. But they also reflect the way that employers regard women as more
"docile", unlike male employees who may become restless in these types of jobs.[15]
In the previous chapter it was shown that the perception of female docility came
through in interviews with managers and supervisors commenting on how it was
much easier to control female employees compared to males, and the unsuitability
of males to assembly line production processes that require a high level of manual
dexterity skills. The recruitment process can also serve to maintain control over
the workforce by relying on word-of-mouth recruitment practices which place
pressure on workers to ensure that the new recruits that they have brought to the
factory will not create problems. HR executives at both Site A and Site B stressed
the usefulness of these informal contacts in securing a supply of workers who will
stay with the firm for the long term, and not take days off, turn up late or act in an
insubordinate manner. The recruitment process seeks to identify workers who
have a temperament suited to assembly line production:

> We will ask a girl in interview something like 'how would you feel if your supervisor
> used a loud voice and makes you feel uncomfortable?'. The right kind of response
> would be that she would discuss the matter with the supervisor later, but the wrong
> response would be that she shouts back. We don't want people like that. So you would
> also ask questions like 'at work, how would you feel if you were told to keep un-picking
> the seam that you are working on?'[16]

The firm also benefits from having numerous family members working within the
same firm not only because these family ties place additional pressure on new
recruits to conform to standards of behaviour and comply with modes of control
already in place within the firm, but also because they contribute to the often
paternalistic employment practices and attitudes displayed by the firm. There are
many examples of the firm implementing workplace practices that are paternalistic
in that they are meant to secure the loyalty of employees through non-wage based

---

[14] Interview with Sewing Department Supervisor, Site A (10th March 1999).
[15] Interview with Cutting Floor Manager, Site A (10th March 1999).
[16] Interview with HR Executive, Site A (3rd March 1999).

rewards (e.g. "employee of the month" schemes) and mutual obligations between the firm and the employees that extend to non-work based activities. The firm operates activities such as "family days" whereby workers and their families are provided with an outing by the company, thus sustaining an association between the firm and familial structures/obligations. HR executives will also visit workers who are off sick and expect workers to come to them if they are experiencing problems in their personal lives. One HR executive that I spoke with went as far as to suggest that women workers are far more likely to speak to her regarding problems at work, than to go through the in-house trade union.[17]

Although labour relations within the firm (at Site A at least) take the form of an in-house union, many workers have not joined the union (especially among Chinese workers) preferring to deal with a matter through the HR department or by directly dealing with supervisors and managers. In terms of the union itself, all key positions (president, vice president and finance officer) are all filled by male employees. It has been suggested that the prevalence of patriarchal norms and values within trade unions creates a barrier to the women's ability to put issues that affect them at the top of union agendas.[18] Women at UKALM were involved in the organising committee of the union but were only found in supporting roles.[19] This lack of female trade union leaders at UKALM, on top of the lack of a union at Site B (a site where almost no men are employed at all given that it is concentrated on sewing production) suggests that the firm has been largely successful in creating an easily controllable female workforce.

This is not to suggest that all women on the factory floor at UKALM conform to the stereotype of the docile and submissive worker. Significantly, It was revealed to me in interviews with the factory managers that the factory had experienced a number of "spirit possession" incidents (bouts of mass hysteria) the worst of which had occurred in 1994. This is a well documented phenomenon in studies of gender and employment in Malaysia – in particular in the studies by Ackerman (1980) and Ong (1987), in which spirit possession incidents are viewed in terms of the difficulties faced by a new female Malay working class to adapt to the rigours of capitalist production. The lack of unionization, or other channels through which to voice their grievances, inevitably leads to a reversion to alternative forms of resistance. The irony is then, that whilst the Malay cultural context is viewed in some ways as turning women into better sewing machinists, rural Malay society is also regarded as a source of (backward) cultural beliefs and practices.

However, this "resistance" to capitalist authority needs to be understood as a phenomenon that (a) does not significantly upset gender roles within the factory and (b) feeds into the construction of the Malay-female as "backward" and "irrational" and therefore unsuited to work that might require more responsibility.

---

[17] Interview with HR Officer, Site A (3rd March 1999).

[18] Interview with members of the women's committee of the MTUC Petailing Jaya, Selangor (12th February 1999). Interview with NGO activist Labour Resources Centre, Bangsar, Kuala Lumpur (12th March 1999).

[19] Interview with in-house trade union president, Site A (18th August 1999).

Thus, the spirit possession incidents act, in certain ways, to confirm the status of rural Malay women as the least advantaged group of workers within the firm. Spirit possession is a form of resistance that does not upset prevailing gender ideologies since it is almost expected of women to behave in such an "irrational" manner – especially if these women are from rural Malay backgrounds. Ackerman, for example, has labelled mass hysteria as a "safety valve institution" claiming that it is a form of industrial conflict, but is never acknowledged as such. Rather:

> The existing structure of relations in the factory is maintained rather than challenged by the ritualization of conflict since no direct confrontation between opposing interests is seen to occur by the workers or management (Ackerman, 1980).

These perceptions that women are more prone to these "irrational" outbursts is, argues Ong, closely linked to fears regarding women's sexuality as women move out of the household and into factory employment (Ong, 1987: 184-185, 220). This view was clearly articulated by the HR director when he suggested that it is not just that women (being the "weaker sex") are more prone to so-called spirit possession, but the "girls" who suffer from these attacks are likely to be young women who do not fit into certain norms of Malay traditional family life.[20] He suggested that they may come from broken homes, they may be experiencing problems with a boyfriend, or have had an abortion. More importance, however, was attached to women who "are making no headway in their social life".[21] He suggested that in Malaysian society getting married is "a critical issue", and "girls aged 23 plus in relationships with guys and not getting married can cause problems".[22] During this conversation, he went on to use the Malay word *bohsia* meaning loose woman to describe some of the women who were particularly susceptible to these attacks.

Concerns regarding the sexuality of young female workers has been an issue in Malaysian public debate since women were first recruited into the export factories in the 1970s (Ariffin, 1994a; Buang, 1993; Fatimah, 1985; Ong, 1987: 181-186). Such concerns, saw the government launch a research project looking into the welfare of new Malay women workers (Ariffin, 1994a: 1-2) and also saw both government and Islamic groups taking action to highlight the supposed "moral threats" that women faced in the new factory environment.[23] Although it has been suggested that "the issue of cultural and social stigmatization of women

---

[20] See also Ackerman (1980: 160, 188) for examples of company managers expressing similar views.
[21] Interview with HR Director, Site A (18th August 1999).
[22] Interview with HR Director, Site A (18th August 1999).
[23] This point is raised by Ong (1987: 182-183) and Jamilah Ariffin (1994: 1-2), and it was also raised in interviews with a women's NGO activist from the organisation *Sahabat Wanita* (19th March 1999). It is apparent that concerns about the moral susceptibility of young women workers have been articulated by nationalist groups within a number of states in which there has been growth in female export-sector factory employment. See, for example, Lynch (2002).

workers is no longer relevant" (Maznah and Ng, 1996: 46), it was clear even from my interviews with mangers that there were still concerns about the way in which entry into full time waged employment could have some form of corrupting effect on the younger girls entering the factory.[24]

One of the most candid conversations that I had whilst visiting the firm, regarding the negative stereotyping that female workers faced, emerged in informal conversations with the HR executive and HR officer over lunch in the staff canteen. A female worker was pointed out to me, she was Malay and in her early twenties and, unlike most of the Malay women in the factory she wore western clothing rather than the traditional dress (known as *tudung*[25]). It was explained to me that this women had been sexually harassed on her way to and from work by a male employee at the factory. The HR executive told me that although she felt that this was a difficult situation, the women should not be dressing in such "sexy" clothing and this was the root of the problem. Sexual harassment, and management's response to charges of sexual harassment, can be regarded as a means through which women who do not fit with a certain image of the traditional Malay female (exemplifying the Islamic ideals of submissiveness and modesty (Ackerman, 1980: 189)) are stigmatized in the factory setting. In this sense, sexual harassment reflects gendered workplace power relations. Although some writers have claimed that sexual harassment is employed in order to ensure that women do not cross gendered occupational boundaries (Stanko, 1988: 91-99), it is difficult to make a case for this on the basis of the limited acknowledgement of sexual harassment that came across in my interviews.

What this case does show, is that young Malay women face considerable pressures to conform to a certain ideal of the diligent worker, an ideal that is so clearly tied up with a whole set of discourses concerning the most appropriate work for women in the factory setting, work that is both low status and low paid compared to that of men working in equivalent occupations. Issues of workplace control are, therefore, closely tied to existing social rules and norms regarding appropriate female behaviour (Ecevit, 1991).

Married women and secondary income earner status

Assumptions of female "irrationality" tend to be applied to a specific group of women workers – young, unmarried and Malay. Yet it was interesting to note that these views exist despite the much greater entry of married women into the workforce. Married women are viewed as unlikely to engage in these superstitious

---

[24] This point was also raised in a numbers of interviews and conversations that I undertook whilst in Malaysia. For example, interview with members of the MTUC Women's Committee, Petailing Jaya, February 12th, 1999; interview with Irene Xavier, *Sahabat Wanita*, 19th March 1999.

[25] This style of dress consists of *baju kurong* (loose tunic and sarong) and *selandang*, a scarf, or *mini-telekung* (veil). A more general discussion of the symbolic importance of this style of dress for debates concerning the position of women in Malay society can be found in Nagata (1995).

acts; therefore it is necessary to consider how gender ideologies within the firm have adapted because of this trend. The employment of married women in the firm creates new problems such as absenteeism due to family responsibilities, time off due to maternity leave and issues of who pays for childcare. Ultimately the firm is able to utilize gendered ideologies regarding the appropriate role and position of married women in order to keep these workers wages as low as possible; viewing the wages that they earn as merely supplementary (or secondary) to the household income.

The control over women workers that the firm is able to operate also reflects how the firm's recruitment strategies have targeted a particular group of women workers for whom opportunities to find paid employment are restricted. The firm recruits women from rural areas, whose formal education is limited and brings them into the factory in company buses. Furthermore, the firm has been forced to employ larger numbers of older married women with children, since younger workers are attracted to the better paying jobs in the electronics sector. These workers are therefore willing to work in fairly low paying jobs that require the performance of repetitive tasks, because alternatives do not exist for them.

Increases in married women's participation in export industries demonstrate a real change from the employment patterns noted in studies of gender and industrialization in Malaysia that emerged in the 1970s and 1980s. It is now no longer possible to view women workers as essentially "factory daughters". In the previous chapter, for example, it was shown that the firm prefers not to employ young school leavers because it believes that these workers will not stay with the firm in the long term. The HR executives claimed that these workers generally seem to be waiting for "better jobs" in the local multinational electronics factories.[26] The younger workers who during the 1970s and 1980s made up the bulk of the workforce in firms such as the Malacca based shoe factory studied by Ackerman (1980: 97) in her research conducted in the 1970s are now less likely to seek employment in the low paying, low technology garment or footwear industries. Ackerman's workers were all young, single women working in the years prior to marriage. It was assumed that most of these workers would leave the factory on marriage, with just 17% of those sampled expressing a desire to work after marriage (Ackerman, 1980: 105). Interviews at UKALM suggested that married women have come to play an increasingly important role at the factory. No data was available on the numbers of married women employed at UKALM although managers estimated that the figure was around 50%. Yet even on the basis of these estimates, it is clear that there has been a considerable shift away from the model of the dutiful factory daughter that characterized accounts of women and industrialization in Malaysia from the 1970s and 1980s (Ackerman, 1980; Ariffin, 1994a; Fatimah, 1985; Ong, 1987) (and accounts of East and Southeast Asian EOI more generally (Arrigo 1980, Salaff, 1981, Wolf, 1990, 1992)).

In most of the conversations that I had with managers regarding the female workforce (especially the sewing machinists) these workers were usually referred

---

[26] Interviews with HR executives at Site A and Site B (March 1999).

to in relation to their husbands. In one of first interviews with the HR director at UKALM, for example, he pointed out that the vast majority of women sewing machinists at the factory will leave the workforce upon marriage:

> Over eighty percent of women leave the workforce on marriage. This is because either they follow their husband when he starts working outside the area, her husband may not like her to work, or it could be a good break after having worked for about five years – especially because for them to get another job is not a problem. To get a blue collar position in this country is no problem.[27]

Thus although many married women will initially leave the workforce of UKALM upon marriage, they will return to this "blue collar" work often very soon after they have had a baby. Indeed, the high numbers of married women at UKALM suggests that many of the women workers have either returned or sought employment at UKALM having had their children. Further questioning of the HR director, suggested that many women do not take much time out to have children at all. Thus the company is happy to recruit soon-to-be-married young women so long as they have some kind of guarantee that the woman will stay working at the firm, maybe returning to the factory after having had children.[28] Young women will generally in their interview be asked whether they have plans to get married. The HR Director commented on this aspect of the interview claiming:

> The girl will get a bit embarrassed here.. and she will start to say 'well actually I'm getting engaged', or 'I'm already engaged'… so then I will ask what her husband's attitude to her working is and if she says he wouldn't have a problem with it then that would be OK.[29]

The trend toward increased levels of married female employment is occurring at a time when the average age of marriage is rising. The overall mean age of marriage rose from 22.3 years in 1971 to 25.3 in 1991. However, it is notable that among Malay women the average age of marriage is somewhat lower at 24 than other ethnic groups where the figure is 26 years for both Chinese and Indian women (Ariffin, 1999). The changing pattern in employment practices away from the exclusive recruitment of unmarried young women reflects a number of different factors. Most important has been a gradually increasing shortage of labour across most sectors of the Malaysian economy, but especially in the lower paying ends of the economy within which the garment industry can be included. The garment industry generally pays lower wages than the big multinational electronics firms, thus in chapter five it was shown how recruiters necessarily have to consider married women with children for operator positions within the factory. Another factor is the natural aging of the workforce (Maznah and Ng, 1996: 16-17). Lie (2000) has also commented on this trend, finding that many of the workers whom she surveyed in 1988 (Lie and Lund, 1994) when they were young and unmarried

---

[27] Interview with HR Director, Site A (3rd March 1999).

[28] Interview with HR Director, Site A (3rd March 1999).

[29] Interview with HR Director, Site A (3rd March 1999).

had, in fact, remained within industrial employment. The women in Lie's study were able to combine motherhood and industrial employment because new factories had opened close to their villages providing transportation to the factories and also because they could rely on maternal grandparents to care for their children.

Ideas relating to women's perceived "secondary status" and why this contributes to how women are devalued in the workplace have a long history, often emerging as part of the socialist feminist critique of liberal feminists' commitment to the market as a gender-neutral space (Barrett, 1980; Ferguson and Folbre, 1991; Hartman, 1979). The construction of systems of payment around the ideal of the male bread-winning household head is a key factor in the grouping of women workers into low waged occupations. Women's entry into "formal" waged employment, therefore is always on an unequal footing to that of men since it is assumed that women do not need to earn the levels of payment available to their male colleagues (Elson, 1983: 7-9; Heyzer, 1989: 35). As has already been discussed in chapter two, feminist economists and earlier socialist feminists have argued that mainstream economics fails to appreciate the interconnections between the labour "market" and the household.[30] This division between the supposedly "real" economy or "public sphere" and a domestic/"private" realm acts to downgrade the significance of women's role as reproducers and un-paid domestic workers (Longino, 1993: 161; Strassman, 1993: 59-60). The lack of value accorded to a woman's domestic role, therefore, acts to consolidate gender subordination within the workplace. When a woman enters into paid employment, she continues to be perceived as essentially part of this domestic realm and her earnings are not regarded as so important as those of her male fellow employees. This feminist position on women and employment raises certain problems with the liberal perspective on the impact of FDI. The assumption in the liberal writings is that women's inequality with men is symptomatic of backward social relations and that greater incorporation into the (gender-neutral) global market economy via employment in MNCs will lead to an economic 'equilibrium' between the sexes. Yet this position ignores (a) the fact that women do not enter the labour market on the same footing as men – in the workplace they are regarded as secondary income earners and their domestic responsibilities are considerably higher than those of men – and (b) the way that market actors, such as firms, draw upon, benefit from and perpetuate gender inequalities. Rather than dwell in any more detail upon these debates, it is useful, to consider how at UKALM, notions of women's secondary status as income earners fed into the construction of women as low paid employees.

One example of this is evident in the problem of high labour turnover among skilled sewing machinist staff. The low rates of pay that these women receive is a factor in the high labour turnover in this sector, with managers admitting that the wages paid at UKALM cannot compete with the higher wages paid in other sectors

---

[30] For an example of the feminist economics argument see Donath (2000). For earlier socialist feminist work see Eisenstein (1979: 26).

of the economy.[31] Yet managers at the firm prefer to see this problem in terms of a woman's family responsibilities getting in the way of her ability to work full time at the factory. In chapter five it was noted that managers will try to ensure that potential female employees who are married have sufficient arrangements in place for child care. The HR executives at Site A, for example, told me that they generally will not recruit women who intend to leave their children with a childminder/babysitter since these sort of arrangements are notoriously unreliable, but if a woman leaves her children with a family member this is considered to be a more stable and sufficient arrangement.[32] The company offers women workers no help with their childcare arrangements since these kinds of policies would raise labour costs significantly (despite recent calls by the Malaysian government for companies to establish on-site childcare facilities).[33] Indeed, the lack of support for childcare at the factory not only reflects the way that the firm would prefer to employ unmarried women, but also the way that the firm seeks to benefit from women's secondary status within the labour market. The firm has identified a segment of the workforce that will work for such low wages – their family responsibilities hold them back from getting the sort of career progression available to male workers. In this sense, it is not in the company's interests to provide workers with childcare arrangements, especially if it can rely on the worker's extended family to provide this service. The HR executives suggested that women are grateful to return to the workforce after having children[34] and other managers at the firm pointed out how married women with young children have been particularly keen to take on the part-time, evening shift work that is available in the cutting and finishing departments.[35]

The assumption that women are secondary workers also helps to explain why male employees are more likely to be employed in jobs where there are good career prospects (e.g. the spreading jobs that provide a stepping stone into the well paid cutting jobs). Even though many at the firm accepted that women are perfectly capable of doing this type of work (evidenced in the recent employment of women in spreading and the employment of a woman as a trainee cutter)[36] there is still a clear preference for men to take on the more technical and craft related better paying jobs at UKALM. In my interview with the cutting floor manager, for example, I was told that men employed in more menial positions would be shifted into spreading jobs when an opportunity opened up. Part of the reason for this lay in the fact that men were unwilling to work for the lower rates of pay in the (piece rated) jobs such as fusing or panel inspection,[37] a position that rests on the

---

[31] Interview with HR Director, Site A (3rd March 1999).

[32] Interviews with HR Executive and HR Officer, Site A (10th March 1999)

[33] Interview with Deputy Director General, Labour Department, Ministry of Human Resources, Kuala Lumpur (27th March 1999).

[34] Interview with HR Executive and HR Officer, Site A (10th March 1999).

[35] Interviews with Cutting and Finishing Managers, Site A (10th March 1999).

[36] Interview with Production Executive, Cutting Department, Site A (10th March 1999).

[37] Interview with Production Executive, Cutting Department, Site A (10th March 1999).

assumption that men are more deserving of higher paid work because of their supposed breadwinner status within the family.

Whatever the causes of this increase in married women's participation in waged employment outside the home, such a process is certainly significant from the point of view of how the recruitment process impacts upon the role and position of women in Malaysian society – especially in terms of the "decomposition" of gendered social practices and norms. The recruitment practices at UKALM have targeted groups of women who would not usually have the opportunity to earn wages and find employment outside of the home or in the informal economy. Multinational firms, and world market factories in general, therefore have played a part in the dismantling of established gender relations in rural areas. For example, writers such as Jamilah Ariffin have discussed the way in which Colonial and immediate post-Colonial state development strategies in Malaysia had shored up the position of women in rural areas as essentially confined to a domestic role (Ariffin, 1999: 10-15).[38] Opening up opportunities for rural women, from the lower social classes, to work outside of the home, has had a real significance for Malaysian society over the past 20 years.

A number of feminist authors have emphasized the importance of securing employment for women in developing countries. The recent work of Amartya Sen, for example, puts forward the argument that paid work outside of the home acts to improve women's status within society (Sen, 1999: 191). The ability of women to earn their own income is, argues Sen, as important as other factors such as education and literacy, and ownership rights in terms of enhancing women's status and position within the existing social order – giving women an identity outside of domesticity and reproduction, and a status as income earner within the household (Sen, 1999: 189-203). Women are thus regarded as "active agents of change" (Sen, 1999: 189) and not the passive victims of an oppressive social order.

Conclusion

Despite the claims that can be made regarding the benefits of industrial employment for many women, questions do need to be raised about the type of jobs that are available to women in export industries. On the one hand, the electronics sector (especially in semi-conductors) has been characterized by considerable rises in wages and working conditions, with writers such as Maznah and Ng (1996: 43) emphasising the more highly skilled job opportunities that are now available to women workers in this sector. On the other hand, however, garment production remains labour intensive and reliant upon low wage labour to

---

[38] The arguments utilised by Jamilah Ariffin concerning the (re)production of gender inequalities via colonial and later by post-colonial economic development strategies reflect those found in a number of key works in the literature on gender and development. See for example Boserup (1970); Mies (1986). A more through examination of the impact of colonial policies on gender relations is found in Ong (1987) and also in Ng and Maznah (1990).

work in low technology, highly controlled production processes. The case study firm was shown to seek out sources of low-cost female labour among married women, crowding these women into low paid sewing machinist positions that lack career progression or status within the firm.

The increased reliance on rural Malay married women with children as a low-cost source of labour is a situation that raises similar issues to the studies of Mexican *maquiladora* industries undertaken by Fussell and Pearson. Arguing against the prevailing notion that industrial employment by and large benefits women workers, these authors have focussed on the way that specific groups of women (in particular relatively uneducated and married women) tend to be confined to sectors of the economy where wages and working conditions are considerably lower. Thus Pearson notes how women working in electronics factories experience better wages and working conditions than those found in the garment sector (Pearson, 1995: 146). Fussell suggests that the *maquiladoras* (usually multinationally owned firms) have moved to employ a section of the labour force that cannot find alternative sources of employment and thus accepts the low levels of pay on offer. Thus these firms are shown to be creating a labour force in which rates of pay are considerably lower compared to other "low skill" employers of female labour (Fussell, 2000: 62-63).

Issues of a worker's ethnicity are again shown to be of crucial importance in terms of the way that the firm has sought to mobilize an appropriate workforce. Malay women are viewed in terms of a gendered set of assumptions relating to female docility and passivity. Yet at the same time, they are viewed as workers that are somehow less likely to display the qualities of rationality that are deemed to be so important in the more male dominated (and better paying) production jobs. By contrast, Chinese women have had access to the better paying jobs within the firm both at the level of the production department, as supervisors, managers and trainers, and within other company departments as managers, administrators and secretaries. Different groups of women are thus affected quite differently by the experience of industrial employment. The criticism of the idea that the firm can have a "progressive" impact by undermining "traditional" gender relations needs to take into account therefore how the firm benefits from social divisions based upon ethnicity cross-cut with gender divisions which are key to the creation of an appropriate labour force.

Conclusion

In this book I have tried to do two things. First, I have highlighted some inadequacies in liberal IPE accounts of the nature of FDI. Secondly, I have put forward the suggestion that a gendered political economy approach to FDI, grounded in empirical research provides a much more nuanced understanding of the impact of FDI. It was shown in the previous chapter how Elson and Pearson's work on the decomposition, recomposition and intensification of gender relations as women enter the factory setting is the starting point for this analysis of the gendered impact of FDI. But this book takes their argument further, suggesting the process of transforming gender relations is actively constituted by MNCs embedded in a culture of "efficiency seeking" managerialism. By exposing the gendered assumptions that lie at the heart of this process, I am then able to raise issue with both the theoretical and empirical assumptions at the heart of the liberal commitment to ideas of the "progressive" nature of FDI on countries in the developing world.

The theoretical critique presented in the book has focussed on the core assumption found in liberal IPE; the ability of the market to operate "freely", as well as many of the wider claims made in the literature regarding the progressive and beneficial impact of FDI. In short, the liberal IPE perspective fails to take into account the way that markets remain embedded in systems of social relations, and are, consequentially, gendered institutions (Elson, 1999). Part of the problem for the economic liberal approaches to FDI is that they are rooted in an understanding of the economy (and more specifically the market) in gender-neutral terms. There is a failure to recognize the way that men and women enter into industrial employment as "gendered subjects", thus labour markets (and, indeed, market-actors such as firms) become "bearers of gender" a discussion that was developed in chapter one.

Such theoretical insights have informed the empirical research undertaken in this book where the focus on recruitment practices in a case study firm demonstrates the way that the MNC actively constitutes an appropriate workforce by drawing upon locally produced gender and ethnic inequalities. Furthermore, the empirical research presented as case-study evidence in chapters four and five of this book is in itself a valuable contribution to debates regarding the impact of FDI.

Contributions and major findings

As noted in the introduction, the primary objective has been to investigate the linkages between export-led development strategies, firms' decisions to invest offshore and the crowding of women workers into low wage, low status employment within export sector MNCs. These connections between state-led economic development strategies, FDI and the role and position of women have often been overlooked in both the mainstream globalization literature and the recent work from within feminist economics and development studies. Writings on women and export-led development have tended to focus on either macro-level studies of the gender inequalities that accompany export-led growth (Seguino, 2000; Standing, 1989, 1999; Wood, 1991) or on women's experiences of industrial employment (often utilising feminist methodologies that emphasize the importance of "women's voices" in understanding the experience of industrial employment (Ecevit, 1991; Lee, 1998; Wolf, 1990, 1992)). What is lacking from both of these dominant feminist perspectives is a specific focus on the multinational firm. This is understandable given that it is not just MNCs that employ women in the export-sector; large numbers of women are employed in locally owned firms or work or as homeworkers in the informal sector (Carr, Alter Chen, and Tate, 2000).

Recent feminist scholarship, therefore, can be contrasted with the earlier NIDL approach, which placed a great deal of emphasis on the role of the MNC in shoring-up structures of inequality (including gender inequality). Writers such as Linda Lim have been particularly critical of the emphasis in the literature on the MNC, suggesting that the levels of pay and working conditions found in MNCs are far superior to those found in local industries and the informal sector (Lim, 1991) (an argument that mainstream development thinking has drawn upon).

However, the research presented in this book suggests that a focus on the MNC remains relevant. Firstly, this is because the MNC has been given such an important role in liberal IPE understandings of globalization. In this sense, by exposing the way that FDI is a gendered process, I am able to comment more widely on the gendered nature of globalization. Secondly, the impact of the MNC on local societies remains a highly topical issue with numerous campaigns targeting the working conditions and employment practices found within MNCs (especially in the garment sector) in the developing world and calling upon these firms to establish codes of conduct regarding employment and environmental standards.[1] These campaigns thus echo Elson and Pearson's view that a focus on the MNC is important not because MNCs are important in terms of the number of women employed, but because MNCs possess a "transformatory potential" (Elson and Pearson, 1989: 2), the ability to significantly improve the role and position for women within the workforce (and indeed society more generally).

This need for a gendered political economy based critique of the role of the MNC in today's global economy is a starting point for the analysis presented in this book. The research itself has looked at the nature of company recruitment practices in order to develop this critique and the major findings from this research are as follows:

Firstly, that the construction of women as a source of low cost labour is an integral feature of both FDI and EOI. These strategies hinge upon implicit assumptions regarding the availability of low cost female labour that characterizes both firms' foreign investment strategies and the decision by states to pursue

---

[1] See for example the websites of the following campaign organizations: Clean Clothes Campaign, www.cleanclothes.org and the Ethical Trading Initiative, http//ethicaltrade.org – see also; Frenkel and Scott (2002), Green (1998) and Sajhau (1998).

export-led growth policies based upon labour intensive industrialization. Thus, for example in chapter three it was shown that the adoption of export-led development and the desire to attract FDI into the export sector were development strategies that depended upon the growth of a female Malay proletariat, a process that was encouraged (albeit indirectly at first) through government policies. Crucially, the role of MNCs in creating the feminization of employment that accompanied EOI must be emphasized in any analysis of the gendered nature of economic development in Malaysia. Thus in chapters five and six, the book provides an insight into how exactly the firm sought to gender employment in export manufacturing. These chapters demonstrate how gender divisions played such an important role in the creation of an appropriate workforce for UK-Apparel.

We need to recognize how firms construct gendered inequalities because otherwise we would merely replicate the assumptions of liberal IPE concerning the innate rationality of market actors (that firms are rational actors who merely draw upon inequalities embedded within the host state). Instead, this book has indicated how the firm fashions inequalities in *new* ways – effectively globalizing the process through the perpetuation of a global gender culture that exists in a global space and yet, is enmeshed with localized cultures of gender and ethnicity.

Secondly, although the liberal IPE perspective on FDI can be challenged on a number of theoretical grounds (see chapters one and two), there is also a need to analyse some of the specific claims that are made in mainstream development thinking regarding the impact of FDI on women and gender relations. In particular the research challenges claims that multinational firms can undermine local "backward" gender inequalities through the increased employment opportunities that they offer to women. Questions need to be raised about the type of work that firms such as UK-Apparel make available to women, and the research presented in chapters four and five clearly indicates that the process of FDI is accompanied by the grouping of women into low paid, low status work. The firm therefore draws upon locally produced gender inequalities in order to sustain the supply of low wage workers that it requires to maintain low production costs.

This leads me onto the third major finding from this study, that in the process of drawing upon gender inequalities, the firm moves to target specific groups of women workers. Thus whereas numerous Chinese women are found in high ranking positions within the case study firm (for example as Finance Director or Operations Manager), the bulk of the firm's female sewing machinists are drawn from the local rural Malay population. It is important to recognize, therefore that the impact of FDI on gender relations needs to be understood in terms of the way that different types of women are affected quite differently by the operations of the MNC in the host economy. The differences between women are shown yet again more clearly in the discussion of the recruitment of married women into industrial employment at UK-Apparel. Moving away from the exclusive recruitment of young unmarried women because the industry is unable to compete with the better paying jobs available to these more economically mobile groups of women, the firm has sought to target another group of women and thus maintain the connection between sewing machine work and low pay. These employment practices are not exclusive to the operations of this particular firm. For example, it was shown in chapter three how the UK based garment sector targeted marginalized, ethnic minority, groups of women to work in the "sweatshop" sector that expanded during the 1980s in Britain.

. Finally, these findings enable me to comment more broadly on some of the debates regarding gender and globalization. Understandings of the multinational firm cannot simply view the firm as an agent of globalization, with globalization defined in terms of a (gender-neutral) process of economic integration around the free market system. Rather, there is need for understandings of FDI (and therefore globalization more generally) to take into account the differential impacts of this process on different groups of people within states (Mehra and Gammage, 1999: 533). In this sense, the research enables me to look at how globalization "is set within multiple contexts" (Germain, 2000: 70), contexts that take account of the specific local sets of social arrangements that underpin global processes.

I have shown how an exploration of the way that both this state and this firm have sought to construct a certain type of (low cost) female worker for employment in export-manufacturing yields a number of contributions (both substantively and theoretically). However, at the same time some research limitations are unavoidable, largely because the research is actor-specific concerned as it is with the role of the firm (UK-Apparel), and the role of the Malaysian State in the process of FDI.

Firstly, the choice of a garment sector firm raises questions regarding the role of low cost female labour in the shift in production from the developed to the developing world that has been taking place since the 1960s. The lack of technological innovation in the production process within garment firms has meant that firms such as UK-Apparel remain dependent upon simple sewing machine technologies that call for labour intensive production processes. Much of the liberal writings on the progressive nature of FDI have emphasized the role that technology transfers play in the ability of firms to both enhance local economic development and improve the skill profile of the workforce. Thus the focus on a garment firm creates certain limitations in the extent to which it is possible to assess the kinds of claims that are made in mainstream literature. On the other hand, the technological innovations that have impacted upon the garment sector most significantly are those communications and transportation technologies that enable firms in the developed world to shift production offshore and engage in the vast subcontracted networks of production that now characterize the global garment industry (Hale, 2000: 406-408). Indeed, the garment industry is often hailed as a model of successful globalized industrialization (Dicken, 1992). An identification of the gendered inequalities that underpin this global shift again raises questions about the nature of the process of globalization and how this has impacted upon the lives of women workers.

Secondly, the research presented in this book has raised issues regarding the model of economic development pursued in Malaysia. Limitations exist in the somewhat atypical nature of EOI as pursued in Malaysia compared to other Asian economies (with the exception of the city states of Singapore and Hong Kong) where there was a much lower reliance on FDI in their EOI strategies. Yet, in examining how the Malaysian state sought to attract sufficient levels of FDI, issues are brought to the fore regarding the role of ethnicity and gender in the pursuit of a labour-intensive model for economic growth. The significance of gender inequality to EOI development strategies has been noted by feminist economists such as Stephanie Seguino (2000), but given that the Malaysian model of economic development was so heavily dependent upon FDI, the research presented in this book suggests that gender inequalities are not only a feature of EOI but also of FDI.

Future directions for research in this area

Some of the limitations of the book identified above could be resolved through future research into the topic of FDI and gender that takes a broader, more comparative approach. For example, on the area of the impact of technology transfers and the role and position of women in the workforce, it would be useful to compare the impact of new production technologies on the recruitment and employment strategies of firms in more technologically advanced sectors. Given that the Malaysian government has, since the Sixth Malaysia Plan (Malaysia, 1991), stressed the need for a shift into more capital intensive industries it would be interesting to examine how industries less dependent upon low wage female labour have altered their recruitment and employment practices. Some research into the impact of the shift to more capital intensive production has been undertaken by feminist scholars and it has been observed that increases in capital intensity are often accompanied by a decline in female employment opportunities (United Nations, 1999: 10). By broadening this research to incorporate a comparison with a MNC operating in a more capital-intensive sector, it would also be possible to look at what sort of women (and men) are being targeted by this firm's recruitment strategies, again raising the issue of how FDI impacts upon different groups within a population in different ways.

In chapter five issues were raised regarding how the garment sector has sought to maintain women as low waged workers and emphasis was placed on the ability of the firm to locate new sources of women that would constitute this workforce (i.e. married women with children). Related to this process is the whole issue of labour migration from neighbouring countries (in particular Indonesia) to be employed in the garment sector. The issue of foreign migrant workers is of considerable importance to the recent political economy of Malaysia, where labour shortages in low paid occupations (in particular the construction, manufacturing and plantation sectors (Business Times, 1999)) have seen the recruitment of workers from neighbouring Asian countries. This was an issue that was not examined in great depth in this book, mainly because all of the workers employed in this case study firm were recruited locally. However, in other multinationally-owned garment firms in Malaysia foreign migrant labour has played an important role. Clearly the issue relating to the recruitment of foreign migrant workers raises issues that are relevant to understandings of how MNCs seek out new sources of low cost labour and the gender and ethnic dimensions of this process. The shift towards increased levels of foreign migrant workers within the Malaysian garment sector, underlines the extent to which the industry is facing difficulties in attracting an appropriate (low wage) workforce. Thus to what extent will these firm remain located in Malaysia whilst neighbouring states such as Indonesia offer significantly lower labour costs? An assessment of the impact of migrant labour on company recruitment strategies in the Malaysian garment sector, would therefore, link into wider discussions concerning the sustainability of export-led growth strategies based upon the promotion of low cost (female) labour.

Bibliography

Ackerman, S. (1980), *Cultural Processes in Malaysian Industrialization: A Study of Women Workers*: PhD Thesis, University of California.

Agathangelou, A.M., and Ling, L.M.H. (2001), *Power, Borders, Security, Wealth: Lessons of Violence and Desire from September 11*, on-line paper available at http://www.maxwell.syr.edu/maxpages/faculty/gmbonham/Ling_signspaper.doc [accessed 01.08.03].

Allen, J. (1995), 'Crossing Borders: Footloose Multinationals', in J. Allen, and C. Hammnett (eds), *A Shrinking World?* Oxford: Open University Press/Oxford University Press, pp. 55-102.

Amis, L. (2003), 'Business and Human Rights: The Risk of Being Left Behind', *New Academy Review*, Vol. 2 (1).

Amoore, L. (2000), 'International Political Economy and the Contested Firm', *New Political Economy*, Vol. 5 (2), pp. 183-204.

Amsden, A. (1989), *Asia's Next Giant: South Korea and Late Industrialization* New York: Oxford University Press.

Anderson, H., Bahia, N., Kaur, S., and Davies, A. (1991), *The Clothes Showdown: The Future of the West Midlands Clothing Industry*, Birmingham: West Midlands Low Pay Unit.

Anson, R. (1999), Exodus: UK firms 'at last going offshore', *Textile Horizons* (April 1999), pp. 14-15.

Anthias, F., and Davies, N.Y. (1983), 'Contextualising Feminism: Gender, Ethnicity and Class Divisions', *Feminist Review*, Vol. 15, pp. 62-75.

Ariffin, J. (1994a), *From Kampung to Urban Factories: Findings from the HAWA Study*, Kuala Lumpur: University of Malaya Press.

Ariffin, J. (1994b), *Reviewing Women's Status: Country Report in Preparation for the 4th UN World Conference on Women*, Kuala Lumpur: University of Malaya Press.

Ariffin, J. (1999), 'Women and Development in Malaysia' in Economic and Social Commission for Asia and the Pacific (ed.), *Gender Dimensions of Population and Development in South-East Asia*, New York: United Nations pp. 33-43.

Ariffin, J., Horton, S., and Sedlacek, G. (1995), 'Women in the Labour Market in Malaysia', in S. Horton (ed.), *Women and Industrialization in Asia*, London: Routledge, pp. 201-243.

Arrigo, L.G. (1980), 'The Industrial Workforce of Young Women in Taiwan', *Bulletin of Concerned Asian Scholars*, Vol. 12(2), pp. 25-30.

Arudsothy, P., and Littler, C.R. (1993), 'State Regulation and Union Fragmentation in Malaysia', In S. Frenkel (ed.), *Organized Labor in the Asia-Pacific Region*, Ithaca, New York: ILR Press, pp. 107-130.

Atalas, S. (1997), *Democracy and Authoritarianism in Indonesia and Malaysia*, Basingstoke: MacMillan.

Balaam, D.M., and Veseth, M. (1996), '"Laissez-Faire", "Laissez-Passer": The Liberal IPE Perspective', in D.M. Balaam, and M. Veseth (eds), *Introduction to International Political Economy*, New Jersey: Prentice Hall, pp. 45-66.

Barker, T. (1999), 'Little Surprise at M&S Warnings', *Financial Times: Companies and Finance* (01.16.99), p. 9.

Barnet, R.J., and Cavanagh, J. (1994), *Global Dreams: Imperial Corporations in the New World Order*, New York: Simon and Schuster.

Barrett, M. (1980), *Women's Oppression Today*, London: Verso Editions.

Beaudat et al. (1993), *Garment Industry Survey of Four ASEAN Countries with Special Reference to Technical and Managerial Skills Development for Women in the Garment Industry*, Vienna: UNIDO.

Beneria, L., and Sen, G. (1981), 'Accumulation, Reproduction and Women's Role in Economic Development: Boserup Revisited', *Signs*, Vol. 8(2), pp. 279-298.

Bhopal, M., and Todd, P. (2000), 'Multinational Corporations and Trade Union Development in Malaysia', in C. Rowley, and J. Benson (eds), *Globalization and Labour in the Asia-Pacific Region*, London: Frank Cass, pp. 193-213.

Block, F. (1990), *Postindustrial Possibilities: A Critique of Economic Discourse*, Berkley: University of California Press.

Block, F., and Sommors, M.R. (1984), 'Beyond the Economistic Fallacy', in T. Skocpol (ed.), *Vision and Method in Historical Sociology*, Cambridge: Cambridge University Press, pp. 47-84.

Blyth, R. (1996), 'Sourcing Clothing Production', in J. Winterton (ed.), *Restructuring Within a Labour Intensive Industry*, Aldershot: Avebury pp. 112-141.

Boserup, E. (1970), *Women's Role in Economic Development*, New York: St Martins Press.

Brah, A. (1992), 'Difference, Diversity, Differentiation' in J. Donald, and A. Rattansi (eds), *Race, Culture and Difference*, London: Sage, pp. 126-149.

Brittan, L., Sir (1995), 'Investment Liberalization: the Next Great Boost to the World Economy', *Transnational Corporations*, Vol. 4(1), pp. 1-10.

Bryne, C. (1998), *The Industrial and Social Impact of New Technology in the Clothing Industry into the 2000s*, Manchester: David Rigby Associates.

Buang, A. (1993), 'Development and Factory Women: Negative Perceptions from a Malaysian Source Area', in J.H. Momsen, and V. Kinnard (eds), *Different Places Different Voices: Gender and Development in Africa, Asia and Latin America*, London: Routledge, pp. 197-210.

Burgess, R.G. (1984), *In the Field: An Introduction to Field Research*, London: Allen and Unwyn.

Business Times (1999), 'Nod for more foreign workers in three sectors', *Business Times*, Kuala Lumpur (from MTUC archives).

Caroli, M.L. (1999), 'Garment Factory Workers in the City of Fez', *Middle East Journal*, Vol. 53(1), p. 28.

Carr, M., Alter Chen, M., and Tate, J. (2000), 'Globalization and Home Based Workers', *Feminist Economics*, Vol. 6(3), 123-142.

Casson, M. (1992), 'Introduction', in M. Casson (ed.), *International Business and Global Integration*, Basingstoke: MacMillan, pp. 1-22.

Caves, R.E. (1997), 'The Multinational Enterprise as an Economic Organisation' in J.A. Friedan, and D.A. Lake (eds), *Perspectives on Global Power and Wealth,* London: Routledge, pp. 139-153.

Chandran, P. (1997), *Study on Multinational Companies in Asia-Pacific: Malaysia. Singapore*, paper presented to the International Confederation of Free Trade Unions – Asia and Pacific Organisation (ICFTU)/JIL Regional Symposium on Multinational Companies, Singapore, July 22-26, 1997.

Chang, H.-J. (1998), 'Globalization, Transnational Corporations and Economic Development: Can the Developing Countries Pursue Strategic Industrial Policy in a Globalizing World?', in D. Baker, G. Epstein, and R. Pollin (eds), *Globalization and Progressive Economic Policy*, Cambridge: Cambridge University Press, pp. 97-114.

Chin, C.B.N. (1998), *In Service and Servitude: Foreign Female Domestic Workers and the Malaysian "Modernity" Project*, New York: Columbia University Press.

Cho, G. (1990), *The Malaysian Economy: Spatial Perspectives*, London: Routledge.

Christerson, B. (1995), *Rags and Riches: The Organisation and Location of Production in the Global Apparel Industry,* PhD Thesis, University of California at Santa Barbara (Department of Sociology).

Cockburn, C. (1985), *Machinery of Dominance: Women, Men and Technical Know-how*, London: Pluto Press.

Cook, J., Roberts, J., and Waylen, G. (2000) 'Towards a Gendered Political Economy', in J. Cook, J. Roberts, and G. Waylen (eds), *Towards a Gendered Political Economy*, Basingstoke: MacMillan, pp. 3-13.

Corner, L. (1999), *Capacity Building for Gender Mainstreaming*, Bangkok: UNIFEM: East and Southeast Asia.

Coyle, A. (1984), *Redundant Women*, London: The Women's Press.

Crinis, V. (2002), 'The Stratification of the Garment and Textile Industries and Labour Movements in Malaysia', in D-S. Gills and N. Piper (eds), *Women and Work in Globalising Asia*, London: Routledge, pp. 154-168.

Crouch, H. (1993), 'Malaysia: Neither Authoritarian nor Democratic', in K. Hewison, R. Robison, and G. Rodan (eds), *Southeast Asia in the 1990s: Authoritarianism, Democracy and Capitalism*, Sydney: Allen and Unwin for the Asian Studies Association of Australia, pp. 133-158.

de la Torre, J., Doz, Y., and Devinney, T. (2001), *Managing the Global Corporation: Case Studies in Strategy and Management*, New York: Irwin/McGraw Hill.

Denny, C. (1999), 'From Maesteg to Dhaka, the same fears', *The Guardian*, London (29.11.99), p. 11.

Deyo, F.C. (1989), *Beneath the Miracle: Labour Subordination in the New Asian Industrialization*, Berkley: University of California Press.

Dicken, P. (1992), *Global Shift: The Internationalization of Economic Activity*, London: Paul Chapman.

Dickerson, K.G. (1999), *Textiles and Apparel in the Global Economy*, New Jersey: Prentice Hall.

Donath, S. (2000), 'The Other Economy: Toward a Distinctively Feminist Economics', *Feminist Economics*, Vol. 6(1), pp. 115-123.

Drapers Record (1998), 'City Predicts M&S to Strengthen Supply Base', *Drapers Record* (11.04.98), p. 2.

Drapers Record (1999a), 'Open Letter to Marks and Spencer: Drapers Record Says Act Now and not in June', *Drapers Record* (20.02.99), p. 6.

Drapers Record (1999b), 'Suppliers face shock waves of Baird Axing', *Drapers Record* (30.10.99), p. 9.

Dunning, J.H. (1977), 'Trade Location of Economic Activity and the Multinational Enterprise: A search for an eclectic approach', in B. Ohlin, P.-o. Hesselbon, and P.M. Wijkman (eds), *International Allocation of Economic Activity*, Basingstoke: MacMillan, pp. 395-418.

Dunning, J.H. (1993a), *The Globalization of Business: The Challenge of the 1990s*, London: Routledge.

Dunning, J.H. (1993b), *Multinational Enterprises in the Global Economy*, Essex: Addison Wesley.

Dunning, J.H. (2000), 'The New Geography of Foreign Direct Investment', in N. Woods (ed.), *The Political Economy of Globalization*, Basingstoke: MacMillan.

Ecevit, Y. (1991), 'Shop Floor Control: The Ideological Construction of Turkish Women Factory Workers', in N. Redclift (ed.), *Working Women: International Perspectives on Labour and Gender Ideology*, London: Routledge.

Economist (2000), 'The World's View of Multinationals', *Economist*, (29.01.00), pp. 21-22.

Eisenstein, Z. (1979), 'Developing a Theory of Capitalist Patriarchy and Socialist Feminism', in Z. Eisenstein (ed.), *Capitalist Patriarchy and the Case for Socialist Feminism*, New York: Monthly Review Press.

Ellis, V. (2001), 'Can Global Business be a Force for Good?' *Business Strategy Review*, Vol. 12(20), pp. 51-20.

Elson, D. (1983), 'Nimble Fingers and Other Fables', in W. Chapkis, and C. Enloe (eds), *Of Common Cloth: Women in the Global Textile Industry*, Amsterdam: Transnational Institute, pp. 5-15.

Elson, D. (1996), 'Male Bias in the Development Process: An Overview', in D. Elson (ed.), *Male Bias in the Development Process*, Manchester: Manchester University Press, pp. 1-28.

Elson, D. (1999), 'Labour Markets as Gendered Institutions: Equality, Efficiency and Empowerment Issues', *World Development*, Vol. 27(3), pp. 611-627.

Elson, D., and Pearson, R. (1981), 'The Subordination of Women and the Internationalization of Factory Production', In K. Young, C. Wolkowitz,

182 *Fashioning Inequality*

and R. McCullagh (eds), *Of Marriage and the Market*, London: CSE Books, pp. 18-40.

Elson, D., and Pearson, R. (1989), 'Introduction: Nimble Fingers and Foreign Investments', in D. Elson, and R. Pearson (eds), *Women's Employment in Multinationals in Europe*, Basingstoke: MacMillan, pp. 1-11.

Enloe, C. (1983), 'Women Textile Workers and the Militarization of Southeast Asia', in J. Nash, and M.P. Fernandez Kelly (eds), *Women, Men and the International Division of Labour*, Albany: SUNY Press, pp. 407-425.

Enloe, C. (1989), *Beaches, Bananas and Bases*, London: Pandora Press.

Estrin, S., Hughes, K., and Todd, S. (1997), *FDI in Central and Eastern Europe: Multinationals in Transition*, London and Washington: Pinter.

Fatimah, D. (1985), *Minah Karan: The Truth about Malaysian Factory Girls*, Kuala Lumpur: Beria Publishing.

Ferber, M.A., and Nelson, J.A. (1993), 'Introduction: The Social Construction of Economics and the Social Construction of Gender', In M.A. Ferber, and J.A. Nelson (eds), *Beyond Economic Man: Feminist Theory and Economics,* Chicago: University of Chicago Press, pp. 1-22.

Ferguson, A., and Folbre, N. (1991), 'The Unhappy Marriage of Patriarchy and Capitalism', In L. Sargent (ed.), *Women and Revolution*, Boston: South End Press, pp. 313-338.

Fernandez Kelly, M.P. (1981), 'Development and the Sexual Division of Labour: An Introduction', *Signs*, Vol. 7(2), pp. 268-278.

Frenkel S.J., and Scott D. (2002), 'Compliance, Collaboration and Codes of Labor Practice: The Adidas Connection', *California Management Journal*, Vol. 45(1), pp. 29-49.

Fröbel, F., Heinrichs, J., and Kreye, O. (1980), *The New International Division of Labour*, Cambridge: Cambridge University Press.

Fussell, E. (2000), 'Making Labor Flexible: The Recomposition of Tijuana's Maquiladora Female Labour Force', *Feminist Economics*, Vol. 6(3), pp. 59-79.

Gallin, R.S. (1990), 'Women and the Export Sector in Taiwan: The Muting of Class Consciousness', In K. Ward (ed.), *Women Workers and Global Restructuring*, Ithaca: ILR Press, pp. 172-192.

Germain, R.D. (2000), 'Globalization in Historical Perspective', in R.G. Germain (ed.), *Globalization and Its Critics,* Basingstoke: MacMillan, pp. 67-90.

Gills, D-S. S. (2002), 'Neoliberal Economic Globalization and Women in Asia', in D-S.S. Gills and N. Piper (eds), *Women and Work in Globalizing Asia*, London: Routledge.

Gomez, E.T. (1990), *Politics in Business: UMNO's Corporate Investments* Kuala Lumpur: Forum.

Gomez, E.T., and Jomo, K.S. (1997), *Malaysia's Political Economy: Politics, Patronage and Profits*, Cambridge: Cambridge University Press.

Goodwin, B. (1997), *Using Political Ideas*, Chichester, UK: John Wiley.

Grace, E. (1990), *Shortcircuiting Labour: Unionising Electronic Workers in Malaysia*, Petailing Jaya, Selangor: INSAN.

Graham, E.G., and Krugman, P.R. (1993), 'The Surge in FDI in the 1980s', in K.A. Froot (ed.), *Foreign Direct Investment*, Chicago and London: Chicago University Press, pp. 16-38.

Green, D. (1998a), *Fashion Victims: Together We Can Clean Up the Clothes Trade: The Asian Garment Industry and Globalization*, London: CAFOD.

Green, D. (1998b), Notes on meeting with UK-Apparel (M&S largest garment supplier) and M&S (unpublished document).

Greenhalgh, S. (1985), 'Sexual Stratification: The Other Side of Growth with Equity in East Asia', *Population and Development Review*, Vol. 11(2), pp. 265-314.

Grown, C., Elson, D., and Catatay, N. (2000), 'Introduction', *World Development*, Vol. 28(7), 1146-1155.

Grunberg, L. (1996), 'The IPE of Multinational Corporations', in D.M. Balaam, and M. Veseth (eds), *Introduction to International Political Economy*, New Jersey: Prentice Hall, pp. 346-368.

Hale, A. (2000), 'Technologies of Control and Resistance: New Technologies and Women Workers in the Globalized Garment Industry', *International Feminist Journal of Politics*, Vol. 2(3), pp. 406-408.

Hale, A., and Shaw, L. (2001), 'Women Workers and the Promise of Ethical Trade in the Globalised Garment Industry: A Serious Beginning?', *Antipode*, Vol. 33(3), pp. 510-530.

Harding, S. (1986), *The Science Question in Feminism*, Milton Keynes: Open University Press.

Hartman, H. (1979), 'Capitalism, Patriarchy, and Job Segregation by Sex', in Z. Eisenstein (ed.), *Capitalist Patriarchy and the Case for Socialist Feminism*, New York: Monthly Review Press.

Held, D., McGrew, A., Goldblatt, D., and Perraton, J. (1999), *Global Transformations*, Cambridge: Polity Press.

Heyzer, N. (1986), *Working Women in Southeast Asian Development: Subordination and Emancipation*, Milton Keynes: Oxford University Press.

Heyzer, N. (1989a), 'The Internationalisation of Women's Work', *Southeast Asian Journal of Social Science*, Vol. 17(2), pp. 25-39.

Heyzer, N. (1989b), 'Asian Women Wage Earners: Their Situation and Possibilities for Donor Intervention', *World Development*, Vol. 17(7).

Higgott, R., Underhill, G., and Bieler, A. (eds) (2000), *Non-State Actors and Authority in the Global System*, London: Routledge.

Hirst, P., and Thompson, G. (1999), *Globalization in Question*, London: Polity Press.

Hooper, C. (2001), *Manly States: Masculinities, International Relations and Gender Politics*, New York: Columbia University Press.

Hua, W.Y. (1983), *Class and Communalism in Malaysia: Politics in a Dependent Capitalist State*, London: Zed.

Hymer, S. (1976), *The International Operations of National Firms: A Study of Foreign Direct Investment*, MIT Monographs in Economics 14, Massachusetts: MIT.

Ibrahim, B. (1989), 'Policies Affecting Women's Employment in the Formal Sector: Strategies for Change', *World Development*, Vol. 1(7), pp. 1097-1107.

ILO (1974), *Yearbook of Labour Statistics 1974*, Geneva: ILO.

ILO (1983), *Yearbook of Labour Statistics 1983*, Geneva: ILO.

ILO (1987), *Yearbook of Labour Statistics 1987*, Geneva: ILO.

ILO (1990), *Yearbook of Labour Statistics 1989/90*, Geneva: ILO.

ILO (1992), *Yearbook of Labour Statistics 1992*, Geneva: ILO.

ILO (2000), *Yearbook of Labour Statistics 2000*, Geneva: ILO.

Institute for Employment Research (1999), *Review of the Economy and Employment*, Coventry: University of Warwick, Institute for Employment Research.

Jennings, A. (1999), 'Dualisms', in J. Peterson and M. Lewis (eds), *The Elgar Companion to Feminist Economics*, Cheltenham: Edward Elgar.

Jenkins, R. (1987a), *Transnational Corporations and Uneven Development: The Internationalisation of Capital and the Third World*, London: Routledge.

Jenkins, R. (1987b), 'Doing Research into Discrimination: Problems of Method, Interpretation and Ethics', in G.C. Wenger (ed.), *The Research Relationship: Practice and Politics in Social Policy Research*, London: Allen and Unwin, pp. 144-160.

Jesudason, J.V. (1990), *Ethnicity and the Economy: The State, Chinese Business and Multinationals in Malaysia*, Singapore: Oxford University Press.

Joekes, S.P. (1987), *Women in the World Economy: An INSTRAW Study*, New York and Oxford: Oxford University Press.

Joekes, S.P., and Weston, A. (1994), *Women and the New Trade Agenda*, New York: United Nations Development Fund for Women (UNIFEM).

Johnson, C. (1982), *MITI and the Japanese Miracle: The Growth of Industrial Policy 1925-1975*, Stanford: Stanford University Press.

Johnson, C. (1987), 'Political Institutions and Economic Performance: The Government business relationship in Japan, South-Korea and Taiwan' in F.C. Deyo (ed.), *The Political Economy of New Asian Industrialism*, Ithaca: Cornell, pp. 136-164.

Jomo, K.S. (1990), *Growth and Structural Change in the Malaysian Economy*, Basingstoke: MacMillan.

Jomo, K.S., and Edwards, C. (1993), 'Malaysian Industrialization in Historical Perspective', in K.S. Jomo (ed.), *Industrializing Malaysia: Policy Performance Profits*, London: Routledge.

Jomo, K.S., and Edwards, C.B. (1998), 'Malaysian Industrialization: Performance, Problems, Prospects' in I. Yussof, and G.I. Abdul (eds), *Malaysian Industrialization: Governance and Technical Change*, Bangi: UKM.

Jomo, K.S., and Todd, P. (1994), *Trade Unions in Peninsular Malaysia*, Kuala Lumpur: Oxford University Press.

Jomo, K.S., and Wad, P. (1994), 'In House Unions: "Looking East" for Industrial Relations' in K.S. Jomo (ed.), *Japan and Malaysian Development: In the Shadow of the Rising Sun*, London: Routledge.

Julius, D. (1990), *Global Companies and Public Policy: The Growing Challenge of Foreign Direct Investment*, London: Pinter.

Julius, D. (1994), 'International Direct Investment: Strengthening the Policy Regime' in P.B. Kenen (ed.), *Managing the World Economy: Fifty Years After Bretton Woods*, Washington DC: Institute for International Economics, pp. 269-286.

Kabeer, N. (1994), *Reversed Realities: Gender Hierarchies in Development Thought*, London: Verso.

Kelegama, S. and Foley, F. (1999), 'Impediments to Promoting Backward Linkages in the Garment Sector in Sri Lanka', *World Development*, Vol. 27(8), pp. 1445-1460.

Khan, J.S. (1997), 'Growth, Economic Transformation, Culture and the Middle Classes in Malaysia', in R. Robison, and D.S. Goodman (eds), *The New Rich in Asia: Mobile Phones, MacDonalds and Middle-Class Revolution*, London: Routledge, pp. 49-75.

Khoo J-J. (1992), 'The Grand Vision: Mahatir and Modernisation', in J.S. Khan, and F.L.K. Wah (eds), *Fragmented Vision: Culture and Politics in Contemporary Malaysia*, Sydney: Allen and Unwin, pp. 44-76.

Kilduff, P. (1997), *The Dynamics of the Global Textile and Clothing Industries*, paper presented at University of Huddersfield Department of Design Conference – The Impact of Off-Shore Manufacturing and Sourcing Upon the UK Textile/Fashion Industry, Huddersfield.

Krugman, P., R., and Obstfeld, M. (2000), *International Economics: Theory and Policy*, Reading, Mass: Addison Wesley.

Lairson, T.J., and Skidmore, D. (1997), *International Political Economy: The Struggle for Power and Wealth*, Forthworth Tx: Harcourt Bruce.

Lal, J. (1996), 'Situating Locations: The Politics of Self, Identity and "other" in Living and Writing the Text', in D.L. Wolf (ed.), *Feminist Dilemmas in Field Work*, Boulder: Westview, pp. 185-214.

Lee, C.K. (1998), *Gender and the South China Miracle: Two Worlds of Factory Women*, Berkley and LA: University of California Press.

Leete, R. (1996), *Malaysia's Demographic Transition: Rapid Development, Culture, and Politics*, Kuala Lumpur: Oxford University Press.

Leifer, M. (1995), *Dictionary of the Modern Politics of South-East Asia*, London: Routledge.

Leung, C.K. (1996), 'Foreign Manufacturing Investment and Regional Economic Growth in Guangdong Province', *Environment and Planning A*, Vol. 28(3), pp. 513-536.

Liddle, J., and Rai, S. (1993), 'Between Feminism and Orientalism', in M. Kennedy, C. Lubelska, and V. Walsh (eds), *Making Connections: Women's Studies, Women's Movements, Women's Lives*, London: Taylor and Francis, pp. 11-23.

Lie, J. (1991), 'Embedding Polanyi's Market Society'. *Sociological Perspectives*, Vol. 34(2), pp. 219-235.

Lie, M. (2000), 'Two Generations: Life Stories and Social Change in Malaysia', *Journal of Gender Studies*, Vol. 9(1), pp. 27-43.

Lie, M., and Lund, R. (1994), *Working Women and Foreign Industry in Malaysia*, Richmond: Curzon.

Lim, L. (1980), 'Women Workers in Multinational Corporations: The case of the Electronics Industry in Malaysia and Singapore', *Michigan Occasional Papers in Women's Studies*, no. IX.

Lim, L. (1985), *Women Workers in Multinational Enterprises*, Geneva: ILO.

Lim, L.L. (1991), 'Women's Work in Export Factories: The Politics of a Cause', in I. Tinker (ed.), *Persistent Inequalities: Women and World Development*, New York and Oxford: Oxford University Press, pp. 101-199.

Lim, L.L. (1993), 'The Feminization of Labour in the Asia-Pacific Rim Countries: From Contributing to Economic Dynamism to Bearing the Brunt of Structural Adjustments', in N. Ogawa, G.W. Jones, and Jeffrey G. Williamson (eds), *Human Resources in Development along the Asia-Pacific Rim*, Singapore: Oxford University Press, pp. 175-209.

Ling, L.M.H. (1999), 'Sex Machine: Global Hypermasculinity and Images of Asian Woman in Modernity', *Positions: East Asia Cultures Critique*, Vol. 7(2), pp. 277-306.

L'Observatoire Européen du Textile et d'Habillement (OETH) (1999), *The EU Textile and Clothing Sector: A Factual Report*, Brussels: OETH.

Longino, H.E. (1993), 'Economics for Whom?' in M.A. Ferber, and J.A. Nelson (eds), *Beyond Economic Man: Feminist Theory and Economics*, Chicago: University of Chicago Press.

Luinstra, A. (2001), *Toil and Sweat: What can be done to improve working conditions in developing countries?* Washington: World Bank.

Lynch, C. (2002), 'The Politics of White Women's Underwear in Sri Lanka's Open Economy', *Social Politics*, Vol. 9(1), pp. 87-125.

Malaysia (1971), *Second Malaysia Plan 1971-1975*, Kuala Lumpur: Government Printers.

Malaysia (1981), *Fifth Malaysia Plan 1981-1985*, Kuala Lumpur: Government Printers.

Malaysia (1991), *Sixth Malaysia Plan 1991-1996*, Kuala Lumpur: Government Printers.

Malaysia (1996), *Seventh Malaysia Plan, 1996-2000*, Kuala Lumpur: Government Printers.

Malaysia, Department of Statistics (1998), *Social Statistics Bulletin: Malaysia 1998*, Kuala Lumpur: Department of Statistics.

Malaysia, Ministry of Human Resources (1997), *Malaysia: Labour and Human Resources Statistics 1992-1996*, Kuala Lumpur: Ministry of Human Resources.

Malaysian Industrial Development Authority (MIDA) (1999), *Malaysia: Investment in the Manufacturing Sector: Policies, Incentives, Procedures*, Kuala Lumpur: MIDA.

Marchand, M.H. (1996), 'Reconceptualising "Gender and Development" in an Era of 'Globalisation', *Millennium: Journal of International Studies*, Vol. 25(3), pp. 577-603.

Market Tracking International (1999), *The UK Fashion Handbook*, London: MTI/EMAP Fashion.

Mauzy, D. (1997), 'The Human Rights and "Asian Values" Debate in Southeast Asia: Trying to Clarify the Key Issues', *Pacific Review*, Vol. 10, pp. 210-236.

Maznah M. (1996), *The Malay Handloom Weavers: A Study of the Rise and Decline of Traditional Manufacture*, Singapore: ISEAS.

Maznah M., and Ng, C. (1996), *New Technologies and Women's Labour: Case Studies of Two Electronics Firms in Malaysia*, Institut Kajian Malaysia dan Antarabangsa (IKMAS) Working Paper, No. 5, Bangi: Universiti Kebangsaan Malaysia.

McMillan, C.H. (1993), 'The Role of Foreign Direct Investment in the Transition From Planned to Market Economies', *Transnational Corporations*, Vol. 2(3), pp. 97-120.

Mehmet, O. (1999), *Westernising the Third World: The Eurocentricity of Economic Development Theories*, London: Routledge.

Mehra, R., and Gammage, S. (1999), 'Trends, Countertrends and Gaps in Women's Employment', *World Development*, Vol. 27(3), pp. 533-550.

Mies, M. (1982), *The Lacemakes of Narsapur: Indian Housewives Produce for the World Market*, Westport: Lawrence Hill.

Mies, M. (1986), *Patriarchy and Accumulation on a World Scale: Women in the International Division of Labour*, London: Zed.

Mies, M., Bennholdt-Thomsen, V., and Welfhof, C.V. (1988), *Women the Last Colony*, London: Zed.

Milne, R.S., and Mauzy, D.K. (1999), *Malaysian Politics Under Mahatir*, London: Routledge.

Mitter, S. (1986), *Common Fate Common Bond: Women in the Global Economy* London: Pluto Press.

Mitter, S. (1988), 'Industrial Restructuring and Manufacturing Homework: Immigrant women in the UK Clothing Industry', *Capital and Class*, No. 27, pp. 37- 80.

Moss, W. (1997), *Clothing the Nation, The Impact of Off-Shore manufacturing and Sourcing upon the UK Textile/Fashion Industry*, paper presented at University of Huddersfield Department of Design Conference – The Impact of Off-Shore Manufacturing and Sourcing Upon the UK Textile/Fashion Industry, Huddersfield.

Murphy, C.N. (1996), 'Seeing Women, Recognising Gender, Recasting International Relations', *International Organisation*, Vol. 50(3), pp. 513-538.

Murphy, J. (1997), *Mainstreaming Gender in World Bank Lending: An Update*, Washington DC: IBRD.

Myrdal, G. (1968), *Asian Drama: An Inquiry into the Poverty of Nations*, Harmondsworth: Penguin.

Nagata, J. (1995), 'Modern Malay Women and the Message of the Veil, in Wazir Jahan Karim (ed.), *"Men" and "Women" in Developing Southeast Asia*, Oxford: Berg Publishers, pp. 101-120.

Nandy, A. (1988), *The Intimate Enemy: Loss and Recovery of Self Under Colonialism*, New Dehli: Oxford University Press.

Nash, J. (1983), 'Introduction', in J. Nash, and M.P. Fernandez Kelly (eds), *Women, Men and the International Division of Labour*, Albany: SUNY Press, pp. vii-xv.

Ng, C., and Maznah, M. (1990), 'Primary But Not Subordinated: Changing Class and Gender Relations in Rural Malaysia' in B. Agarwal (ed.), *Structures of Patriarchy: The State, Community and the Household*, London: Zed, pp. 52-82.

Nobuyaki, Y. (1991), 'Malaysia's New Economic Policy and the Industrial Co-ordination Act', *The Developing Economies*, Vol. 29(4), pp. 330-349.

North, D.C. (1990), *Institutions, Institutional Change and Economic Performance*, Cambridge: Cambridge University Press.

O'Brien, L. (1988), 'Between Capital and Labour: Trade Unionism in Malaysia', in T.M. Shaw (ed.), *Labour and Unions in Africa and Asia*, Basingstoke: MacMillan, pp. 136-170.

O'Brien, L. (1993), *The Economic Climate for Joint Ventures in Malaysia*, Policy paper no. 4, Asia Research Centre, Murdoch University.

O'Conner, D. (1993), 'Textiles and Clothing: Sunrise or Sunset Industry' in K.S. Jomo (ed.), *Industrializing Malaysia: Policy, Performance, Prospects*, London: Routledge, pp. 234-271.

OECD (1990), *Foreign Trade by Commodities, 1988*, Paris: OECD.

OECD (1999), *Foreign Trade by Commodities, 1992-1997*, Paris: OECD.

OECD (2002), *Multinational Enterprises in Situations of Violent Conflict and Human Rights Abuses*, OECD Directorate for Financial, Fiscal and Enterprise Affairs, Working Papers on International Investment, No. 2001/1.

Office for National Statistics (1986), *Business Monitor 1986, Report on the Census of Production, PA453: Clothing, Hats and Gloves*, London: HMSO.

Office for National Statistics (1992), *Business Monitor 1992, Report on the Census of Production, PA453: Clothing, Hats and Gloves*, London: HMSO.

Ohmae, K. (1990), *The Borderless World: Power and Strategy in the Interlinked Economy*, London: Collins.

Ong, A. (1987), *Spirits of Resistance and Capitalist Discipline: Factory Women in Malaysia*, Albany: SUNY Press.

Ostrovsky, A. (1998), 'Keeping Manufacturers Alive – At a cost', *Financial Times* (21.5.91), p. 1.

Ostry, S. (1992), 'The Domestic Domain: The New International Policy Arena', *Transnational Corporations*, Vol. 1(1), pp. 7-26.

Pearson, R. (1988), 'Multinational Companies and Women Workers', in R. Pahl (ed.), *On Work*, Oxford: Blackwell.

Pearson, R. (1992), 'Gender Issues in Industrialization'. In T. Hewitt, H. Johnson, and D. Wield (eds), *Industrialization and Development*. Milton Keynes: Open University Press.

Pearson, R. (1995), 'Male Bias and Women's Work in Mexico's Border Industries', In D. Elson (ed.), *Male Bias in the Development Process*, Manchester: Manchester University Press, pp. 133-163.

Pearson, R. (1998), 'Nimble Fingers Revisited: Reflections on Women and Third World Industrialization in the Late Twentieth Century', in C. Jackson, and R. Pearson (eds), *Feminist Visions of Development: Gender Analysis and Policy*, London: Routledge, pp 171-188.

Peterson, V.S. (1996), 'Shifting Ground(s): Epistemological and Territorial Remapping in the Context of Globalisation(s)' in E. Kofman, and G. Youngs (eds), *Globalisation: Theory and Practice*, London: Pinter, pp. 11-28.

Peterson, V.S., and Sisson Runyan, A. (1993), *Global Gender Issues*, Boulder, Co: Westview.

Pettman, J.J. (1996), *Worlding Women: A Feminist International Politics*, London: Routledge.

Phillips, A., and Taylor, B. (1980), 'Sex and Skill: Notes Towards a Feminist Economics', *Feminist Review*, Vol. 6, pp. 79-88.

Phizacklea, A. (1990), *Unpacking the Fashion Industry: Gender, Racism and Class in Production*, Routledge: London.

Phongpaichit, P. (1990), 'Two Roads to the Factory: Industrialization Strategies and Women's Work in Southeast Asia', in B. Agarwal (ed.), *Structures of Patriarchy: The State, The Community and the Household*, London: Pinter, pp. 11-28.

Polanyi, K. (1957), *The Great Transformation: The Political and Economic Origins of our Time*, Boston: Beacon Press.

Pringle, R., and Watson, S. (1998), '"Women's interests" and the Poststructuralist State', in A. Phillips (ed.), *Feminism and Politics*, Oxford: Oxford University Press, pp. 203-223.

Pyle, J.L. (1994), 'Economic Restructuring in Singapore and the Changing Roles of Women: 1957 to the Present', in N. Aslanbeigui, S. Pressman, and G. Summerfield (eds), *Women in the Age of Economic Transformation: Gender Impact of Reforms in Post-Structuralist and Developing Countries*, London: Routledge, pp. 129-144.

Rai, S. (1996), 'Women and the State in the Third World', in H. Afshar (ed.), *Women and Politics in the Third World*, London: Routledge, pp. 25-39.

Rai, S. (1998), *Engendered Development in a Global Age?* CSGR Working paper No. 20/98, December 1998, Centre for the Study of Globalisation and Regionalisation, University of Warwick.

Rai, S. (2002), *Gender and the Political Economy of Development: From Nationalism to Globalization*, Cambridge: Polity.

Ram, M. (1996),'Unravelling the Hidden Clothing Industry: Managing the Ethnic Minority Garment Sector'. In I.M. Taplin, and J. Winterton (eds), *Restructuring Within a Labour Intensive Industry*, Aldershot: Avebury, pp. 409-433.

Ram, M., Gilman, M., Arrowsmith, J., and Edwards, P. (2003), 'Once More into the Sunset? Asian Clothing Firms after the National Minimum Wage', *Environment and Planning C*, Vol. 21(1), pp. 71-88.

Rannie, A.F. (1984), 'Combined and Uneven Development in the Clothing Industry' *Capital and Class*, Vol. 22 (Spring), pp. 141-157.

Rasiah, R. (1993), 'Competition and Governance: Work in Malaysia's Textile and Garment Industry'. *Journal of Contemporary Asia*, Vol. 23(1), pp. 3-23.

Rasiah, R. (1997), 'Class, Ethnicity and Economic Development in Malaysia', in G. Rodan, K. Hewison, and R. Robison (eds), *The Political Economy of South-East Asia: An Introduction*, Melbourne: Oxford University Press.

Razavi, S. (1999a), 'Export-Oriented Employment Poverty and Gender: Contested Accounts', *Development and Change*, Vol. 30(3), pp. 653-683.

Razavi, S. (1999b), 'Gendered Poverty and Well-being: Introduction', *Development and Change*, Vol. 30(3), pp. 417-421.

Reich, R.B. (1992), *The Work of Nations: Preparing Ourselves for 21st Century Capitalism*, New York: Vintage Books.

Rhee, Y. W. (1990), 'The Catalyst Model of Development – Lessons from Bangladesh's Success with Garment Exports', *World Development*, Vol. 18(2), pp. 333-346.

Richter, J. (2001), *Holding Corporations Accountable: Corporate Conduct, International Codes and Citizen Action*, London: Zed.

Robison, R., Rodan, G., and Hewison, K. (1997), 'Introduction', in G. Rodan, K. Hewison, and R. Robison (eds), *The Political Economy of South-East Asia*, Melbourne: Oxford University Press.

Rock, M. (2001), 'Globalization and Bangladesh: The Case of Export-Oriented Garment Manufacture', *South Asia – Journal of South Asian Studies*, Vol. 24(1), pp. 201-225.

Rodan, G. (1989), *The Political Economy of Singapore's Industrialization: National State and International Capital*, Basingstoke: MacMillan.

Rostow, W.W. (1959), *The Stages of Economic Growth*, London: MacMillan.

Rushe, D. (1998), 'Final Cut', *Sunday Times: Business* (13.09.98), p. 8.

Safa, H.I. (1981), 'Runaway Shops and Female Employment The Search for Cheap Labour', *Signs*, Vol. 7(2), pp. 418-433.

Sajhau, J.-P. (1998), *Business Ethics in the Textile, Clothing and Footwear(TCF) industries: Codes of Conduct*, Working paper ILO: Geneva.

Salaff, J. (1981), *Working Daughters in Hong Kong*, Cambridge: Cambridge University Press.

Scheffer, M. (1994), *The Changing Map of European Textiles*, Bruxelles: L'Observatoire Européen du Textile et de l'Habillement.

Scott, E., and Shah, B. (1993), 'Future Projects/Future Theorizing in Feminist Research Methods: Commentary on a Panel Discussion', *Frontiers*, Vol. 13(3), pp. 90-103.

Seguino, S. (2000), 'Gender Inequality and Economic Growth: A Cross Country Analysis', *World Development*, Vol. 28(7), pp. 1211-1230.

Sen, A. (1999), *Development as Freedom*, Oxford: Oxford University Press.

Sen, G. (2001), *Gendered Labour Markets in Asia*, Occasional Paper, UNCTAD/UNDP.

Sha'ban Muftah Isma'il (1997), *Women, Economic Growth and Development in Malaysia*, Petailing Jaya, Malaysia: IBS Buku.

Shamsulbahriah Ku Ahmad (1999), What *Are We Trying to Measure? Conceptualising Ethnic and Gender Inequality in Malaysia*, unpublished manuscript provided by the author.

Shanin, T. (1997), 'The Idea of Progress', in M. Rahnema, and V. Bawtree (eds), *The Post Development Reader*, London: Zed, pp. 65-72.

Shari, I. (2000), 'Economic Growth and Income Inequality in Malaysia' *Journal of the Asia-Pacific Economy*, Vol. 5(1/2), pp. 122-144.

Smith, A. (1970), *The Wealth of Nations,* Harmondsworth: Penguin.

Smith, A. (2003), 'Power Relations, Industrial Clusters, and Regional Transformations: Pan European Integration and Outward Processing in the Slovak Clothing Industry', *Economic Geography*, Vol. 79(1), pp. 17-40.

Smith, W.A. (1994), 'A Japanese Factory in Malaysia: Ethnicity as a Management Ideology', in K.S. Jomo (ed.), *Japan and Malaysian Development: In the Shadow of the Rising Sun*, London: Routledge, pp. 154-181.

Spero, J.E. (1990), *The Politics of International Economic Integration*, London: Allen and Unwin.

Standing, G. (1989), 'Global Feminization Through Flexible Labor', *World Development*, Vol. 17(7), pp. 1077-1095.

Standing, G. (1999), 'Global Feminization Through Flexible Labor: A Theme Revisited', *World Development*, Vol. 23(3).

Stanko, E. (1988), 'Keeping Women in and Out of Line: Sexual Harassment and Occupational Segregation', in S. Walby (ed.), *Gender Segregation at Work*, Milton Keynes: OU Press, pp. 91-99.

Stansfield, J.R. (1980), 'The Institutional Economics of Karl Polanyi', *Journal of Economic Issues*, Vol. 13(3), pp. 593-614.

Stiglitz, J.E. (1989), 'Markets, Market Failures and Development', *The American Economic Review*, Vol. 79(2), pp. 197-203.

Stivens, M. (1996), *Matrilinity and Modernity: Sexual Politics and Social Change in Rural Malaysia*, St Leonards NSW: Allen and Unwin.

Stopford, J., and Strange, S., with Henley, J.S. (1991), *Rival States, Rival Firms: Competition for World Market Shares*, Cambridge: Cambridge University Press.

Strassman, D. (1993), 'Not a Free Market: The Rhetoric of Disciplinary Authority in Economics', in M.A. Ferber, and J.A. Nelson (eds), *Beyond Economic Man: Feminist Theory and Economics*, Chicago: Chicago University Press, pp. 54-68.

Strober, M.H. (1994), 'Can Feminist Thought Improve Economics? Rethinking Economics Through a Feminist Lens', *American Economic Review*, Vol. 84(2), pp. 143-147.

Swedberg, R. (1987), 'Economic Sociology Past and Present', *Culture and Society*, Vol. 35(1), pp. 1-221.

Swedberg, R., and Granovetter, M. (1992), 'Introduction', in M. Granovetter, and R. Swedberg (eds), *The Sociology of Economic Life*, Boulder: Westview.

Sylvester, C. (1994), *Feminist Theory and International Relations in a Postmodern Era*, Cambridge: Cambridge University Press.

Tinker, I. (1976), 'The Adverse Impact of Development on Women', in I. Tinker, and M. Bramsen (eds), *Women and World Development*, Washington DC: Equity Policy Center, pp. 3-13.

Troung, T-D. (1999), 'The Underbelly of the Tiger: Gender and the Demystification of the Asian Miracle', *Review of International Political Economy*, Vol. 6(3), pp. 133-65.

Tzannos, Z. (1999), 'Women and Labour Market Changes in the Global Economy: Growth Helps, Inequalities Hurt and Public Policy Matters', *World Development*, Vol. 27(3), pp. 551-569.

UNCTAD (1994), *World Investment Report 1994: Transnational Corporations, Employment and the Workplace*, New York: United Nations.

UNCTAD (1995), *World Investment Report 1995: Transnational Corporations and Competitiveness*, New York: United Nations.

UNCTAD (1999), *World Investment Report 1999: Foreign Direct Investment and the Challenge of Development*, New York: United Nations.

UNCTC (1992), *World Investment Report 1992: Transnational Corporations as Engines of Growth*, New York: United Nations.

Underhill, G.R.D. (1998), *Industrial Crisis and the Open Economy: Politics, Global Trade and the Textile Industry in the Advanced Economies*, Basingstoke: MacMillan.

United Nations (1999), *1999 World Survey of the Role of Women in Development: Globalization, Gender and Work*, New York: United Nations.

United Nations Industrial Development Organisation (1991), *Malaysia: Sustaining the Industrial Investment Momentum*, Cambridge MA: Basil Blackwell.

Uriminsky, M.(2001), *Self regulation in the Workplace: Codes of Conduct, Social Labelling and Socially Responsible Investment*, Management and Corporate Citizenship Working Paper No. 1, Geneva: ILO.

Vernon, R. (1966), 'International Investment and International Trade in the Product Cycle', *Quarterly Journal of Economics*, Vol. 80(1), pp. 190-207.

Viotti, P.R., and V, K.M. (1997), *International Relations and World Politics: Security, Economy, Identity*, New Jersey: Prentice Hall.

Visvanathan, N. (1997), 'Introduction to Part 1', in N. Visvanathan, L. Duggan, L. Nisonoff, and N. Wiegersma (eds), *The Women, Gender and Development Reader*, London: Zed, pp. 17-33.

Wad, P. (1997), *Enterprise Unions and Structural Change in Malaysia: Preliminary Research Findings*, Institut Kajian Malaysia dan Antarabangsa (IKMAS) Working Papers, No. 13, Bangi: Universiti Kebangsaan Malaysia, 1997.

Wade, R. (1990), *Governing the Market: Economic Theory and the Role of Government in East Asian Industrialization*, Princeton: Princeton University Press.

Walsh, J. (1991), 'The Performance of UK Textiles and Clothing: Recent Controversies and Evidence' *International Review of Applied Economics*, Vol. 5(3), pp. 297-303.

Waylen, G. (1997), 'Gender Feminism and Political Economy' *New Political Economy*, Vol. 2(2), pp. 205-220.

Waylen, G. (1998), 'Gender Feminism and the State: An Overview' in V. Randall, and G. Waylen (eds), *Gender, Politics and the State*, London: Routledge pp. 1-17.

Whitehead, M. (1994), 'Marks and Spencer: Britain's Leading Retailer: Quality and Value Worldwide' *Management Decision*, Vol. 32(3), pp. 38-41.

Whitworth, S. (1997), *Feminism and International Relations*, Basingstoke: MacMillan.

Williams, C.L. (1993), 'Introduction', in C.L. Wiliams (ed.), *Doing "Women's Work": Men in Non-Traditional Occupations*, California: Sage.

Winterton, R., and Barlow, A. (1996), 'Economic Restructuring of UK Clothing', in I.M. Taplin, and J. Winterton (eds), *Restructuring Within a Labour Intensive Industry,* Aldershot: Avebury, pp. 25-47.

Wolf, D.L. (1990), 'Linking Women's Labor with the Global Economy: Factory Workers and their Families in Rural Java', in K. Ward (ed.), *Women Workers and Global Restructuring*, Ithaca NY: Cornell, pp. 25-47.

Wolf, D.L. (1992), *Factory Daughters: Gender, Household Dynamics and Rural Industrialization in Java*, Berkley and LA: University of California Press.

Wolf, D.L. (1996), *Feminist Dilemmas in Fieldwork*, Boulder: Westview.

Wood, A. (1991), 'North-South Trade and Female Labour in Manufacturing: An Asymmetry', *The Journal of Development Studies*, Vol. 27(2), pp. 168-189.

World Bank (1990), *World Development Report 1990*, Washington DC: Oxford University Press.

World Bank (1991), *World Development Report 1991*, New York: Oxford University Press.

World Bank (1993), *The East Asian Miracle: Economic Growth and Public Policy*, Oxford: Oxford University Press.

World Bank (1994), *Enhancing Women's Participation in Economic Development: A World Bank Policy Paper*, Washington DC: World Bank.

World Bank (1995), *World Development Report*, New York: Oxford University Press.

World Bank (2001), *Engendering Development: Through Gender Equality in Rights, Resources and Voice*, A World Bank Policy Research Paper, Oxford: Oxford University Press for the World Bank.

Youngs, G. (1996), 'Dangers of Discourse: The Case of Globalisation', in E. Kofman, and G. Youngs (eds), *Globalisation: Theory and Practice*, London: Pinter.

Yuval-Davis, N., and Anthias, F. (1989), *Woman-Nation-State*, Basingstoke: Macmillan.

Zalewski, M. (1998), 'Where is Woman in International Relations? To Return as a Woman and be Heard', *Millennium: Journal of International Studies*, Vol. 27(4), pp. 847-867.

Zeitlin, J., and Totterdill, P. (1989), 'Markets, Technology and Local Intervention: The Case of Clothing', in P. Hirst, and J. Zeitlin (eds), *Reversing Industrial Decline? Industrial Structure and Policy in Britain and her Competitors*, Oxford: Berg.

Index

UK-Apparel Ladieswear Malaysia
(UKALM) 1, 6, 112-146
   careers
      cutting 134-135, 169-170
      finishing 133, 135
      managerial 142
      sewing 112, 123-126, 136
      spreading 149
   company structure 115-116
   employee of the month scheme
      163
   Human Resources department
      109-110
      Director of Human
         Resources 63, 109-111,
         117-119, 121, 128, 130-
         132, 140-145, 148, 152,-
         153, 164, 167
   job descriptions
      Cutters 133-134
      Fusing 134
      Panel inspection 134
      Pinning 134
      Pressers 135-136
      QC 121, 139
      Sewers 122-126
      Spreaders 133-134
      Supervisors 130, 138-139,
         141
      Trainer 138-139, 150
      Vac Pac operators 150
   lack of childcare facilities 169
   management structure 117-119
   operations Department 109, 115,
      142
   paternalism 162-163
   pay 150-160
      daily rated staff 152
      in male dominated jobs 134,
         150, 158-159

      monthly rated staff 150, 152
      non-wage benefits 162-163
      piece-rate bonus system
         124, 150, 152, 162
      sewers and cutters compared
         156-159
   production department 133
      cutting floor 115, 133-135
      sewing floor 115
      finishing floor 115, 135-137
   recruitment practices (see
      Recruitment)
   relationship between HR in
      Malaysia and the UK 109-110
   relationship with parent company
      107-111
   training School 109, 115
UMNO 50, 52, 68
UN Conference on trade and
   development (UNCTAD) 2, 4
   Corporations 11
   Journal *Transnational*
   World investment reports 4, 19-
      25
UNCTC 9, 13
UNIDO 57
Urbanization, in Malaysia 52-53
USA 91

Vernon, R 11

Washington Consensus, end of 22
Waylen, Georgina 28-27, 48
Wolf, D. 1, 122, 161, 166
William Baird PLC 83
'Woman' as a category 29, 33
Women in Development (WID) 28
World Bank 9,19, 22, 24
   East Asian Miracle report 19, 47
   World Bank and Gender 24